HISTORY'S GREATEST MYSTERY
The Improbable Convergence of Four Images of Christ

Paul F. Caranci

Foreword by Fr. Christopher M. Mahar, pastor of Saint Augustine Church, Providence, RI, former Vatican Official, Dicastery for Promoting Integral Human Development

History's Greatest Mystery:
The Improbable Convergence of Four Images of Christ
Copyright © 2024 Paul F. Caranci.

Produced and printed by Stillwater River Publications.
All rights reserved. Written and produced in the United
States of America. This book may not be reproduced
or sold in any form without the expressed, written
permission of the author and publisher.

Visit our website at
www.StillwaterPress.com
for more information.

First Stillwater River Publications Edition.
ISBN: 978-1-965733-05-9

1 2 3 4 5 6 7 8 9 10
Written by Paul F. Caranci.
Published by Stillwater River Publications,
West Warwick, RI, USA.

*The views and opinions expressed
in this book are solely those of the author
and do not necessarily reflect the views
and opinions of the publisher.*

DEDICATION

For Margie, and our unending love.

Table of Contents

Foreword - Fr. Christopher Maher i

Acknowledgments v

Introduction - Why This Book? Why Now? vii

Part I – The Facts

    Chapter 1 – The Passion and Crucifixion of Jesus 1

    Chapter 2 – Material Evidence of the Passion, Death, and
        Resurrection 48

    Chapter 3 – The Veil of Veronica 55

    Chapter 4 – The Shroud of Turin 71

    Chapter 5 – The Sudarium of Oviedo 89

    Chapter 6 – The Image of Divine Mercy 99

Part II – The Science

    Chapter 7 – What Science Reveals About the Shroud of Turin . 111

    Chapter 8 – What Science Reveals About the
        Sudarium of Oviedo 172

    Chapter 9 – What Science and Tradition Reveal About the Veil
        of Veronica and the Image of Divine Mercy 184

Part III – The Truth and the Faith

    Chapter 10 – Scientific Studies Produce Theories on the Creation
        of the Image on the Shroud 193

    Chapter 11 – The Four Images Are One 201

    Chapter 12 - The Shroud, the Veil of Manoppello, the Sudarium
        of Oviedo and Eucharistic Miracles 215

Conclusion 225

Appendix A
  Traditional Catholic Prayers to The Holy Face 233
  The Chaplet of Divine Mercy 243
Bibliography **245**
About the Author **255**

FOREWORD

St. John Henry Newman, in one of his *Parochial and Plain Sermons*, writes of Christ and the hidden splendor of the Incarnation. "He was born of a poor woman," Newman explains, "laid in a manger, brought up to a lowly trade, that of a carpenter; and when He began to preach the Gospel He had not a place to lay His head: lastly, He was put to death, to an infamous and odious death, the death which criminals suffered."[1] Newman masterfully cements the connection between the crib and the cross, the Incarnation and the crucifixion of Jesus Christ. Our Lord was born into the world so that He could offer His life for our salvation.

For us Christians, the Incarnation and the cross lead quite naturally to adoration as we fall down in worship and awe before the God who loved us "to the end" (John 13:1). We contemplate Christ and the wounds that He bore for us and we pray in adoration with St. Thomas in the Gospel: "My Lord and my God!" (John 20:28). The manifestation of the Incarnate God moves us to worship and adore Him in the Blessed Sacrament of the Eucharist, in His Body and Blood poured out for us on the cross.

Adoration, of course, is closely connected to veneration. There is a compelling scene described in three Gospels in which a woman with an issue of blood approached Jesus in order to be healed (see Matthew 9:20-22; Mark 5:25-34; and Luke 8:43-49). She reached out to Him and devoutly "touched the fringe of his garment" (Luke 8:44), and she was cured. Another object of great interest is the seamless garment that Jesus wore, a tunic taken from Him in the

---

[1] John Henry Newman, "Sermon XVI-Christ Hidden from the World," *John Henry Newman Selected Sermons*, Ed. Ian Ker, Paulist Press (New York, 1994), p. 246.

passion. These were garments that belonged to the Lord, and rightly do we attach our devotion and attention to them.

The book, "History's Greatest Mystery" by Paul Caranci leads us through the same journey of faith which flows from the Incarnation. The body of Jesus has been revealed for us to adore and His sacrifice of love on the cross has widened our hearts so that we can quickly run in the way of His commandments (see Psalm 119:32). Like the woman with the issue of blood, however, we are also drawn to the garments of Christ, to the articles of clothing associated with His passion and to the images that lead us more deeply into love with Him.

The Veil of Veronica takes us back to the journey of Christ who stumbles through the Via Dolorosa on His way to Calvary. Veronica lovingly wipes the blood and sweat away from Jesus' face, leaving us with a perpetual remembrance of His passion. The Incarnation leads us, naturally, to venerate this sacred cloth that places us physically in the presence of Jesus' sacrifice.

Similarly, the Shroud of Turin allows us to be physically close to the death and resurrection of our Lord and Savior. Joseph of Arimathea, a picture of love and courage, took the linen cloth and covered Jesus' body at His deposition. Duly and with devotion do we venerate that sacred shroud that clothed the Incarnate God in that solemn moment as He anticipated the resurrection.

The Sudarium of Oviedo, like the Shroud of Turin, gives us access to the passion of Christ in a tangible and unforgettable way. The "napkin" (John 20:7) that covered the beautiful face of our Lord allows us to contemplate Him and draw ever closer to the God made visible in Jesus of Nazareth.

In the Image of Divine Mercy, we are given a description from Christ Himself on the meaning and significance of His sacrifice. Two rays of light emanate from His heart, one pale and the other red. Jesus tells St. Faustina the purpose of these rays of light and their intimate connection with His passion: "These two rays issued forth from the depths of My tender mercy when My agonized Heart was opened by a lance on the cross" (St. Faustina, Diary, 299). The blood and water that brought forth new life for souls in Baptism and the Eucharist are wonderfully depicted in this sacred image that communicates God's infinite mercy for souls.

Paul Caranci, in this excellent book, provides the history of these four images associated with Jesus and explores the scientific studies that help us to verify their significance for our times. The Eucharistic miracles provide further evidence for the authenticity of these cloths and images that place us in direct contact with the living God. All four of these images draw us more deeply into the mystery of the Incarnation and put us in contact with God made visible. The *Incarnation* leads to *adoration* and *veneration* as we seek to deepen our devotion to Jesus Christ. Ultimately, the pages of this book motivate us to embrace a robust *imitation* of the love of God, a true passion for His Passion, and a desire to emulate that generosity Christ displayed for us on the cross. May "History's Great Mystery" lead us ever closer to the God who never ceases to give Himself totally to us.

—**Reverend Christopher M. Mahar**
Pastor, St. Augustine Church
Providence, R.I.

Acknowledgments

Sometime around the spring of 2020, Joseph Petrarca, the brother of a very good friend, John Petrarca, approached me with some photos he had taken during his visit to Italy. Those photos showed the face of Christ on something called the Veil of Manoppollo. Joe told me that of the various veils thought to be the Veil used by Veronica to wipe the face of Jesus as He carried His cross to Cavalry, this one has proven to be authentic. Evidence gathered in my own research of the Veil supported Joe's assertion. But then I discovered evidence that the facial image on that Veil was nearly identical to the facial image on the Shroud of Turin. Both of those images shared many points of congruence with the blood stains on the Sudarium of Oviedo, and all three of those, were very similar to the image of Divine Mercy painted under the direction of Sister Faustina, with divine guidance from Jesus.

For me, this was far too interesting a story to pass over, and so, I started the research for this book in 2021. It seemed, however, that each time I began to put pen to paper I was presented with a different opportunity to engage in another writing project; one that stole my attention. In 2022, Tim Purcell, the leader of my favorite cover band, Foxes & Fossils, finally responded to many correspondences that I had sent over the prior six months asking for permission to write the band's biography. I thought I would need about twelve months to complete that book, but twelve months turned into eighteen before the book was finally published.

With the completion of *Ear Candy: The Inside Story of Foxes & Fossils, America's #1 Cover Band,* written with band member, Sammie Purcell, I once again turned my attention to writing about the four images of Jesus, only to be sidetracked once again. This time it was my good friend and fellow author Julien Ayotte who called. He read a Providence Journal article about a young man who received the Silver Star for Valor while serving our country in the jungles of Vietnam. Having saved the lives of nearly the entire front unit of men who were caught in the Vietcong's u-shaped ambush, Phil Salois kept a promise to God and became a Catholic priest. For the next 40 years, he ministered to Vietnam veterans who suffered from PTSD saving far more lives than he did in that distant land. Julien, an award-winning mystery-thriller novelist, asked if I would help him write the authorized biography of Fr. Phil. Once again, the offer was too good to pass on, and that very moving story became *In The Shadows of Vietnam: The Gallant Life of Father Phil Salois*.

With the publication of *In the Shadows of Vietnam*, I was finally ready to complete the research and begin writing this book. Though distracted several times with other projects and offers, I was determined to bring to light the story of these four images, a story that so urgently needs to be told.

I am grateful to Joe Petrarca for alerting me to the story of the Veil of Manoppollo back in 2020, and to John Marcello, who first made me aware of the phenomenon of Eucharistic Miracles. I also acknowledge my family, especially my wife, Margie, for the constant encouragement that I always receive. I am grateful to Fr. Christopher Mahar, for agreeing to take time from his busy schedule to write the book's preface. Finally, my gratitude is extended to Steve and Dawn Porter, and all the good people at Stillwater River Publications who worked so hard to bring this book to publication. They are simply the best!

Introduction

Miracles happen every day. They are all around us though some don't see them, and others refuse to acknowledge them. Miraculous events are sometimes reported by those who experience them while others simply accept them as a matter of faith with little or no fanfare. Miracles are almost never acknowledged by science despite the absence of any logical scientific explanation of an event. If a sightless person can suddenly see following a visit to the place of the apparition of Our Lady of Lourdes in France, doctors might say simply that they are at a loss to explain it. People of faith, however, have come to understand the lack of scientific commitment as a possible miracle.

There have been hundreds of Marian apparitions, and all are miraculous to those who believe, even when the Catholic Church has been cautious in giving its formal approval, such as in the case of the apparitions at Medjugorje. Yet these same apparitions are simply termed inexplicable events to unbelievers or to those who await scientific scrutiny. This phenomenon is exemplified in the events that took place on October 13, 1917, in Fatima, Portugal, an event now known as the miracle of the sun.

Jacinta, (left) Lucia, (middle) and Francisco (right) pose for a photo in 1917. The three children suffered greatly following the first Apparition on May 13th. They were ridiculed, interrogated by clergy and government officials and threatened with a torturous death if they wouldn't recant their stories of the Marian Apparitions.

An estimated 70,000 people gathered at the Cova da Iria in Fatima, Portugal on October 13, 1917, in anticipation of a miracle promised by Our Lady of the Rosary. Here, they watch in amazement as the sun began to first spin in the sky, and then fall toward Earth, before returning to its normal position in the sky.

    This public miracle followed a promise that the Virgin Mary made to Lucia Dos Santos, and her cousins Francisco and Jacinta Marto, the three visionaries of Fatima, four months earlier. During the Virgin's third appearance to the children in July 1917, Lucia, the oldest of the three visionaries, requested a public miracle so that others would believe. Our Lady told the children that She would perform a miracle for all to see on October 13, 1917. The children told everyone about the promise and over seventy-thousand people turned out at the Cova-de-Iria on that rainy October day. Despite the rain and several inches of mud, even secular journalists, most of whom were there only for the purpose of dispelling the visions as fake, were in attendance that day.

    Following the events witnessed, those atheistic journalists had no choice but to report what they had seen; the sun dancing in the sky and then falling toward the Earth causing the muddy ground and people's rain-soaked clothing to dry instantly, moments later, the sun returned to its usual position of stability in the afternoon sky. Despite overwhelming agreement by those who witnessed the occurrence, there were still some who refused to acknowledge that a miracle had taken place. As is typical of such events, science had no explanation, and some who were not present even denied that it happened. Other deniers called it a mass hallucination.

In the 11th century Saint Thomas Aquinas noted, "'To one who has faith, no explanation is necessary. To one without faith, no explanation is possible.' This seemingly simple yet thought-provoking statement encapsulates the tension between the realms of belief and skepticism, inviting us to contemplate the nature of faith itself. At its core, Aquinas's quote suggests that faith is an experiential certainty, grounded in personal conviction and a deep sense of understanding."[2]

Miracles happen even if one refuses to believe in them. And, unlike the miracle of the sun in Fatima, not all miracles are fleeting. Some produce lasting evidence, and some come with tangible proof in the form of imagery. On December 11, 1531, Our Lady of Guadalupe provided the miracle of the flowers, but also left behind, for all to see, Her own image on the tilma of Saint Juan Diego. The image on that cheap cactus fiber cloak remains today and can be observed, by all who wish to see it, in a cathedral in Mexico City located near the hill at Tepeyac where the several apparitions of Our Lady to Juan Diego took place.

The image itself, imprinted on a tilma meant to last only a few years, contains no paint or other pigments. The image is truly miraculous, but the features of the image contain several more miracles, many of which were discovered hundreds of years later

---

[2] The Socratic Method, St. Thomas Aquinas, October 7, 2023, https://www.socratic-method.com/quote-meanings/thomas-aquinas-to-one-who-has-faith-no-explanation-is-necessary-to-one-without-faith-no-explanation-is-possible. **Page 1.**

when scientific advancement presented new equipment not available in the 14th century. For example, with the advent of optometry and ophthalmology, it was discovered that the pupils of Mary's eyes open

The image of Our Lady of Guadalupe as it appears on the tilma of Juan Diego. An explanation of the many miracles discovered over the years associated with this image have been added in the circles.

and close with the introduction of light. The eyes of the image are "alive"; The pupils reflect the image of all those who were present at the unfurling of the tilma on that December day in 1531, thirteen people in all. These images are undetectable with the naked eye and were discovered only after the invention of the microscope; the stars on Mary's mantle reflect the exact constellation in the sky at the moment that Juan Diego unfurled his tilma to Bishop Zumarraga and the others present. The point of view, however, is not from someone standing on Earth looking up at the sky, but rather of someone positioned above the stars looking down; further, when the mantle is laid flat and a musical graph is placed over it, the stars, regarded as musical notes, create the most harmonious and heavenly sound imaginable. If the stars had reflected the constellation as it appeared in the sky either two minutes before, or two minutes after Juan Diego unfurled the tilma, the "note" placement produces nothing but discordant noise. The image of Our Lady of Guadalupe contains many additional miracles, far more than can be recounted here.[3] Science is at a loss to explain how the image was produced or why the tilma on which it is displayed has lasted for almost five hundred years despite being made of cheap cactus fibers meant to last only a few years. Yet, despite the overwhelming evidence of the miraculous, there are still those who deny that a miracle has taken place.

Likewise, the image of Our Lady on a rock wall within the canyon of the Guáitara River in Ipiales, Nariño Department, Colombia, presents another miracle that can still be observed today. The image below was left by Our Lady of Las Lajas (Our Lady of the Rocks) in 1754.

---

[33] NOTE: All of the miracles of the image on the tilma are discussed in detail in the book Heavenly Portrait: The Miraculous Image of Our Lady of Guadalupe, written by the author of this book and published by Stillwater River Publications in November 2019.

Our Lady, holding the Christ Child, appeared with St. Francis and St. Dominic leaving this image on the rock wall of the cave in Columbia. The apparition has been permanently imprinted on the rock and has actually become the rock itself.
This file is licensed under the Creative Commons Attribution-Share Alike 3.0 Unported license.

"In the beautiful image, Our Lady is holding the Child Jesus and handing St. Dominic a rosary; the Child Jesus is extending a friar's cord to St. Francis of Assisi." Initially it was thought that someone of extraordinary talent painted the image on the rock. "Geologists have since bored core samples from several places in the rock and discovered that there is no paint, dye, or pigment on the surface of the rock. The colors of the mysterious image are the colors of the rock itself and extend several feet deep inside the rock!"[4] After these extensive scientific investigations, civil authorities and scientists determined that the scene was not a painting at all. The image has miraculously become part of the rock itself!

There are many examples of these enduring miracles that can still be seen today by anyone moved to visit the sites. This book discusses four miraculous images. Three of them are ancient cloths with impressions inexplicably imprinted upon them. The fourth is a painting, the details of which were directed by the hand of Jesus Himself through the visions of a lowly nun in the year 1934. Each of the four images offers a study of the miraculous, but taken together, they document the extent of Jesus' suffering and perhaps even provide proof of His resurrection.

---

[4] Calloway, Fr. Donald, MIC, The Miraculous Image of Our Lady of Las Lajas. Catholic Exchange, March 29, 2017. https://catholicexchange.com/miraculous-image-lady-las-lajas/.

PART I
THE FACTS

CHAPTER I

THE PASSION AND CRUCIFIXION OF JESUS

A Brief History of Crucifixion

Death by crucifixion is one of the most painful forms of chastisement imaginable, and it was a form of punishment that was used liberally by the Romans from the 1st Century BC to the 1st Century AD. While it may be argued that the Roman Empire perfected the art of crucifixion, the Romans were certainly not the first to employ its use as a form of execution. Crucifixion was introduced to the Roman Empire by Greece, where Alexander the Great had been a major proponent of this choice of punitive instrument many years earlier. The origins of crucifixion, however, can be traced all the way back to the Bronze Age and the Assyrian

Empire, meaning that the cross may predate the establishment of the Roman Empire by some 2,000 years.

The process of Roman crucifixion typically began with the criminal being stripped naked and scourged. The victim was forced to stretch his arms around a pillar, boulder or another large object, typically at a forward-leaning angle. His hands were then "bound ... with thongs" (Acts 22:25) tightly on the other side of the pillar or boulder so that his arms were distended, and his back stretched taut. He was then whipped with the Roman flagrum or flagellum, which is a whip with two or three long leather strips attached to a short wooden handle. Knotted in along the leather strips were pieces of metal and bone."[5]

While the flagrum was typically used in the scourging process that preceded crucifixion, there were other, more lethal types of whips that were sometimes employed. Meant to increase the intensity of the pain, the scorplana, for example, "contained metal hooks at the tip of the leather that caused the flesh to tear away from the body. These hooks dug into and then tore out flesh during the whipping, which shredded the victim's back from the neck to the buttocks. It wasn't uncommon for the victims of the Roman scourge to die from the ensuing blood loss and/or shock."[6] Depending on the force applied to the scourging by the executioner, and the type of whip used, the process could tear significant amounts of flesh from the victim's body.

Once scourged to Roman satisfaction, the condemned person would be driven through the city streets naked and forced to carry the transverse beam of the cross to the place of execution. The beam, known as the patibula, typically weighed between seventy-five and one hundred-twenty-five pounds. While bearing the weight of the cross, the victim was whipped by the Romans and stoned and spat upon by some onlookers.

---

[5] BibleVerseStudy.com, Roman Scourge, Roman Scourge & Flagellum, 2023, https://www.bibleversestudy.com/acts/acts22-roman-scourge.htm
[6] Ibid.

Upon arriving at the site of the execution, the victim would be nailed to the patibula while still lying on the ground. Five-to-nine-inch steel nails were driven through the wrists and into pre-fashioned holes of the beam. Once securely fastened to the wood, the patibula, bearing the victim, was raised and secured to the upright beam, known as the stipe, and dropped into place.

During the raising process, the victim would hang from the nailed hands which would be made to bear the entire weight of his body. The three major nerves of this region, the median, radial, and ulnar nerves, would all be impacted by the pressure of the nail causing excruciating pain to radiate through the hands and arms of the victim. To ensure as much pain as possible, the soldiers would use several blows to drive the nail making the "process slow, clumsy and intimately agonizing."[7]

When dropped into place on the stipe, the flesh of the victim's scourged back was scraped against the rough wood of the stipe causing additional agony. The condemned person would hang by the nails in his wrists until the feet were crossed one over the other and secured to the stipe with a single seven-to-nine-inch nail. The Romans employed a variety of imaginative ways to hang their victims on the cross, and they had options for attaching them as well. Sometimes, for example, two separate nails were used to secure the feet to the stipe with one nail being driven through each of the victim's heels, placing one on either side of the stipe. Nails, however, were expensive to produce, so Roman's liked to use them sparingly. They often recycled the nails for use in subsequent crucifixions.

The agony of crucifixion did not end with the process of affixing the victim to the cross. Rather, the victim was left to die slowly over a period of several days while their naked bodies were

---

[7] YouTube video, Crucifixion: The Process and the Monstrous Logic Behind It. The Reality of Roman Crucifixion. April 2023, https://www.youtube.com/watch?v=Emk21WbOFo0.

exposed to the elements, the sun, wind, rain, and the wildlife. The physical pain during those final days was intense and each breath contributed greatly to the agony. A full inhalation required the victim to raise himself up against the wood of the cross increasing the pressure against the nails and causing the torn flesh of their flayed back to scrape against the course and splintered wood of the cross. The lifting motion increased the pressure of the nails against the nerves causing excruciating pain in the wrists, arms, legs, feet and torso. Exhaling was equally difficult and required the victim to lower himself back down in another excruciatingly painful exercise. This process had to be repeated several times per minute.

"By the time thirst and hunger set in the victim had doubtlessly long been wishing for death, but that could still be days away. The process pushed the human body to the brink meaning that the causes of death could vary widely,"[8] and include, among other causes, blood loss, heart failure, asphyxiation, and shock.

The Suffering of Jesus in His Final Hours

In many ways the crucifixion of Jesus was atypical of a conventional Roman Execution. Unlike any other crucifixion in recorded history, the passion of Jesus began the night before and continued unabated for some twenty hours.

Thursday, April 6, 30 A.D.
The Agony in the Garden of Gethsemane

The punishing physical stresses applied to the body of Jesus began on Thursday of Passover week in about the year 30 A.D.,[9]

---

[8] Ibid.

[9] "Owing to various adjustments in the calendar, the years of Jesus birth and death remain controversial. However, it is likely that Jesus was born in either 4 or 6 BC and died in 30 AD. During Passover observance in 30 AD, the Last Supper would have been observed on Thursday, April 6 [Nisan 13]. And Jesus would have

following his sharing of the Passover meal with his twelve disciples in the upper room of a home in southwest Jerusalem. It was about 11:00 on the night of Thursday, April 6, 30 A.D. After singing the hallel (Praise Ye), but before drinking the fourth and final cup of wine traditional of the Jewish Passover meal, the eleven remaining disciples (Judas had departed for his meeting of betrayal with the Sanhedrin) walked with Jesus to the Mount of Olives, a garden across the Kidron valley located to the northeast of the city.

According to evangelist Matthew: "Then Jesus went with them to a place called Gethsemane, and he said to his disciples, 'Sit here, while I go over there and pray.' And taking with him Peter and the two sons of Zebedee, he began to be sorrowful and troubled. Then he said to them, 'My soul is very sorrowful, even to death; remain here, and watch with me.' And going a little farther he fell on his face and prayed."[10]

The evangelist Luke described it this way in his Gospel account: "…And he came out, and went, as was his custom, to the Mount of Olives; and the disciples followed him. And when he came to the place he said to them, 'Pray that you may not enter into temptation.' And he withdrew from them about a stone's throw, and knelt down and prayed, 'Father, if you are willing, remove this chalice from me; nevertheless, not my will, but yours, be done. And there appeared to him an angel from heaven, strengthening him. And being in an agony, he prayed more earnestly; and his sweat became like great drops of blood falling down upon the ground. And when he rose from prayer, he came to the disciples and found them sleeping for

---

been crucified on Friday, April 7 [Nisan 14]. Source: The Journal of the American Medical Association (JAMA), Edwards, William D.; Gabel, Wesley J., MDiv; Hosmer, Floyd E. MS, AMI, On the Physical Death of Jesus Christ. JAMA, March 21, 1986, Vol. 255, No. 11. Page 1455.

[10] The Holy Bible - New Testament, Matthew 26:36-39. The Great Adventure Bible, Revised Standard Version, Second Catholic Edition, Ascension Press, West Chester, PA. Page 1304.

sorrow, and he said to them, 'Why do you sleep? Rise and pray that you may not enter into temptation.'"[11]

While it may seem like an exaggeration for Luke, a physician, to describe Jesus sweat as "great drops of blood," there is actually significant scientific and medical evidence of this phenomenon which is known as Hematidrosis.

"Hematidrosis, or hematohidrosis, is a very rare *(only a few handfuls of cases were confirmed in medical studies in the 20th century)* medical condition that causes one to ooze or sweat blood from the skin when not cut or injured. ...It usually happens on or around the face, but the skin might be lining the inside of the body, too, like in the nose, mouth or stomach. The skin around the bloody area may swell temporarily. Hematidrosis can look like blood, bloody sweat, or sweat with droplets of blood in it."[12] Hematidrosis can occur "in highly emotional states or in a person suffering from a bleeding disorder. Knowing the type of death Jesus was about to suffer, he was clearly in an intense emotional state when he entered the garden, as he said to Peter and James and John, the two sons of Zebedee, before withdrawing to a place of private prayer, "My soul is very sorrowful, even to death; remain here and watch with me."[13]

It is believed that during hematidrosis, the "blood vessels that taper in capillaries become distressed and burst under the skin and exit out of sweat glands, leaving the skin [very fragile] and sensitive to touch. Even a breath against the skin is painful."[14] Though blood

---

[11] Ibid. Luke 22:39-46. Page 1376.
[12] WebMD, Editorial Contributors, Medically Reviewed by Debra Jaliman, MD on January 26, 2022. https://www.webmd.com/a-to-z-guides/hematidrosis-hematohidrosis
[13] The Holy Bible - New Testament, Matthew 26:38. The Great Adventure Bible, Revised Standard Version, Second Catholic Edition, Ascension Press, West Chester, PA. Page 1304. Also Mark 14:34, Page 1329.
[14] YouTube video, The Man of the Shroud Lecture Series, The Sufferings of the Man of the Shroud, Fr. Andrew Dalton, May 19, 2023.

loss from Hematidrosis is typically minimal, "in the cold night air, it may have produced chills."[15]

The Betrayal by Judas and the Arrest of Jesus

It was to this sensitive skin that Judas affixed the kiss that betrayed Jesus to the clutches of Caiaphas the High Priest. Typically a sign of friendship, that kiss became a sign of betrayal "registering in Christ's body as physical pain."[16]

Luke continues: "While he was still speaking, Judas came, one of the Twelve, and with him a great crowd with swords and clubs, from the chief priests and the elders of the people. Now the betrayer had given them a sign, saying, 'The one I shall kiss is the man; seize him.' And he came up to Jesus at once and said, 'Hail, Master!' And he kissed him. Jesus said to him, 'Friend, why are you here?' Then they came up and laid hands on Jesus and seized him. ...Jesus said..., 'Have you come out as against a robber, with swords and clubs to capture me? Day after day I sat in the temple teaching, and you did not seize me. But all this has taken place, that the Scriptures of the prophets might be fulfilled.' Then all the disciples deserted him and

---

https://video.search.yahoo.com/yhs/search?fr=yhs-tro-freshy&ei=UTF-8&hsimp=yhs-freshy&hspart=tro&p=youtube+video%2C+the+sufferings+of+the+man+of+the+shroud&type=Y219_F163_204671_102220#id=1&vid=27149d850f4e485514276857ab5387b1&action=click.

[15] The Journal of the American Medical Association (JAMA), Edwards, William D.; Gabel, Wesley J., MDiv; Hosmer, Floyd E. MS, AMI, On the Physical Death of Jesus Christ. JAMA, March 21, 1986, Vol. 255, No. 11. Page 1456.

[16] YouTube video, The Man of the Shroud Lecture Series, The Sufferings of the Man of the Shroud, Fr. Andrew Dalton, May 19, 2023.
https://video.search.yahoo.com/yhs/search?fr=yhs-tro-freshy&ei=UTF-8&hsimp=yhs-freshy&hspart=tro&p=youtube+video%2C+the+sufferings+of+the+man+of+the+shroud&type=Y219_F163_204671_102220#id=1&vid=27149d850f4e485514276857ab5387b1&action=click.

fled."[17] Luke ads, "Then they seized Jesus, bound him and led him away."[18]

While Luke points out that Jesus was bound before being led away, he does not provide any description as to how Jesus might have been bound. Neither do any of the other Gospel writers, nor any period historians describe this process. However, for purposes of understanding how Jesus may have been bruised or injured in the process of being bound, it is important to have a basic understanding of what may have taken place during his arrest in the Garden of Gethsemane. Such an account was provided by a seventeenth century Franciscan Abess and mystic by the name of Mary of Jesus of Agreda.[19]

As a result of a series of mystical encounters with the Virgin Mary, she brings to life the way Jesus was bound by his captors. "The signal of the kiss having been given by Judas, the Lord with his disciples and the soldiers, who had come to capture him, came face to face, forming two squadrons the most opposed and hostile that ever

---

[17] The Holy Bible - New Testament, Matthew 26:47-56. The Great Adventure Bible, Revised Standard Version, Second Catholic Edition, Ascension Press, West Chester, PA. Pages 1304-1305.

[18] Ibid. Luke 22:54. Page 1377

[19] Wikipedia, Mary of Jesus of Agreda. Mary of Jesus of Agreda, also known as the Abess of Agreda (2 April 1602 – 24 May 1665), was a Franciscan abbess and spiritual writer, known especially for her extensive correspondence with King Philip IV of Spain and reports of her bilocation between Spain and its colonies in New Spain (what is today, Texas and Mexico). She was a noted mystic of her era. María de Ágreda's best known single work is the Mystical City of God, consisting of eight books (six volumes). This related her revelations about the terrestrial and heavenly life, reportedly received directly from the Blessed Virgin Mary. The books include information about the relationship of the 'Blessed Virgin' with the Triune God, as well as the doings and Mysteries performed by Jesus. The narrative contains extensive details and covers the New Testament timeline. It also relates advice given by the Holy Mother on how to acquire true sanctity.
https://en.wikipedia.org/wiki/Mary_of_Jesus_of_%C3%81greda#:~:text=Mary%20of%20Jesus%20of%20%C3%81greda%20%28Spanish%3A%20Mar%C3%ADa%20de,between%20Spain%20and%20its%20colonies%20in%20New%20Spain.

the world saw. For on one side was Christ our Lord, true God and man, as the captain of all the just, supported by his eleven Apostles the chieftains and champions of his Church with innumerable hosts of angelic spirits full of adoring wonder at this spectacle. On the other side were Judas, the originator of the treason, filled with hypocrisy and hatred, and many Jews and gentiles, bent on venting their malice with the greatest cruelty....The first one who hastened to approach him in order to lay hands on the Master of life, was a servant of the high priests named Malchus....Thereupon they fell upon the most meek lamb like fierce tigers, binding him securely with ropes and chains in order thus to lead him to the house of the high priest....They bound him in the garden, adding to the chains and ropes insulting blows and vilest language; for like venomous serpents they shot forth their sacrilegious poison...They left the garden of Olives in great tumult and uproar, guarding the Savior in their midst. Some of them dragged him along by the ropes in front and others retarded his steps by the ropes hanging from the handcuff's behind. In this manner, with a violence unheard of, they sometimes forced him to fall; at others they jerked him backwards; and then again, they pulled him from one side to the other, according to their diabolical whims. Many times, they violently threw him to the ground and as his hands were tied behind. He fell upon [his face] and was severely wounded and lacerated. In his falls they pounced upon him, inflicting blows and kicks, trampling upon his body and upon his head and face. All these deviltries they accompanied with festive shouts and opprobrious insults."[20] It was just after midnight on Friday, April 7, 30 AD.

---

[20] Agreda, Mary of, Venerable, The Mystical City of God, Volume III, The Transfixion. Tan Books, Charlotte, NC, 1914, Translated from the Original Authorized Spanish Edition by Fiscar Marison (Rev. George J. Blatter), Begun in 1902. Pages 496, 498, and 528.

Early Morning Hours of Friday, April 7, 30 AD
First Stop, The House of Annas and
the First Trial of Jesus

He may have passed the title on to his son-in-law, Caiaphas, but Annas still wielded the real power over the Sanhedrin. He once held the title for himself, "and [was] for years, the 'power behind the throne,' the ruling spirit of Jewry. He had himself been high priest; five of his sons had been high priests after him, as well as a son-in-law, Caiaphas, and a grandson. He was a Sadducee by profession and was hard; an unbeliever in spite of his dignity, as were others of his class. Annas was his own god, his own beginning and end, cool, calculating, determined, successful, wise with the wisdom of the children of men. Indeed, he was the wise man of Jerusalem; the independent man who was never ruffled, the prudent man who would always in the end secure his own way, who could promote men to office and let them govern as they would, yet somehow through it all his own will was done…Both history and the Gospels indicate that Caiaphas owed his priesthood to Annas. It was common almost natural, especially if it was known that Annas wished it, to bring important cases before him for a preliminary judgement, and the case of Jesus of Nazareth was surely one of these. For this reason, when they came to the gate of Annas's court, the guard almost instinctively turned in."[21]

Annas, though not so keen of his belief in the significance of Jesus, "was well acquainted with the Law and the Prophets; the practice of the Temple, and the meaning of that practice."[22] Therefore, like Herod, the King at the time of the birth of Jesus, Annas was suspicious of him and concerned about the actions of his disciples

---

[21] Goodier, Alban, Archbishop, The Passion and Death of Our Lord Jesus Christ. Sophia Institute Press, Manchester, NH. 2022, First Edition published by Burns Oates & Washbourne, London & Ireland. 1933. Page 154.
[22] Ibid.

once Jesus was gone. Clearly, he would have been more comfortable if all of Jesus' disciples were arrested with him. But in the current reality, Annas would have to be cunning. That explains why at the trial before Annas, there "were no witnesses brought, and no sentence passed. Jesus was not asked to pronounce his own condemnation; he was questioned only about those things in which Annas himself was interested.

Jesus stood bound before this merciless, masterful, far-seeing, calculating man. That he would be ultimately condemned, Annas had no doubt at all; he could safely leave that to his more eloquent and self-righteous son-in-law, who knew well enough already…Annas's mind. But his own examination went deeper; he looked through Jesus, as it were, and beyond him, making nothing of him, making much of what might follow after he was dead."[23] Who Jesus thought he was did not concern Annas in the least. "What mattered more was the influence he possessed, the sway over other men that was pitted against his own; who and how many, and of what kind, were his followers; what was the secret of his teaching that gave him his power, not only over friends but also over enemies. Annas called for no other evidence"[24] and focused only on the answers to those questions.

John's Gospel records the exchange between Annas and Jesus. In response to Annas' questions about the disciples, Jesus could not be outsmarted. "'I have spoken openly to the world; I have always taught in the synagogues and in the temple, where all Jews come together. I have said nothing secretly. Why do you ask me? Ask those who have heard me, what I said to them; they know what I said.'"[25] Jesus knew the heart of Annas and wasn't about to give him any information that might bring harm to his disciples. "Annas was

---

[23] Ibid. Pages 154 - 155.
[24] Ibid. Page 155.
[25] The Holy Bible - New Testament, John 18:20-21., The Great Adventure Bible, Revised Standard Version, Second Catholic Edition, Ascension Press, West Chester, PA. Page 1407.

silenced and had failed; for once he had met one who dared to defy and challenge him. He could do no more. He could not condemn, for that was not within his office; even if he could, he would not, for that might compromise him. But his sycophants in the room read the mind of their master well, and willingly supplied what he was too cautious of himself to do. They saw that he had been worsted, and they would avenge him; be he right or wrong, that this lord of theirs should be defied was not to be endured. Honest defense there was none; there remained only that of brutality, that commonest resort of might and cowardice in high places. So, when he had said this, one of the officers standing by struck Jesus with his hand, saying, 'Is that how you answer the high priest?'"[26]

In frustration, "Annas then sent him bound to Caiaphas the high priest."[27] The time was about 12:45 AM, Friday, April 7, 30 AD.

About 12:45 AM, Friday, April 7, 30 AD
Trial Before Caiaphas and Other Dignitaries
The Second Trial of Jesus

Jesus was taken to the high priest where he was questioned by Caiaphas, and some of the scribes and distinguished men of the Jews. It was now about 1:00 in the morning. "The law indeed forbade that trials should take place after nightfall, but this night all law and justice were scattered to the winds."[28] At this trial, many witnesses testified falsely against him, as Jesus stood in silence. But even their perjured testimony was inconsistent and contradictory, leading Caiaphas to become impatient. According to Mark's Gospel account the high priest stood and asked Jesus, "'Have you no answer to make?' But he

---

[26] Ibid. John 18:22. Page 1407.
[27] Ibid. John 18:24. Page 1407.
[28] Goodier, Alban, Archbishop, The Passion and Death of Our Lord Jesus Christ. Sophia Institute Press, Manchester, NH. 2022, First Edition published by Burns Oates & Washbourne, London & Ireland. 1933. Page 154.

was silent and made no answer. Again, the high priest asked him, 'Are you the Christ, the Son of the Blessed?' And Jesus said, 'I Am; and you will see the Son of man sitting at the right hand of Power and coming with the clouds of heaven.' And the high priest tore his clothes, and said, 'Why do we still need witnesses? You have heard his blasphemy. What is your decision?' And they all condemned him as deserving death. And some began to spit on him, and to cover his face, and to strike him, saying to him, 'Prophesy!' And the guards received him with blows."[29]

The Confinement of Jesus Before the Trial by the Sanhedrin

As anxious as Caiaphas was to condemn Jesus, he knew that before he could proceed, he would need to hold a trial before the full Sanhedrin, giving every member an opportunity to question Jesus and to hear for themselves his blasphemous words. Under the law, however, that couldn't happen until morning. Once again, it is Mary of Agreda who provides a detailed account of what took place between the two trials. "As it was already past midnight, the whole council of these wicked men resolved to take good care, that [Jesus] be securely watched and confined until the morning, lest he should escape while they were asleep. For this purpose, they ordered him to be locked, bound as he was, in one of the subterranean dungeons, a prison cell set apart for the most audacious robbers and criminals of the state. Scarcely any light penetrated into this prison to dispel its darkness. It was filled with such uncleanness and stench that it would have infected the whole house if it had not been so remote and so well enclosed; for it had not been cleaned for many years, both because it was so deep down and because of the degradation of the criminals that

---

[29] The Holy Bible - New Testament, Mark 14:60-65, The Great Adventure Bible, Revised Standard Version, Second Catholic Edition, Ascension Press, West Chester, PA. Page 1407. Pages 1329-1330.

were confined in it; for none thought it worthwhile making it more habitable than for mere wild beasts, unworthy of all human kindness."[30]

Mary of Agreda noted that during the time he was imprisoned in the dungeon Jesus remained "bound with the fetters laid upon him in the garden, these malicious men freely exercised all the wrathful cruelty with which they were inspired by the prince of darkness; for they dragged him forward by the ropes, inhumanely causing him to stumble, and loading him with kicks and cuffs amid blasphemous imprecations. From the floor in one corner of the subterranean cavern protruded part of a rock or block, which on account of its hardness had not been cut out. To this block, which had the appearance of a piece of column, they now bound and fettered [Jesus] with the ends of the ropes, but in a most merciless manner. For they forced him to approach it and tied him to it in a stooping position, so that he could neither seat himself nor stand upright for relief, forcing him to remain in a most painful and torturing posture. Thus, they left him bound to the rock, closing the prison-door with a key and giving it in charge of one of the most malicious of their number."[31] That guard, filled with the spirit of Lucifer, invited other soldiers and servants to enter the dungeon. They released him from the rock so as to taunt Jesus with cruel blasphemies, further tormenting his spirit. "In their diabolical infatuation they continued to practice their insulting mockery and tortures upon the person of Christ, until they noticed that the night had already far advanced; then they again tied him to the column and, leaving him thus bound, they departed."[32] The time was about 5:00 AM on Friday, April 7, 30 AD.

---

[30] Agreda, Mary of, Venerable, The Mystical City of God, Volume III, The Transfixion. Tan Books, Charlotte, NC, 1914, Translated from the Original Authorized Spanish Edition by Fiscar Marison (Rev. George J. Blatter), Begun in 1902. Pages 554.
[31] Ibid. Page 555.
[32] Ibid. Page's559-560.

About 6:00 AM on Friday, April 7, 30 AD.
The Sanhedrin and the Third Trial of Jesus

"Soon after daybreak, presumably at the temple, Jesus was tried before the religious Sanhedrin (with the Pharisees and the Sadducees) and again was found guilty of blasphemy, a crime punishable by death."[33]

The Gospels of Matthew (27:1), Mark (15:1) and Luke (22:66) all reference the fact that Jesus was taken out of the dungeon to face the Sanhedrin, but only Luke provides specifics, though they are scant. Mary of Agreda, however, details how the "ancients, the chief priests, and scribes, who according to the law were looked upon with greatest respect by the people, gathered together in order to come to a common decision concerning the death of Christ. This they all desired, however they were anxious to preserve the semblance of justice before the people."[34] It was about 6:00 AM on Friday, April 7, 30 AD, and "Once more they commanded him to be brought from the dungeon to the hall of the council in order to be examined. The satellites of justice rushed below to drag him forth bound and fettered as he was; and while they untied him from the column of rock, they mocked him with great contempt saying: 'Well now Jesus of Nazareth, how little have thy miracles helped to defend thee…Having freed [Jesus] from the rock, they dragged him up to the council. [He] did not open his lips; but the torturers, the blows, and the spittle, with which they had covered him and which he could not wipe off on account of his bonds, had so disfigured him, that he now filled the

---

[33] The Journal of the American Medical Association (JAMA), Edwards, William D.; Gabel, Wesley J., MDiv; Hosmer, Floyd E. MS, AMI, On the Physical Death of Jesus Christ. JAMA, March 21, 1986, Vol. 255, No. 11. Page 1456.

[34] Agreda, Mary of, Venerable, The Mystical City of God, Volume III, The Transfixion. Tan Books, Charlotte, NC, 1914, Translated from the Original Authorized Spanish Edition by Fiscar Marison (Rev. George J. Blatter), Begun in 1902. Pages 565.

members of the council with a sort of dreadful surprise, but not with compassion. Too great was their envious wrath conceived against [him]. They again asked him to tell them, whether he was the Christ, that is, the Anointed. Just as all their previous questions, so this was put with the malicious determination not to listen or to admit the truth, but to culminate and fabricate a charge against him. But [Jesus], being perfectly willing to die for the truth, denied it not; at the same time, he did not wish to confess it in such a manner that they could despise it, or borrow out of it some color for their calumny; for this was not becoming his innocence and wisdom. Therefore he veiled his answer in such a way, that if the pharisees chose to yield to even the least kindly feeling, they would be able to trace up the mystery hidden in his words; but if they had no such feeling, then should it become clear through their answer, that the evil which they imputed to him was the result of their wicked intentions and lay not in his answer. He therefore said to them: 'If I tell you that I am he of whom you ask, you will not believe what I say; and if I shall ask you, you will not answer, nor release me. But I tell you, that the Son of man, after this, shall seat himself at the right hand of the power of God.' The priest answered: 'Then thou art the Son of God?' and [Jesus] replied: You say that I am.' This was as if he had said: 'You have made a very correct inference, that I am the Son of God; for my works, my doctrines, and your own Scripture, as well as what you are now doing with me, testify to the fact, that I am the Christ, the One promised in the law.'"[35]

Having just confirmed what he had said previously at his earlier trial before Caiaphas, those assembled yelled, "'What further testimony do we need? We have heard it ourselves from his own lips?'"[36] And "they immediately came to the unanimous conclusion

---

[35] Ibid. Pages 566-567.
[36] The Holy Bible - New Testament, Luke 22:71, The Great Adventure Bible, Revised Standard Version, Second Catholic Edition, Ascension Press, West Chester, PA. Page 1377.

that he should, as one worthy of death, be brought before Pontius Pilate, who governed Judea in the name of the Roman emperor and was the temporal Lord of Palestine."[37] Despite the Sanhedrin's two votes to put Jesus to death, they were powerless to do so. Crucifixion was a penalty reserved only for the Romans. Caiaphas had to appeal to Pontius Pilate, the Roman Procurator.

The Appeal to Pontius Pilate for the Execution and the Fourth Trial of Jesus

The sun had already risen, and the City of Jerusalem was teaming with people who were not residents of the city, but rather belonged to Palestine and other provinces near and far. They were in the great city to celebrate the Passover and the "great Pasch of the Lamb and of the unleavened bread."[38]

Rumors of the arrest of Jesus had already been circulating through the crowds, and as Jesus had developed a reputation far and wide as a holy man and a healer, many gathered in the streets to catch a glimpse of him as he passed by. They were told that he was bound with chains, the same chains that fettered him since his arrest some eight or nine hours earlier.

As is the case with any man, Jesus evoked a multitude of emotions within the hearts of others and there was a very mixed reaction among those gathered. As Jesus was led past, "some of them shouted out: Let him die, let him die, this wicked impostor, who deceives the whole world. Others answered: His doctrines do not appear to be so bad, nor his works; for he has done good to many. Still others, who had believed in him, were much afflicted and wept."[39]

---

[37] Agreda, Mary of, Venerable, The Mystical City of God, Volume III, The Transfixion. Tan Books, Charlotte, NC, 1914, Translated from the Original Authorized Spanish Edition by Fiscar Marison (Rev. George J. Blatter), Begun in 1902. Pages 569.

[38] Ibid. Page 568.

[39] Ibid. Page 569.

The sight of him could not help but "break one's heart; for by buffets and blows and by the spittle, his most beautiful countenance [was] so disfigured and defiled, that [it was difficult] to recognize him with [their] own eyes…the whole city was in confusion and uproar concerning the Nazarene."[40]

Jesus, and the entourage leading him, finally arrived at the house of Pilate. Many in the crowd followed behind them. The Jews, however, could not enter the Praetorium as it was Passover and, as Luke notes in his Gospel, Jewish law prevented them from entering the house of a Pagan before eating the Passover meal. "Pilate, although a heathen, yielded to their ceremonious scruples, and seeing that they hesitated to enter his praetorium, he went out to meet them."[41] According to the formality customary among the Romans, he asked them, "'What accusation do you bring against this man?'"[42] They answered him, "We found this man perverting our nation, and forbidding us to give tribute to Caesar, and saying that he himself is Christ a king." Pilate asked Jesus if he were a king to which Jesus replied, "You have said so."[43]

Pilate addressed the chief priest and those assembled telling them that he could find no fault in Jesus, but they insisted that they wanted him punished, noting, "He stirs up the people, teaching throughout all Judea, from Galilee even to this place."[44] The word 'Galilee' piqued Pilate's curiosity and "he asked whether the man was a Galilean."[45] Learning that he was, Pilate realized he had an opportunity to rid himself of the Jesus problem.

---

[40] Ibid. Page 570
[41] Ibid. Page 573.
[42] The Holy Bible - New Testament, John 18:29, The Great Adventure Bible, Revised Standard Version, Second Catholic Edition, Ascension Press, West Chester, PA. Page 1407.
[43] Ibid. Luke 23:3.
[44] Ibid.
[45] Ibid.

Questioned and Mocked by Herod, Jesus Undergoes His Fifth Trial

Pilate instructed Caiaphas to appeal to Herod, under whose jurisdiction Galilee fell. So, in his weakened, bound and beaten state, Jesus was taken by the scribes, the priests and a multitude of soldiers from the house of Pilate to the palace of Herod. Those who held Jesus captive dragged him "along by the ropes and cleared the streets, which had been filled with multitudes of the people to see the spectacle. The military broke their way through the crowds; and as the servants and priests were thirsting so eagerly for the blood of [Jesus] and wished to shed it on this very day, they hastened with Jesus through the streets nearly on a run and with great tumult."[46]

Meanwhile, Herod, who heard Jesus was on his way to the palace, waited impatiently. He knew that Jesus was a close friend of the Baptist whom he had put to death and had heard about the miracles of Jesus and his preaching. When Jesus finally arrived, Herod "received him with loud laughter as an enchanter and conjurer...He commenced to examine and question Jesus. Persuaded that he could thereby induce him to work some miracle to satisfy his curiosity...But Jesus answered him not a word."[47] The priests repeated to Herod the same charges they had explained to Pilate and still, Jesus stood in silence. "Herod was much put out by the silence and meekness of [Jesus]...but tried to hide his confusion by mocking and ridiculing [Him] with his whole cohort of soldiers...[Herod] ordered Him sent back to Pilate...He informed Pilate, that he found no cause in him, but held him to be an ignorant man of no consequence whatever."[48]

---

[46] Agreda, Mary of, Venerable, The Mystical City of God, Volume III, The Transfixion. Tan Books, Charlotte, NC, 1914, Translated from the Original Authorized Spanish Edition by Fiscar Marison (Rev. George J. Blatter), Begun in 1902. Page 584.
[47] Ibid. Page 585.
[48] Ibid. Page 586.

Pilate Questions Jesus a Second Time, His Sixth Trial, and Offers the Release of One Prisoner

Mary of Agreda writes that during travel from the palace of Herod to Pilate's praetorium the maltreatment of Jesus worsened. "On account of the crush of the people and on account of the haste, they tripped him up and threw him on the ground several times. By their cruel pulling at the ropes with which he was bound, they caused the blood to flow from his veins. His hands being tied, he could not easily help himself to rise from his falls. Therefore, the multitudes of the people, who followed and who were neither able, nor cared to stop in their onward rush, stepped upon [Jesus], treading him under foot and kicking him. The blows and wounds he thus received, instead of stirring the compassion of the soldiers, only excited them to loud laughter; for…they had become devoid of all human compassion, no less than so many wild beasts."[49] Eventually, Jesus was delivered to the Governor.

Once again Pilate was confronted with Jesus in his palace, and he was again "bestormed by the Jews to condemn him to death on the cross."[50] The Governor, however, was still convinced that Jesus was innocent of the charges that Caiaphas was alleging. Pilate was beside himself. He thought that he had taken care of this Jesus problem, but Caiaphas was still insisting that Jesus be put to death. The Procurator had Jesus taken inside the praetorium where he spoke to him yet again. This time Jesus answered him, but nothing Jesus said could be deemed by Pilate as a threat to Rome or the people of Jerusalem. Despite his questioning, Pilate could find no guilt in the prisoner.

Pilate thought quickly how he might placate the Jews in different ways. He first pointed out to the crowd that even Herod found no fault with Jesus. Caiaphas was unmoved. He then offered to release to the crowd one criminal in conformance with the Jewish

---

[49] Ibid. Pages 587-588.
[50] Ibid. Page 590.

Passover custom. "The custom of giving freedom to an imprisoned criminal at this great solemnity of the Pasch was introduced by the Jews in grateful remembrance of the release of their forefathers from servitude by their passage through the Red Sea, when the Almighty freed them from the power of Pharaoh by killing the first-born children of the Egyptians and afterwards annihilating him and his armies in the waters of the Red Sea. In gratitude for this favor the Jews always sought out the greatest malefactor and pardoned him his crimes; while they refused such clemency to those who were less guilty. In their treaties with the Romans, they expressly reserved this privilege; and the governors complied with it. But in the present instance they failed to follow out in their demands what they were so loudly proclaiming in regard to Jesus."[51] Pilate, therefore, proposed to free either Barrabas, a thief, insurrectionist and murderer, or Jesus, the man so reviled by Caiaphas and the others as the most dangerous of all criminals. Surely, he thought, the Jews would, in conformance with their own religious beliefs, choose Jesus. But driven into a frenzy by Caiaphas and others in the Sanhedrin, the crowd called for the release of Barrabas. This attempt by Pilate also failed to placate the Jews' thirst for the blood of Jesus.

Pilate Sentences Jesus to Be Scourged and Released

Pilate had one more option. He agreed to "chastise [Jesus] and release him,"[52] and with a ceremonial washing of his hands, relinquished himself of all responsibility telling the Jews that they were answerable for what was about to occur. The Jews accepted the responsibility saying, "His blood be on us and on our children!"[53] "Then, according to the Gospel of John, Pilate had Jesus scourged.

[51] Ibid. Page 591.
[52] The Holy Bible - New Testament, Luke 23:16, The Great Adventure Bible, Revised Standard Version, Second Catholic Edition, Ascension Press, West Chester, PA. Page 1378.
[53] Ibid. Matthew 27:25. Page 1306.

The Procurator hoped that an intense beating would leave Jesus so battered and torn that Caiaphas might be moved to pity.

The scourging of Jesus, therefore, was intended to be far more severe than the normal scourging that might precede crucifixion, since, when the order was given, it was intended to be the sole punishment that Jesus would receive. Therefore, the normal concern about the severity of the scourging was absent in Jesus' case. His scourging was much more intense than that of one sentenced to death by crucifixion. Jewish law prevented a criminal from receiving more than thirty-nine blows during a scourging. But this was not a Jewish punishment. It was being carried out under the authority of Rome which was bound by no such restriction. And the Romans were very good at their job!

Roman scourging was meant to be as humiliating as it was punishing. Therefore, Jesus was stripped naked before being shackled to the pillar as is customary for such beatings. Jesus was scourged from his neck to his ankles and on both his back and his front most likely with a flagrum. It is not certain exactly how many times Jesus was whipped, but some estimates place the number at about one-hundred-twenty, evenly distributed from either side suggesting that the beating was administered by two soldiers standing opposite from one another and alternating lashes for maximum impact. Mary of Agreda, in her visions, noted that after the initial wounds covered his body, additional blows were administered to areas already egregiously wounded, making it impossible to count wounds accurately. She described the flogging of Jesus very vividly. "They first took off the white garment with not less ignominy than when they clothed Him therein in the house of the adulterous homicide, Herod. In loosening the ropes and chains, which He had borne since His capture in the garden, they cruelly widened the wounds which His bonds had made in His arms and wrists. "Thus, [Jesus] stood uncovered in the presence of a great multitude and the six torturers bound Him brutally to one of the columns in order to chastise Him so much the more at their ease. Then, two and two at a time, they began to scourge Him with such inhuman cruelty…The first two scourged [Jesus] with hard and thick cords, full of rough knots, and in their sacrilegious fury strained all the powers of their body to inflict the blows. This first scourging raised…great welts and livid tumors, so that the sacred blood gathered beneath the skin and disfigured His entire body. Already it began to ooze the wounds. The first two having at length desisted, the second pair continued the scourging in still greater emulation; with hardened leather thongs they leveled their strokes upon the places already sore and caused the discolored tumors to break open and shed forth sacred blood until it bespattered and drenched the garments of the…torturers, running down also in streams to the pavement. Those two gave way to the third pair of scourgers, who commenced to beat [Jesus] with extremely tough rawhides, dried hard like osier twigs. They scourged Him still more cruelly, because they were wounding, not so much His body, as cutting into the wounds already produced by the previous scourging…As the veins of [His] body had now been opened and His whole person seemed but one continued wound, the third pair found no more room for new wounds. Their ceaseless blows inhumanly tore the…flesh of [Jesus] and scattered many pieces of it about the pavement; so much so that a large portion of the shoulder-bones were exposed and showed red through the flowing blood; in other places also the bones were laid bare larger than the palm of the hand…They beat Him in the face and in the feet and hands, thus leaving unwounded not a single spot in which they could exert their fury and wrath against [Him]…The scourging in the face, and in the hands and feet, was unspeakably painful, because these parts are so full of sensitive and delicate nerves. His…countenance became so swollen and wounded that the blood and the swellings blinded him. In addition to their blows the executioners spurted upon His person their disgusting spittle and loaded Him with insulting epithets. The exact number of blows dealt out to [Jesus] from head to foot was 5,115."[54]

With the beating complete, the executioners unbound Jesus. Mary of Agreda continues, "and with imperious and blasphemous presumption commanded Him immediately to put on His garment. But while they had scourged [Him] one of his tormentors had hidden his clothes out of sight, in order to prolong the nakedness and exposure…for their derision and sport…During this protracted nakedness [Jesus] had, in addition to the wounds, suffered greatly from the cold of that morning as mentioned by the Evangelists Mark, Luke and John."[55] Some of the blood on his open wounds had begun to coagulate, "compressing the wounds, which had become inflamed and extremely painful; the cold had diminished His powers of resistance."[56]

Jesus is "Crowned" With a Cap of Thorns and Beaten

The torturers were not done having their fun with Jesus. Once He was dressed, they approached Pilate saying, "This seducer and deceiver of the people, Jesus of Nazareth, in His boasting and vanity, has sought to be recognized by all as the king of the Jews. In order that His pride may be humbled, and His presumption be confounded, we desire your permission to place upon Him the royal insignia merited by His fantastic pretensions."[57] Pilate relented to their request, and they proceeded to further mock the Nazarian. "…They took Jesus to the praetorium where with the same cruelty and contempt, they again despoiled Him of his garments and in order to

---

[54] Agreda, Mary of, Venerable, The Mystical City of God, Volume III, The Transfixion. Tan Books, Charlotte, NC, 1914, Translated from the Original Authorized Spanish Edition by Fiscar Marison (Rev. George J. Blatter), Begun in 1902. Pages 609-610.
[55] Ibid. Page 610.
[56] Ibid.
[57] Ibid.

deride Him before all the people as a counterfeit king, clothed Him in a much torn and soiled mantle of purple color. They placed also upon His head a cap made of woven thorns, to serve Him as a crown. This cap was woven of thorn branches and in such a manner that many of the hard and sharp thorns would penetrate into the skull, some of them to the ears and others to the eyes…Instead of a scepter they place into His hands a contemptible reed. They also threw over His shoulders a violet-colored mantle, something of the style of capes worn in churches; for such a garment belonged to the vestiture of a king. In this array of a mock king the perfidious Jews decked out Him."[58]

According to the Gospel of Matthew, "They stripped Him and put a scarlet robe upon Him and plaiting a crown of thorns they put it on His head and put a reed in His right hand. And kneeling before Him they mocked Him, saying, 'Hail, King of the Jews!' And they spat upon Him and took the reed and struck Him on the head."[59] The evangelist John adds that in addition to beating Him with the reed, the Roman soldiers also struck Jesus with their hands.

Pilate's Final Attempt to Release Jesus
The Seventh Trial of Jesus

The Gospel of John further states that Pilate, in an effort to spare Jesus the death penalty, stood before the assembly yet again "and said to them, "Behold, I am bringing him out to you, that you may know that I find no crime in him. So, Jesus came out wearing the crown of thorns and the purple robe. Pilate said to them, 'Here is the man!' When the chief priests and the officers saw him, they cried out, 'Crucify him, crucify him!' Pilate said to them, 'Take Him yourselves and crucify Him, for I find no crime in Him.' The Jews answered him,

---

[58] Ibid. Pages 610-611.
[59] The Holy Bible - New Testament, Matthew 27:28-31, The Great Adventure Bible, Revised Standard Version, Second Catholic Edition, Ascension Press, West Chester, PA. Pages 1306 – 1307.

"We have a law, and by that law He ought to die, because He has made himself the Son of God.' When Pilate heard these words, he was even more afraid; he entered the praetorium again and said to Jesus, 'Where are You from?' But Jesus gave no answer. Pilate therefore said to him, 'You will not speak to me? Do you not know that I have the power to release You, and power to crucify You?' Jesus answered him, 'You would have no power over me unless it had been given you from above; therefore, he who delivered me to you has the greater sin.'

Upon hearing this Pilate sought to release him, but the Jews cried out, 'If you release this man, you are not Caesar's friend; everyone who makes himself a king sets himself against Caesar. When Pilate heard these words, he brought Jesus out and sat down on the judgement seat at a place called The Pavement, and in Hebrew, Gabbatha. Now it was the day of Preparation of the Passover; it was about the sixth hour. He said to the Jews, 'Here is your King!' They cried out, 'Away with him, away with him, crucify him!' Pilate said to them, 'Shall I crucify your King?' The chief priests answered, 'We have no king but Caesar.'"[60]

There was nothing, it seemed, that Pilate could do or say that would squelch the high priest's, and the crowd's, thirst for Jesus' blood.

Pilate Sentences Jesus a Second Time
This Time the Sentence is Death

Pilate's attempt to "move, and fill with shame, the hearts of that ungrateful people" by making a spectacle of a man so illtreated, had failed. The "priests and pharisees, in their eager and insatiable hostility, were irrevocably bent upon taking away the life" of this

---

[60] Ibid. John 19:4-16. Page 1408.

innocent man, "that nothing but His death would content or satisfy them."[61]

Antonio Ciseri's famous depiction of Pontius Pilate's plea to the Jews, The work is entitled "Ecce Homo" and was painted in 1871.

In an act of final desperation, Pilate rid himself of the Jesus issue and handed Him over to be crucified in accordance with the wishes of the crowd. Beaten, hungry, thirsty and scourged until His flesh was a bloody mess, Jesus was now forced to pick up His cross.

Jesus Carries His Cross to His Crucifixion
Just after 9:00 AM on Friday, April 7, 30 AD

The ordinary number of inhabitants of the city had been increased by the gathering of many out of towners who were in

---

[61] Agreda, Mary of, Venerable, The Mystical City of God, Volume III, The Transfixion. Tan Books, Charlotte, NC, 1914, Translated from the Original Authorized Spanish Edition by F scar Marison (Rev. George J. Blatter), Begun in 1902. Pages 6612-613.

Jerusalem to celebrate Passover. Word of the Nazarian's death sentence spread quickly through the city and the streets were filled with onlookers; the curious, the depraved, those anxious for the death of this blasphemer, and those who were unable to fathom the injustice of the death sentence doled out to such a peaceful man of God. "In the sight of these multitudes they brought forth [Jesus] in his own garments and with a countenance so disfigured by wounds, blood and spittle, that no one would have again recognized Him as the one they had seen or known before."[62]

Upon seeing Jesus, some in the crowd, those who benefited from His healings and teachings, wept. Others were simply confused by what was taking place in their sight. Still others cheered with a vengeance and were almost giddy at the thought of such a dangerous and despicable human being facing the road to death.

When the murmurs, wails, and cheers of those assembled had dimmed, the death sentence was read aloud for all to hear:
"'I Pontius Pilate, presiding over lower Galilee and governing Jerusalem, in fealty to the Roman Empire, and being within the executive mansion, judge, decide, and proclaim, that I condemn to death, Jesus, of the Nazarene people and a Galilean by birth, a man seditious and opposed to our laws, to our senate, and to the great emperor Tiberius Caesar. For the execution of this sentence I decree, that his death be upon the cross and that He shall be fastened thereto with nails as is customary with criminals; because, in this very place, gathering around Him every day many men, poor and rich, He has continued to raise tumults throughout Judea, proclaiming Himself the son of god and king of Israel, at the same time threatening the ruin of this renowned city of Jerusalem and its temple, and the sacred Empire, refusing tribute to Caesar; and because He dared to enter in triumph this city of Jerusalem and the temple of Solomon, accompanied by a great multitude of the people carrying branches of palms. I command

---

[62] Ibid. Page 621.

the first centurion, called Quintus Cornelius, to lead Him for his greater shame through the said city of Jerusalem, bound as He is, and scourged by my orders. Let Him also wear His own garments, that He may be known to all, and let Him walk through all the public streets between two other thieves, who are likewise condemned to death for their robberies and murders, so that this punishment be an example to all the people and to all malefactors.

I desire also and command in this my sentence, that this malefactor, having been thus led through the public streets, be brought outside the city through the pagora gate, now called the Antonian portal, and under the proclamations of the herald, who shall mention all the crimes carried out in my sentence, He shall be conducted to the summit of the mountain called Calvary, where justice is wont to be executed upon wicked transgressors. There, fastened and crucified upon the cross which He shall carry as decreed above, His body shall remain between the aforesaid thieves. Above the cross, that is, at its top, He shall have placed for Him His name and title in the three languages; namely in Hebrew, Greek and Latin; and in all and each one of them shall be written: This is Jesus of Nazareth, King of the Jews, so that it may be understood by all and become universally known.[63]

At the same time, I command, that on one, no matter of what condition, under pain of the loss of his goods and life, and under punishment for rebellion against the Roman Empire, presume audaciously to impede the execution of this just sentence ordered by me to be executed with all rigor according to the decrees and laws of

---

[63] The sign on which the condemned man's name and crime were displayed is called the 'titulus'. It was generally carried by one of the soldiers walking ahead of the condemned man as he carried his cross and was later attached to the top of the cross for all to see. Taken from the Journal of the American Medical Association (JAMA), Edwards, William D.; Gabel, Wesley J., MDiv; Hosmer, Floyd E. MS, AMI, On the Physical Death of Jesus Christ. JAMA, March 21, 1986, Vol. 255, No. 11. Page1459.

the Romans and Hebrews. Year of the creation of the world 5233, the twenty-fifth day of March.' Pontius Pilate, Judge and Governor of lower Galilee for the Roman Empire, who signed the above with his own hand."[64]

With the official reading of the sentence completed, Jesus was given His cross. The bonds holding His hands were loosened and the cross was placed upon His tender and battered shoulders. The other ropes that bound him were left in place so that Jesus could be tugged and dragged through the streets with ease. "In order to torment Him the more they drew two loops around his throat."[65]

Jesus did not protest the cross. Rather, he willingly embraced it saying, "O cross, beloved of My soul, now prepared and ready to still My longings, come to Me, that I may be received in thy arms, and that, attached to them as on an altar, I may be accepted by the eternal Father as the sacrifice of His everlasting reconciliation with the human race. In order to die upon thee, I have descended from heaven and assumed mortal and passible flesh; for thou art to be the scepter with which I shall triumph over all My enemies, the key with which I shall open the gates of heaven for all the predestined (Isaiah 22:22), the sanctuary in which the guilty sons of Adam shall find mercy, and the treasure house for the enrichment of their poverty. Upon thee I desire to exalt and recommend dishonor and reproach among men, in order that My friends may embrace them with joy, seek them with anxious longings, and follow Me on the path which I, through thee, shall open up before them. My Father and eternal God, I confess thee as the Lord of heaven and earth (Matthew 11:25), subjecting Myself to thy power and to thy divine wishes, I take upon My shoulders the wood for the sacrifice of My innocent and passible humanity, and I

---

[64] Agreda, Mary of, Venerable, The Mystical City of God, Volume III, The Transfixion. Tan Books, Charlotte, NC, 1914, Translated from the Original Authorized Spanish Edition by Fiscar Marison (Rev. George J. Blatter), Begun in 1902. Pages 624-625.
[65] Ibid. Page 626.

accept it willingly for the salvation of men. Receive thou, eternal Father, this sacrifice as acceptable to thy justice, in order that from today on they may not any more be servants, but sons and heirs of thy kingdom together with Me"[66] (Romans 8:17).

Jesus Carries His Cross, Falls and is Aided by a Woman

Roman executioners were merciless and seemingly devoid of human compassion. They shoved Jesus along the road, beating Him with whips and hurling insults at Him with every step. Using the ropes, they dragged or jerked Him causing Him to stumble under the weight of the cross.

The Evangelist, John, tells the story this way: "So they took Jesus, and He went out, bearing His own cross, to the place of the skull, which is called in Hebrew, Golgotha." The three Synoptic Gospel writers note that along the way, a Cyrene by the name of Simon, the father of Alexander and Rufus, was made to assist Jesus by carrying his cross. He walked behind Jesus bearing the cross on his shoulders. Though early medieval art depicts Jesus carrying the entire cross, it is more probable that he carried only the patibula, as the stipe was likely already in place atop the hill called Golgotha. The weight of the entire cross would have been very difficult for most men to carry, even had they not been beaten and scourged and deprived of food, water and sleep.

In addition to the description of the crucifixion of Jesus provided in the four Gospels, Christian tradition also points out that Jesus fell three times on his way to Golgotha. The falls are described in a Christian devotion known as The Stations of the Cross.[67] Though

---

[66] Ibid. Page 626.
[67] Encyclopedia Britannica On-Line edition. Stations of the Cross, Christianity. November 7, 2023, Written and fact checked by the editors of Encyclopedia

the devotion evolved over time it is believed that Mary, the mother of Jesus, visited the scenes of the Lord's passion daily, retracing the steps of Her son as He carried His cross from the Praetorium to the point of his execution. Once Emperor Constantine legalized Christianity "in the year 312, this pathway (upon which Jesus carried His cross) was marked with its important stations. St. Jerome (342-420), living in Bethlehem during the later part of his life, attested to the crowds of pilgrims from various countries who visited those holy places and followed the Way of the Cross."[68]

The Stations of the Cross not only record the number of times that Jesus fell on His way to Golgotha, they also describe how a woman named Veronica approached Jesus as He walked along Via Dolorosa or the Sorrowful Way, as the path has come to be known, and wiped the face of Jesus, leaving behind a miraculous image of His face on the cloth.

Since the condemned man's arms were typically bound to the patibula as the victim carried the cross beam to the place of execution, each fall would have caused significant injury to the victim's knees and face as there would be no way for the falling man to brace himself. While the Gospels are not clear on the point at which Simon was forced to carry the cross for Jesus, reason would dictate that it was probably after one or more of the falls under the weight of the cross.

Britannica and most recently revised and updated by Amy Tikkanen. **Stations of the Cross**, a series of 14 pictures or carvings portraying events in the Passion of Christ from his condemnation by Pontius Pilate to his entombment. The series of stations is as follows: (1) Jesus is condemned to death, (2) he is made to bear his cross, (3) he falls the first time, (4) he meets his mother, (5) Simon of Cyrene is made to bear the cross, (6) Veronica wipes Jesus' face, (7) he falls the second time, (8) the women of Jerusalem weep over Jesus, (9) he falls the third time, (10) he is stripped of his garments, (11) he is nailed to the cross, (12) he dies on the cross, (13) he is taken down from the cross, and (14) he is placed in the sepulcher.

[68] Saunders, Fr. William, EWTN, How Did the Stations of the Cross Begin. 2023. https://www.ewtn.com/catholicism/library/how-did-the-stations-of-the-cross-begin-1155.

The Gospels, however, lack any substantial detail of Jesus carrying His cross to Calvary other than the mention of Simon being pressed into service.

The Crucifixion of Jesus

Crucifixion was such a common occurrence during the first century that it required no description by those who lived at the time of its use as a torturous instrument of death. Accordingly, the Gospel writers didn't provide any detailed account of the actual procedure.

"Christ Crucified Between the Two Thieves: The Three Crosses" by Rembrandt van Rijn, 1653

All four Gospels writers, Matthew, Mark, Luke and John, speak to the unusual way that the garments of Jesus were divided among the soldiers, and to some of the conversation that took place between

Jesus, the onlookers, and the two criminals executed with him on that first Good Friday.

And while there are significant references to the type of death that Jesus experienced throughout historical writings,[69] history, too, is relatively silent regarding the details of Christ's actual crucifixion. This is not surprising since very little historical text is preoccupied with a particular description of the life of any individual 'peasant'. History, though, is rich with specifics of the general crucifixion procedure, especially, as discussed earlier, the various methods of Roman crucifixion.

Likewise, the American Medical Association published a report which appeared in a 1986 edition of JAMA, the Journal of the American Medical Association. The report describes the specific type of death Jesus may have suffered at the hands of Roman crucifixion and provides a worthy account of the style of execution, the suffering, and the death of Jesus.

The Slow, Agonizing Death of Jesus from Crucifixion

Evidence as gleaned from archaeological and historical records indicate that the low Tau cross was the one preferred by the

---

[69] The source material relied upon for the preparation of this review "includes the writings of ancient Christian and non-Christian authors, the writings of modern authors, and the Shroud of Turin. Using the legal-historical method of scientific investigation, scholars have established the reliability and accuracy of the ancient manuscripts.... ...Contemporary Christian, Jewish, and Roman authors provide additional insight concerning the first-century Jewish and Roman legal systems and the details of scourging, and crucifixion. Seneca, Livy Plutarch, and others referred to crucifixion practices in their works. Specifically, Jesus (or his crucifixion) is mentioned by the Roman historians Cornelius Tacitus, Pliny the Younger, and Suetonius, by non-Roman historians Thallus and Phlegon, by the satirist Lucian of Samosata, by the Jewish Talmud, and by the Jewish historian Flavius Josephus." Source: The Journal of the American Medical Association (JAMA), Edwards, William D.; Gabel, Wesley J., MDiv; Hosmer, Floyd E. MS, AMI, On the Physical Death of Jesus Christ. JAMA, March 21, 1986, Vol. 255, No. 11. Pages 1455-1463.

Romans who occupied Palestine during the first century, though the Latin cross and other forms were used as well. The use of the low cross is implied in the Gospel of John, who wrote that when Jesus was near the end, he said, "I thirst". In response, the soldiers "put a sponge full of the vinegar on hyssop and held it to his mouth"[70]. The stalk of a hyssop plant is approximately twenty inches in length. Even a soldier standing six feet tall, with an additional arm-reach of two feet, and holding a twenty-inch hyssop stalk upward to the mouth of Jesus, would put the top of the cross at a height just over about nine and a half feet.

"Outside the city walls was permanently located the heavy upright wooden stipes[71]* on which the patibulum would be secured. In the case of the Tau cross, this was accomplished by means of a mortise and tenon joint, with or without reinforcement by ropes. To prolong the crucifixion process, a horizontal wooden block or plank, serving as a crude seat (sedile or sedulum) was often attached midway down the stipe. Only very rarely and probably later than the time of Christ, was an additional block (suppedaneum) employed for the transfixion of the feet."[72] Subsequently, the chances are high that the head of Jesus, once crucified, was only nine feet off the ground, with his feet crossed and nailed directly to the bottom of the patibulum.

---

[70] The Holy Bible - New Testament, John 19:28, The Great Adventure Bible, Revised Standard Version, Second Catholic Edition, Ascension Press, West Chester, PA. Page 1409.

[71]* The wooden stipes generally weighed well over three hundred pounds, and for that reason, were typically not carried by the condemned man. He, instead, was forced to carry only the crossbar or the patibulum, which weighed a more manageable seventy-five to one-hundred-twenty-five pounds.

[72] Journal of the American Medical Association (JAMA), Edwards, William D.; Gabel, Wesley J., MDiv; Hosmer, Floyd E. MS, AMI, On the Physical Death of Jesus Christ. JAMA, March 21, 1986, Vol. 255, No. 11. Page 1459.

Jesus is Nailed to the Cross
Just Before 12:00 PM on Friday, April 7, 30 AD

It was almost Noon when Jesus arrived at the summit of Calvary, exhausted, disfigured, and wasted. Owing to an eclipse, the sky began to darken. The executioners had certainly mastered the art of causing pain, and every opportunity was taken to inflict as much as possible on Jesus. It was customary for victims of crucifixion to be hung on the cross naked. This added to the shame and humility of the experience, ensuring that the suffering was as much mental as physical. Jesus was quickly stripped naked. "As the tunic was large and without opening in front, they pulled it over the head of Jesus without taking off the crown of thorns; but on account of the rudeness with which they proceeded, they inhumanely tore off the crown with the tunic. Thus, they opened anew all the wounds of His head, and in some of them remained the thorns, which, in spite of their being so hard and sharp, were wrenched off by the violence with which the executioners despoiled Him of his tunic and, with it, of the crown. With heartless cruelty, they again forced it down upon His head, opening up wounds upon wounds. By the rude tearing off of the tunic were renewed also the wounds of His whole body, since the tunic had dried into the open places and its removal was…adding new pains to His wounds…To all these sufferings was added the confusion of being bereft of His garments in the presence of his most blessed Mother, of Her pious companions, and in full sight of the multitudes gathered around."[73]

As was typical of crucifixions, in fact as was required by Roman law, Jesus was offered wine mixed with myrrh, but He refused it. By now, the patibulum was already on the ground and the

---

[73] Agreda, Mary of, Venerable, The Mystical City of God, Volume III, The Transfixion. Tan Books, Charlotte, NC, 1914, Translated from the Original Authorized Spanish Edition by Fiscar Marison (Rev. George J. Blatter), Begun in 1902. Pages 642 & 645.

executioners shoved Jesus weakened body to the ground near it and dragged Him across the ground and into position on the beam, they then stretched His arms along the patibulum, and His hands were quickly nailed to the beam. Based on archeological records, the nails used by the Romans in crucifixion were tapered iron spikes each about five to nine inches in length. They had a square shaft that measured about three eighths of an inch near the base and reduced to a dull point at the tip.

Medical evidence presented to JAMA in a report issued by Doctors William D. Edwards, Wesley J. Gabel, and Floyd E. Hosmer, described the process of Jesus' crucifixion as follows: "With arms outstretched, but not taut, the wrists were nailed to the patibulum. It has been shown that the ligaments and bones of the wrist can support the weight of a body hanging from them, but the palms cannot. Accordingly, the iron spikes probably were driven between the radius and the carpals or between the two rows of carpal bones, either proximal to or through the strong bandlike flexor retinaculum and the various intercarpal ligaments.

Although a nail in either location in the wrist might pass between the bony elements and thereby produce no fractures, the likelihood of painful periosteal injury would seem great. Furthermore, the driven nail would crush or sever the rather large sensorimotor median nerve. The stimulated nerve would produce excruciating bolts of fiery pain in both arms. Although the severed median nerve would result in paralysis of a portion of the hand, ischemic contractures and impalement of various ligaments by the iron spike might produce a clawlike grasp."[74]

Once Jesus was securely fastened to the patibulum, it, with the victim hanging from it, was hoisted onto the stipe. During the raising

---

[74] Journal of the American Medical Association (JAMA), Edwards, William D.; Gabel, Wesley J., MDiv; Hosmer, Floyd E. MS, AMI, On the Physical Death of Jesus Christ. JAMA, March 21, 1986, Vol. 255, No. 11. Page 1460.

process, the body hung freely, suspended only by the nails in the wrists. Then, when the mortice of the stipe was aligned with the tenon of the patibulum and dropped into place. Jesus' body was jolted, causing severe pain in his hands and arms.

Once the two sections of the cross were attached, Jesus' feet were quickly nailed to the stipe. Although there were many ways in which a victim's feet could be secured to the cross, the evidence suggests that both of Jesus' feet were crossed, and a single nail was used to pierce them and fasten them to the stipe. According to the JAMA report, "the feet were fixed to the front of the [stipe] by means of an iron spike driven through the first or second intermetatarsal space, just distal to the tarsometatarsal joint. It is likely that the deep peroneal nerve and branches of the medial and lateral plantar nerves would have been injured by the nails."[75] This too, would have caused Jesus to suffer excruciating pain. Though the scourging of Jesus resulted in significant blood loss, crucifixion itself was a relatively bloodless procedure according to the JAMA report.

As soon as the nailing was complete, a soldier hung the titulus, noting the condemned man's name and crime, near the top of the stipe.

Aside from the excruciating pain caused by the nails driven through the hands and feet, crucifixion caused interference with normal respiration, and in particular, with exhalation. The weight of Jesus' body, "pulling down on the outstretched arms and shoulders, would tend to fix the intercostal muscles in an inhalation state and thereby hinder passive exhalation. Accordingly, exhalation was primarily diaphragmatic, and breathing was shallow. It is likely that this form of respiration would not suffice, and that hypercarbia would soon result. The onset of muscle cramps or tetanic contractions, due to fatigue and hypercarbia, would hinder respiration even further."[76]

---

[75] Ibid. Pages 1460 – 1461.
[76] Ibid. Pages 1460-1461.

For Jesus, this meant that in order to exhale adequately, he had to lift his body by pushing up on the feet and flexing the elbows, bringing the shoulders toward the body. This maneuver, however, placed Jesus' entire body weight on the bones of the foot, producing a searing pain. Likewise, flexing the elbows caused the wrists to rotate around the nails triggering equal pain along the damaged median nerve of both of Jesus' wrists. In addition, the action of lifting the body caused a scraping of his tattered back against the rough wood of the stipe adding to the wracking pain that Jesus now experienced. Speaking from the cross was difficult and could occur only during exhalation, therefore, any speech had to be short, and it was extremely painful.

Regardless, Jesus had not yet finished his business, so through the pain he had several short conversations. The first was with one of the criminals crucified with Jesus. After being mocked by the criminal on his right, the thief to his left said, "'Do you not fear God, since you are under the same sentence of condemnation? And we indeed justly; for we are receiving the due reward of our deeds; but this man has done nothing wrong.' And he said, 'Jesus, remember me when you come in your kingly power.' And [Jesus} said to him, *'Truly, I say to you, today you will be with me in Paradise.'*" Then taking notice of his mother and his disciple John, he said to his mother, *"'Woman, behold, your son!'* Then he said to his disciple, *'Behold your mother!'"*

The Death of Jesus
3:00 PM, Friday, April 7, 30 AD

Death from crucifixion could come in any number of ways; "dehydration, stress-induced arrhythmias, and congestive heart failure with the rapid accumulation of pericardial and perhaps pleural effusions." The most prominent causes of death from crucifixion, however, were "hypovolemic shock and exhaustion asphyxia".[77] If the executioners wanted to hasten death, they would break the legs of the victim below the knees, a process known as crucifracture. This made it impossible for a victim to raise and lower himself on the cross bringing about asphyxic death within minutes. Without such intervention, it was possible for a victim to hang on the cross for many hours and even days.

The Gospels make it clear, however, that Jesus died relatively quickly. The moment of death was the ninth hour, 3:00 in the afternoon of Friday, April 7, 30 AD and the executioners recognized the exact moment that Jesus took his last breath. The evangelist Mark writes, "And at the ninth hour Jesus cried with a loud voice, *'Elo-i, Elo-i, Lama sabach-thani?'* Which means, 'My God, my God, why have you forsaken me?'"[78] Evangelist Luke adds these final words of Jesus, *'Father, into your hands I commit my spirit.'*"[79]

To prevent the bodies from hanging on the cross during the Sabbath, which would begin in just a few hours at 6:00 PM that evening, the Jews asked Pilate to break the legs of the victims to hasten death and take the bodies away. Pilate gave the order, and the executioners began the process, "but when they came to Jesus, and saw that he was already dead, they did not break his legs. But one of the soldiers, Longinus by name, pierced his side with a spear, and at once there came out blood and water."[80] The JAMA report notes that the blood was most likely from a "perforation of the distended and thin-walled right atrium or ventricle," meaning that the lance probably pierced Jesus on the right side. The water from the wound likely "represented serous pleural and pericardial fluid and would have

---

[77] Ibid. Page 1461.
[78] The Holy Bible - New Testament, Mark 15:33-37, The Great Adventure Bible, Revised Standard Version, Second Catholic Edition, Ascension Press, West Chester, PA. Page 1331. Also, Matthew 27:46. Page 1307.
[79] Ibid. Luke 23:46. Page 1379.
[80] Ibid. John 19:33-34. Page 1409.

preceded the flow of blood and been smaller in volume than the blood."[81]

The Cause of Jesus' Death

There is little question that the two men crucified along with Jesus died of asphyxia after their legs were broken by the executioners. That Jesus died after hanging on the cross for only three hours, and without having his legs broken, surprised everyone, however, even the Procurator, Pontius Pilate.

It is still unclear what killed Jesus, but Doctors Edwards, Gabel and Hosmer propose a few possibilities. "The fact that Jesus cried out in a loud voice and then bowed his head and died, suggests the possibility of a catastrophic terminal event. One popular explanation has been that Jesus died of cardiac rupture. In the setting of the scourging and crucifixions with associated hypovolemia, hypoxemia, and perhaps an altered coagulable state, friable non-infective thrombotic vegetations could have formed on the aortic or mitral valve. These then could have dislodged and embolized into the coronary circulation and thereby produced an acute transmural myocardial infarction. Thrombotic valvular vegetations have been reported to develop under analogous acute traumatic conditions. Rupture of the left ventricular free wall may occur, though uncommonly, in the first few hours following infarction.

However, another explanation may be more likely. Jesus' death may have been hastened simply by his state of exhaustion and by the severity of the scourging, with its resultant blood loss and pre-shock state. The fact that he could not carry his patibulum supports this interpretation.

The actual cause of Jesus' death, like that of other crucified victims, may have been multifactorial and related primarily to

---

[81] The Journal of the American Medical Association (JAMA), Edwards, William D.; Gabel, Wesley J., MDiv; Hosmer, Floyd E. MS, AMI, On the Physical Death of Jesus Christ. JAMA, March 21, 1986, Vol. 255, No. 11. Pages 1462 – 1463.

hypovolemic shock, exhaustion asphyxia, and perhaps acute heart failure. A fatal cardiac arrhythmia may have accounted for the apparent catastrophic terminal event."[82]

The important thing is not necessarily what caused the death of Jesus, but rather that he did, in fact, die. "Clearly the weight of historical and medical evidence indicates that Jesus was dead before the wound to his side was inflicted and supports the traditional view that the spear of the soldier Longinus, thrust between his right ribs, probably perforated not only the right lung but also the pericardium and heart and thereby ensured his death."[83]

The Burial of Jesus
Between 3:30 and 6:10 PM on Friday, April 7, 30 AD

After the death of Jesus, but while his body was still on the cross, a sudarium (a Latin word for a 'sweat cloth' used to wipe a face clean) was used to cover his face. First century Jewish law forbade the movement of a dead body without first covering it. If the person's face was damaged in any manner, the law required that it, too, should be covered with a cloth so that people do not have to see it. For this reason, a sudarium was used to cover the postmortem face of Jesus as He hung on the cross.[84] The covering of the rest of the body could not be accomplished until it was removed from the cross.

Though lacking detail on the removal of His body from the cross, the Gospel writers are in general agreement as to how the burial of Jesus came about. A rich member of the Sanhedrin, Joseph of Arimathea was a secret disciple of Jesus and requested that Pilate release Jesus' body to him for burial. Pilate agreed "And Joseph took the body, and wrapped it in a clean linen shroud, and laid it in his own new tomb, which he had hewn in the rock; and he rolled a great stone

---

[82] Ibid. Page 1463.
[83] Ibid.
[84] YouTube video, The Significance of the Folded Napkin, Fairview Church of Christ, May 30, 2023. https://www.youtube.com/watch?v=dNy65pKZS34.

on the door of the tomb and departed. Mary Magdalene and the other Mary were there, sitting opposite the tomb."[85]

Mark's Gospel notes that it was Joseph who removed the body of Jesus from the cross, "wrapped him in the linen shroud, and laid him in a tomb which had been hewn out of rock."[86] Mark also confirms that "the other Mary" referred to by Matthew, Luke and John, was Mary, the mother of Joses who was with Mary Magdalene at the tomb. Luke adds that the two women "saw the tomb and how his body was laid; then they returned, and prepared spices and ointments. On the sabbath they rested according to the commandment."[87]

Rembrandt's 1650-1652 Rendition of "The Descent from the Cross".

The writings of the evangelist John, the disciple whom Jesus loved, and who was an eyewitness to all the events of the crucifixion,

---

[85] The Holy Bible - New Testament, Matthew 27:57-61, The Great Adventure Bible, Revised Standard Version, Second Catholic Edition, Ascension Press, West Chester, PA. Pages 1307 - 1308.
[86] Ibid. Mark 15:46. Page 1331.
[87] Ibid. Luke 23:55-56. Page 1379.

complements the other Gospel writers and adds that along with Joseph of Arimathea, "Nicodemus also, who had at first come to [Jesus] by night, came bringing a mixture of myrrh and aloes, about a hundred pounds' weight. They took the body of Jesus, and bound it in linen cloths with the spices, as is the burial custom of the Jews. Now in the place where he was crucified there was a garden, and in the garden a new tomb where no one had ever been laid. So, because of the Jewish day of Preparation, as the tomb was close at hand, they laid Jesus there."[88]

In 1603 – 1604, Caravaggio painted "The Entombment of Christ" for one of the chapels (the second chapel on the right) in Santa Maria in Vallicella (the Chiesa Nuova), a church built for the Oratory of Saint Philip Neri.

---

[88] Ibid. John 19:39-42. Page 1409.

The Resurrection of Jesus and the Empty Tomb
From Sometime on Saturday April 8, 30 AD
To the Early Morning Hours of Sunday April 9, 30 AD

The high priest was concerned. He knew, once the body of Jesus had been released to the family, that his followers might try to steal the body and proclaim Jesus risen from the dead, something Jesus had spoken about during his ministry. "The next day, the chief priests and the Pharisees gathered before Pilate and said, 'Sir, we remember how that imposter said, while he was still alive, 'After three days I will rise again.' Therefore, order the tomb to be made secure until the third day, lest his disciples go and steal him away, and tell the people, 'He has risen from the dead, and the last fraud will be worse than the first.' Pilate said to them, 'You have a guard of soldiers; go, make it as secure as you can.' So, they went and made the tomb secure by sealing the stone and setting a guard."[89]

In the early morning hours of the third day, that is, on Sunday, April 9, 30 AD, according to the evangelist Matthew, "Mary Magdalene and the other Mary (identified as Mary, the mother of James, in the Gospel of Mark, who also adds that Solome was there, too) went to see the tomb. And behold, there was a great earthquake; for an angel of the Lord descended from heaven and came and rolled back the stone and sat upon it. His appearance was like lightning, and his clothing white as snow. And for fear of him the guards trembled and became like dead men. But the angel said to the woman, 'Do not be afraid; for I know that you seek Jesus who was crucified. He is not here; for he has risen, as he said. Come, see the place where he lay. Then go quickly and tell his disciples that he has risen from the dead, and behold, he is going before you to Galilee; there you will see him. Behold, I have told you.' So, they departed quickly from the tomb with fear and great joy and ran to tell his disciples. And behold, Jesus

---

[89] Ibid. Matthew 27:62-66. Page 1308.

met them and said, 'Hail!' And they came up and took hold of his feet and worshiped him. Then Jesus said to them, 'Do not be afraid; go and tell my brethren to go to Galilee, and there they will see me.'"[90]

The Gospel of Mark differs slightly in the details as it states, that upon the arrival of the three women, the stone was already rolled back. Mark writes, "And entering the tomb, they saw a young man

"The Resurrection of Christ, The Easter Tomb or The Triumph of Christ over Death and Sin" is a painting by Peter Paul Rubens, executed c. 1616.

sitting on the right side, dressed in a white robe; and they were amazed. And he said to them, 'Do not be amazed; you seek Jesus of Nazareth, who was crucified. He is not here; see the place where they laid him. But go, tell his disciples and Peter that he is going before

---

[90] Ibid. Matthew 28:1-10. Page 1308.

you to Galilee; there you will see him, as he told you. And they went out and fled from the tomb: for trembling and astonishment had come upon them; and they said nothing to anyone, for they were afraid."[91]

The Evangelist Luke more closely conforms to the account written by Mark but notes that there were two angels inside the tomb. "…And they found the stone rolled away from the tomb, but when they went in, they did not find the body. While they were perplexed about this, behold, two men stood by them in dazzling apparel; and as they were frightened and bowed their faces to the ground, the men said to them, 'Why do you seek the living among the dead? He is not here but has risen. Remember how he told you, while he was still in Galilee, that the Son of man must be delivered into the hands of sinful men, and be crucified, and on the third day rise. And they remembered his words, and returning from the tomb they told all this to the Eleven and to all the rest. Now it was Mary Magdalene and Jo-anna and Mary the mother of James and the other women with them who told this to the apostles; but these words seemed to them an idle tale, and they did not believe them. But Peter rose and ran to the tomb; stooping and looking in, he saw the linen cloths by themselves; and he went home wondering at what had happened."[92]

Finally, the Gospel of John, the only Gospel account written by an eyewitness to the suffering, death and aftermath of the events that took place between Jesus' arrest and resurrection, provides this detail. "Now on the first day of the week, Mary Magdalene came to the tomb early, while it was still dark, and saw that the stone had been taken away from the tomb. So she ran, and went to Simon Peter and the other disciple, [John] the one whom Jesus Loved, and said to them, 'They have taken the lord out of the tomb, and we do not know where they have laid him.' Peter then came out with the other disciple, and they went toward the tomb. They both ran, but the other disciple

---

[91] Ibid. Mark 16:4-8. Page 1332
[92] Ibid. Luke 24: 2-12. Page 1373.

outran Peter and reached the tomb first; and stooping to look in, he saw the linen cloths lying there, but he did not go in. Then Simon Peter came, following him, and went into the tomb; he saw the linen cloths lying, and the napkin, which had been on his head, not lying with the linen cloths but rolled up in a place by itself. Then the other disciple, who reached the tomb first, also went in and he saw and believed; for as yet, they did not know the scripture, that he must rise from the dead. Then the disciples went back to their homes.

CHAPTER II

MATERIAL EVIDENCE OF THE PASSION, DEATH, AND RESURRECTION

The previous chapter references three cloths. The first is a veil that a woman traditionally called "Veronica" used to wipe the face of Jesus as he carried His cross along the road to Cavalry. This cloth, according to Christian tradition, bears a miraculous image of Jesus as He appeared during His passion. The other two cloths are the burial cloths of Jesus found in His otherwise empty tomb by the disciples Peter and John, the three women, and perhaps others.

As noted, the shroud in which Jesus was wrapped, and the "napkin" which had been laid on His head, were the only items remaining in the tomb upon the arrival of the woman, and subsequently by the two apostles, in the early morning hours of Sunday, April 9, 30 AD, the day of the Resurrection. It was the first thing that the evangelist John noticed when he entered the tomb and it was of such vital significance to him that he felt compelled to include some seemingly irrelevant details about it in his Gospel. Something about the first sight of the smaller cloth was so provocative that immediately upon seeing it, John believed. What was it that John saw that brought sudden clarity and understanding to him about the absence of Jesus' body from the tomb?

There are only three possible explanations for the missing body of Jesus. The first is that his body was stolen. That was a legitimate fear of the high priest when he approached Pontius Pilate and asked for the placement of Roman guards at the entrance of the tomb for three days. The fear that Caiaphas relayed to Pilate stemmed from Jesus' own proclamation that he would rise from the dead after three days. Whether Pilate was convinced of the legitimacy of the concern or simply placating the high priest is unknown. Either way, the request was granted and at least two guards, most probably more were placed at the entrance of the tomb. Stealing the body of Jesus, therefore, would have required a conspiracy of believers, who wanted to give the impression of a resurrection, and Roman soldiers, who would have faced execution for their role in the plot.

The second possibility to explain the missing body is that the guards simply slept while believers entered the tomb and stole the body. This explanation, however, offers only a remote possibility as it would be virtually impossible, even if the soldiers slept from exhaustion, that they would not have been awakened by the sound of several men rolling away the heavy stone that sealed the tomb and then carrying the body right past them as they fled.

In fact, the Gospel of Matthew recounts, "While they [the disciples] were going, some of the guard went into the city and told the chief priest everything that had happened. After the priests had assembled with the elders, they devised a plan to give a large sum of money to the soldiers, telling them, 'You must say, 'His disciples came by night and stole him away while we were asleep.' If this comes to the governor's ears, we will satisfy him and keep you out of trouble.' So they took the money and did as they were directed. And this story is still told among the Jews to this day."[93]

The venerable Bishop Fulton Sheen noted, "The bribery of the guard was really a stupid way to escape the fact of the Resurrection. First of all, there was the problem of what would be done with His body after the disciples had possession of it. All that the enemies of the Lord would have had to do to disprove the Resurrection would be to produce the body. Quite apart from the fact that it was very unlikely that a whole guard of Roman soldiers slept while they were on duty, it was absurd for them to say that what had happened, happened when they were asleep; and yet they were so awake as to have seen thieves and to know that they were disciples. If all of the soldiers were asleep, they could never have discovered the thieves; if a few of them were awake, they should have prevented the theft. It is equally improbable that a few timid disciples should attempt to steal their master's body from a grave closed by stone, officially sealed, and guarded by soldiers without awakening the sleeping guards. The orderly arrangement of the burial cloths afforded further proof that the body was not removed by his disciples.

The secret removal of the body would have been to no purpose so far as the disciples were concerned, nor had any of them even thought of it; for the moment, the life of their master was a failure and a defeat. The crime was certainly greater in the bribers than in the bribed; for, the council was educated and religious; the soldiers were untutored and simple. The Resurrection of Christ was officially proclaimed to the civil authorities; the Sanhedrin believed in the Resurrection before the Apostles. It had bought the kiss of Judas; now it hoped it could buy the silence of the guards."[94]

---

[93] The Holy Bible – New Testament, The Word on Fire Bible, The Gospels. New Revised Standard Version. Matthew 28:11-15. Brandon Vogt, General Editor. Word on Fire, Park Ridge, IL. 2020. Pages 166 & 168.

[94] Ibid. Pages 167 – 168.

The Reverand Christopher M. Mahar, Pastor of The Church of Saint Augustine in Providence, RI, former Vatican official, and author of the best-selling book, *Finding God in Suffering*, noted that the tale fabricated and circulated by the Sanhedrin may be "the earliest known example of fake news".

The third and final explanation is that Jesus actually rose from the dead and those who guarded the tomb were powerless to prevent it.

These same possibilities had to have quickly passed through the minds of the disciples and the women who discovered the empty tomb. Somehow, the disciple John, after seeing the linens, was convinced that option three, the resurrection of Jesus, was in fact the reason for the empty tomb.

There were two "cloths" noticed by John as he entered the tomb. It is likely that the larger cloth referenced by the evangelist, the one in which the body of Jesus was wrapped, is the burial cloth which today is commonly referred to as the Shroud of Turin. There is a second cloth, however, and it was not with the burial cloth, but instead lying rolled up in a separate place by itself. This is the cloth that was used to cover the face of Jesus while He was still attached to the cross. This cloth is referred to by John as a "napkin," but today is known as the Sudarium of Oviedo. For John to believe that Jesus had risen from the dead, he would also need to believe that Jesus rolled the Sudarium and separated it from the shroud. But why would Jesus take the time to do such an insignificant thing at the moment of His resurrection?

The answer may lie in first century Jewish custom. According to Fr. Chrystian Shankar, a Brazilian priest serving at the diocesan shrine dedicated to Friar Galvão in Divinopolis, "The rolling up and placement of this cloth ties up to a Jewish custom at the time. After a servant had prepared the dining table for his master, he would stand to the side, out of sight of the master, but very attentive to his master as he eats. He wouldn't dare to return to the table until his master had finished his meal. When the master finished his meal, he would rise, clean his mouth [and] fingers, and leave the 'napkin' crumpled on the table. The wrinkled, discarded napkin means 'I have finished.' If, for whatever reason, the master left the table with the intention of coming back to the table, then he would crease the napkin into folds and leave it beside the dishes. This was a message for the servants not to touch anything on the table, given that the master had indicated, 'I am returning.'

This could be the reason for John's attention to the detail of our Lord's face cloth. Jesus promised to His disciples that the Son of Man would return. That Easter Sunday morning, He fulfilled His promise, with the very symbolic sign of leaving His face cloth neatly and carefully rolled to the side, thereby assuring that He did not leave for good and will 'come back' again. Jesus was very clear to His disciples before he left... 'Do not let your hearts be troubled or afraid. You heard me tell you, 'I am going away, and I will come back to you.'"[95] (John 14:27-28)

There are those who believe, however, that because a napkin-folding custom is not preserved in historical writings, that it may have been a fabrication and not a real first century Jewish custom. Despite that assertion, there were many ancient customs that were not written but rather, passed down orally. Some were simply considered too insignificant to write about. This would not be unusual, specifically at a time when few people could read or write and writing implements were not easily found among the peasantries. It is also possible that it was a custom specific to a particular region and not exceptionally widespread. A lack of written documentation, especially from an era where few things were written and oral tradition was relied upon heavily, should not signify a lack of truth.

For those who require it, however, there is another explanation that was offered in a homily by a cleric of the early Church. "St. John

---

[95] Catholic Bellator, YouTube video, Why Did Jesus Fold the Cloth That Covered His Face in the Tomb? https://www.youtube.com/watch?v=L7San7bOSD0.

Chrysostom (c. 347 – 14 September 407) was an important early [Catholic] church father who served as archbishop of Constantinople. He is known for his preaching and public speaking, [and] his denunciation of abuse of authority by both ecclesiastical and political leaders."[96] Chrysostom notes,

"If any persons had removed the body of Jesus, would they have stripped it before doing so? Or if anyone had stolen it, would they have taken the trouble to remove the cloth, and roll it up, and lay it in a place by itself? They would have taken the body as it was. On this account John tells us, by anticipation, that the body of Jesus was buried with much myrrh, which glues linen to the body even more firmly than lead. So when you hear that the linen wrappings lay apart, you may not endure those who say that the body of Jesus was stolen. For a thief would not have been so foolish as to spend so much trouble on a superfluous matter. Why should he undo the cloths? And how could he have escaped detection if he had done so? He would probably have spent much time in so doing and be found out by delaying and loitering. But why do the cloths lie apart, while the cloth was folded together by itself? That you may learn that it was not the action of men in confusion or haste, the placing some on one place, some in another, and then wrapping them together. From this the disciples believed in the Resurrection. On this account Christ afterwards appeared to them, when they were convinced by what they had seen."[97]

The empty tomb signifies to Christians the world over that Jesus had in fact risen from the dead. That reality is supported by over five hundred eyewitnesses who saw Him, spoke to Him, touched Him, and ate with Him, after he had already died and been buried. These witnesses included his eleven Apostles, His Mother, some of His close

---

[96] Wikipedia, John Chrysostom, https://en.wikipedia.org/wiki/John_Chrysostom. Page 1.
[97] The Word on Fire Bible, The Gospels. New Revised Standard Version. John 20:1-10. Brandon Vogt, General Editor. Word on Fire, Park Ridge, IL. 2020. Page 575.

disciples, and hundreds of ordinary converts all of whom saw Jesus, and many of whom witnessed His ascension into heaven.

All three of the cloths described here share fascinating similarities, and all three testify to the fact that Jesus suffered, was crucified, died, and was buried in the manner described by the authors of the four Gospels. These three cloths also give testimony to the resurrection of Jesus in a most extraordinary way. Two of them bear the image of the man that they touched and the third holds enough evidence to be inexplicably connected to the other two. In the subsequent chapters, each of the cloths, in the chronological order of appearance in the tradition of Christianity, will be the subject of greater evaluation.

CHAPTER III

THE VEIL OF VERONICA

The first cloth encountered in the Passion of Jesus comes, not from the Gospel accounts, but rather from Christian tradition. It derives from a popular devotion of Jesus' walk on the path from Pontius Pilate's Praetorium to the hill of Golgotha upon which He was crucified and subsequently carried to the tomb of Joseph of Arimathea where He was buried. Ancient Christian tradition holds that the devotion known as The Stations of the Cross was popularized by Jesus' Mother Mary who is said to have retraced the steps of her Son on a regular basis in commemoration of His suffering.

Fr. William Saunders, the 1994 President of Notre Dame Institute and associate pastor of Queen of Apostles Parish in Alexandria, VA, wrote that when Christianity was legalized in the early fourth century by the Roman Emperor Constantine, the pathway upon which Jesus walked during His Passion was marked with some of the more important points of interest. It was an English pilgrim by the name of William Wey who coined the term "stations" in reference to the important points along the path. "Prior to this time, the path usually followed the reverse course of ours today – moving from Mount Calvary to Pilate's house. At this time, the reverse – going from Pilate's house to Calvary – seems to have taken hold."[98] While the actual "stations" have changed over the years, twelve of the current fourteen stations were popularized in a book written in the sixteenth century by Adrichomius. A bit later, devotional books began to appear which contained the fourteen stations currently displayed in churches around the world and included a prayer for each one.

It is the sixth of the fourteen stations where a woman who has come to be known as Veronica, was moved with pity at the site of Jesus carrying His cross to the place of the skull. She gave Him her veil to wipe his brow. Jesus accepted the veil, held it to His face and returned it to the woman, leaving behind a veil on which the face of Christ appears. While the four Gospels make no mention of this woman, there is reference to a woman similarly named Beronike in the apocryphal Gospel of Nicodemus. The name Veronica is itself a Latinization of this ancient Macedonian name. The story was later elaborated in the eleventh century by adding that Christ gave her a portrait of himself on a cloth, with which she later cured the Roman Emperor Tiberius."[99] It was not until circa 1380 that a popular book titled, *Meditations on the Life of Christ*, that the two stories were connected.

In 1884, a Carmelite nun and a visionary in Tours, France, by the name of Marie of St. Peter, had a vision in which she reported seeing "Veronica wiping away the spit and mud from the face of Jesus

---

[98] Saunders, William Fr., How did the Stations of the Cross Begin? Arlington Catholic Herald, March 10, 1994. Page 1.
https://www.ewtn.com/catholicism/library/how-did-the-stations-of-the-cross-begin-1155.

[99] Wilson, Ian, Holy Faces, Secret Places. Doubleday, Garden City, Page 175.
https://archive.org/details/isbn-9780385261050/page/175.

with her veil on the way to Calvary."[100] Marie reported that Jesus instructed her to start a devotion to His Holy Face in reparation for sacrilege and blasphemy. Her apparitions were approved by Pope Leo XIII the following year.

This scene of the sixth station, Veronica Wipes the Face of Jesus, is at the National Shrine of Divine Mercy in Stockbridge, MA. The magnificent bronze statues in all fourteen stations were the work of renowned master sculptor Timothy Schmalz. The work was formally dedicated at the Shrine on Friday September 14, 2012. (photographed by the author.)

Mary Jane Zuzolo, author of the book, *Unveiling the Sixth Station of the Cross: Reparation to the Holy Face, Mother of All Devotions*, notes that the devotion to the Holy Face "is prefigured in the book of Job, compliments Fatima and other Marian apparitions, encompasses the spirituality of St Therese, crowns the insights of the

---

[100] Ibid. Wikipedia, Saint Veronica. Page 2.
https://en.wikipedia.org/wiki/Saint_Veronica.

great Carmelite mystics, affirms the Mariology of St. Louis de Montfort, and has generated more miracles than the Sanctuary of Our Lady of Lourdes. Words of Christ from approved private revelations describe the Holy Face Devotion as 'the most beautiful work under the sun' and 'the greatest source of grace second to the sacraments.'"[101]

A Brief Study of the Woman Called Veronica

As mentioned previously, the four Gospels make no reference to a woman named Veronica or to her pious actions along the road to cavalry, popularly known as the Via Dolorosa. In fact, there is no allusion to this incident anywhere in Scripture. This should not be considered unusual as there were hundreds of people lining the road as Jesus passed. There was a great deal of confusion; soldiers trying to rush the condemned to the site of their crucifixion, other soldiers trying to control the crowd, many onlookers yelling insults, spitting and perhaps even throwing objects at the condemned men as they passed. Some tried to reach in and grab them while sympathizers and family members tried to help them. This type of chaos was typical of first century Roman crucifixions. With so much happening it is possible that few noticed a woman stepping forward toward Jesus for a few seconds. It is also likely that, even if noticed, few would have regarded her actions as worthy of annotation at the time. It was, after all, a relatively insignificant gesture, made toward an ostensibly unimportant man, during a very tumultuous moment in time. It is not surprising then, that sacred tradition, and not the Gospels, recall an incident where a first century woman from Jerusalem approached Jesus as he was being led to his crucifixion, and wiped His face with her veil. The actions are described in the devotion of the Way of the Cross, commonly referred to as the Stations of the Cross.

---

[101] Zuzolo, Mary Jane, Unveiling the Sixth Station of the Cross: Reparation to the Holy Face, Mother of All Devotions. Sophia Institute Press, Manchester, New Hampshire, 2024.

Even the name of the woman who wiped the face of the condemned man has been the subject of controversy. As noted earlier, the name "Veronica is the Latinization of an ancient Macedonian name,"[102] as some references have been made to the name Berenike. Others explain the name as the derivative of the Latin word, 'vera,' meaning 'truth', and the Greek word 'eikon' meaning 'image'. Still other academics suggest that the veil bearing the image of Christ was known as the 'vera icon' in Latin and that an adaptation of these words was used to develop the name, Veronica. Regardless of its origin, this name was later given to the unidentified woman who wiped the face of Jesus, the action that produced the image on the veil.

In addition, tradition holds that a small chapel on the Via Dolorosa in Jerusalem, known as the Chapel of the Holy Face, is the former home of Veronica and the place where she approached Jesus as He walked to his crucifixion.

As a question of history, it matters little what the woman who used her veil to wipe the bloody face of Jesus is called. The only issue of significance is the veil itself, and even that has been the subject of significant controversy.

The Veil of Veronica: Multiple Accounts and Images

The provenance of the Veil said to belong to Veronica is shrouded in as much historical mystery as the woman herself, and that makes it difficult to determine the authenticity of the various cloths thought to be the one used by Veronica to wipe the face of Jesus. While the cloth can be traced initially, it becomes lost to history for a time. Consequently, when it re-emerges, historians are left to rely on legend to determine authenticity. Therefore, there is no agreement among historians as to which of the various "cloths" is the original. What follows are three of the more popular accounts used to expound on the veil's authenticity.

---

[102] Ibid.

The first official "Church" mention of the image is when the cloth appeared in Rome under rather mysterious circumstances during the Papacy of John VII (705-707).

The next reference to the veil does not appear until the early eleventh century when it was said that "Christ gave [Veronica] a portrait of Himself on a cloth, with which she later cured the Roman Emperor Tiberius."[103]

In the year 1208, "Pope Innocent III established a special procession on the Sunday following the Octave of Epiphany which started at St. Peter's and arrived at the nearby Church of the Holy Spirit (Santo Spirito in Sassia) and its adjoining hospital."[104] A procession followed the image of the Holy Face and the pilgrims joined in song and canticles. They recited psalms and carried lit candles providing the patients with an extraordinary opportunity for faith in their recovery. It was also an opportunity to solicit funds needed for the operation of the hospital, which was then rebuilt and expanded in accordance with the wishes of Innocent III, who was later described as "the founder of the cult of Veronica"[105].

The success of the pilgrimage, both as an expression of faith and as a fundraiser, "led Pope Boniface VIII to proclaim the first Jubilee in 1300. On this occasion, the veil of Veronica was publicly displayed and became one of the 'wonders of the city' for the pilgrims who visited Rome." There are several descriptions of the cloth from that time, and each identifies the veil similarly. The material of the veil, they say, is "so fine that a breeze can pass through – with an image stamped on both its sides of a still living person with eyes wide

---

[103] Ibid.
[104] Bini, Antonio, The Holy Face: From Manoppello to the World. Supplemento a "IL Volto Santo di Manoppello" Anno CI – n. 1, 2016. Page 9
[105] Ibid. Page 11

open, a face full of suffering and with evident blood spots."[106] Dante Alighieri, the author of the narrative poem *Divine Comedy*, wrote about the veil in verses 103-111 of his Italian classic. Dante began work on that poem in 1308 and completed it just prior to his death in 1321.

In the year 1350, the hospital published a manuscript titled, *Liber Regulae Sancti Spiritus in Saxia,* which contained the rules of the hospital. That manuscript also included "an interesting pictorial description of what was then the religious life and practical assistance to the sick and needy. At the bottom of the first page of the Liber is one of the oldest illustrations of the Veronica, which shows Pope Innocent III with the Veronica in his right hand and the Rule granted to the brothers in the hospital in his left."[107]*

The first formal link between the Passion and the image on the veil was made in a French version of the Bible translated by Roger d'Argenteuil in the thirteenth century. In circa 1380, an internationally popular book titled, *Meditations on the Life of Christ,* caused the story of the veil to gain in popularity throughout Europe, and it is believed

---

[106] Gaspari, Antonio, Has Veronica's Veil Been Found?, Urbi et orbi Communications, November 1999. CatholicCulture.org, Inside the Vatican, Martin de Porres lay Domincan Community, KY. Trinity Communications, 2024. Page 2. https://www.catholicculture.org/culture/library/view.cfm?recnum=2856

[107] Bini, Antonio, The Holy Face: From Manoppello to the World. Supplemento a "IL Volto Santo di Manoppello" Anno CI – n. 1, 2016. Pages 10-11.

*For centuries, the historical value of this depiction was lost to the world. That changed on the eve of the Great Jubilee of 2000 when the manuscript resurfaced and Pope John Paul II "gave an extraordinary thrust to recovering two thousand years of history, starting again from the centrality of the historical figure of Christ. The Liber was in fact displayed in the important exhibition 'Rome & Jubilees: the medieval pilgrimage to Saint Peter's,' held at the Palazzo Venezia, Rome, from October 29, 1999 to February 26, 2000." Here, the document was on full display during the final exhibition of the Jubilee which was entitled, *The Face of Christ*, held at the Palazzo delle Esposizioni in Rome from December 9, 2000 to April 16, 2001.

that what is currently known as the sixth station, *Veronica wiping the face of Jesus*, was then added to the Stations of the Cross.

This version of the Sixth Station is from the Shrine and Grotto of Our Lady of Lourdes in Litchfield, CT. The figures are made of painted steel and were sculpted by an unidentified artist. (photographed by the author.)

Following the death of Innocent III, many of his successors continued to support the operation of the hospital, especially Eugene IV and Sixtus IV under whom the facility was refurbished and expanded.

Vatican support of the hospital continued unabated until 1527, when during the sack of Rome, the Church of Santo Spirito was destroyed and all the sick who were being treated in the adjacent hospital were killed. At the same time, the veil of Veronica disappeared.

Multiple Veils Venerated: The Vatican Veronica

One popular opinion is that the piece of fabric thought to be the Veil of Veronica is Preserved in St. Peter's Basilica in Rome where it is kept under lock and key. "It is shown from the balcony above the statue of Saint Veronica once a year on the fifth Sunday of Lent. It is otherwise kept in a chapel in a vault [built] inside a pillar."[108] The Vatican claims that the cloth, other than on the fifth Sunday of Lent each year, has been secured in that vault since it left the Church of the Santo Spirito in 1527. The cloth held at the Vatican does depict an image of a face of a person with shoulder-length hair and a beard.

The framed Veil, claimed by the Vatican to be the authentic Veil of Veronica, is kept in a vault built into a column of a chapel at the Vatican in Rome, Italy. While the photo appears as a silhouette, a face can be seen when the image is held at a certain angle and under certain lighting.

---

[108] EWTN News Nightly, Veils of Veronica: Cloth Shows the Face of Jesus. YouTube Video, May 1, 2020.

The Holy Face on the Veil of Manoppollo

There is speculation that during the sack of Rome in 1527, the veil containing the image was brought to the remote Italian village of Manoppello to protect it from the carnage. Professor Heinrich Pfeiffer disagrees with that assessment, though he doesn't disagree that the Manoppollo Veil is authentic.

Pfeiffer believes "that the veil was stolen from the Vatican in the years following the Holy Year of 1600 when St. Peter's was in the chaotic phase of being rebuilt, and he notes that the veil appeared in Manoppello at that time."[109] Cardinal Fiorenzo Angelini, who served as cardinal deacon of Santo Spirito for almost twenty-five years, and in 1997 founded the International Institute for Research on the Face of Christ, agrees with Pfeiffer's "thesis regarding the identification of the mysterious image of Manoppello."[110]

In 1608, during the papacy of Paul V, the chapel in which the veil of Veronica was kept was destroyed. Pfeiffer believes that the veil may have been stolen during that time. As partial evidence in support of his thesis, Pfeiffer notes that during the restoration of St. Peter's in 1606, Pope Paul V prohibited copies of Veronica's veil from being made. Pfeiffer claims that this canon of St. Peter's Basilica suggests that the precious relic was no longer in the possession of the Vatican. "In fact, all the copies made after this period showed the image of Christ with his eyes closed, though earlier images show Christ with his eyes open."[111] Pope Urban VIII, who served as Bishop of Rome from 1623 to 1644, went a step further. In addition to prohibiting additional copies of Veronica's veil from being made, he "also

---

[109] Bini, Antonio, The Holy Face: From Manoppello to the World. Supplemento a "IL Volto Santo di Manoppello" Anno CI – n. 1, 2016. Pages 10-11.
[110] Bini, Antonio, The Holy Face: From Manoppello to the World. Supplemento a "IL Volto Santo di Manoppello" Anno CI – n. 1, 2016. Page 14.
[111] Gaspari, Antonio, Has Veronica's Veil Been Found?, Urbi et orbi Communications, November 1999. CatholicCulture.org, Inside the Vatican, Martin de Porres lay Domincan Community, KY. Trinity Communications, 2024. Page 2. https://www.catholicculture.org/culture/library/view.cfm?recnum=2856

ordered all existing copies to be destroyed. Pfeiffer argues that this action also suggests the veil had been lost or stolen."[112]

Perhaps the best evidence of the veil leaving the control of the Vatican is a 1618 inventory of all the objects held by the Vatican at the old St. Peter's. The inventory, made by Giacomo Grimaldi, the Vatican archivist, is compelling in its nature. "On his list [is] the reliquary containing Veronica's veil, but, [Grimaldi] writes, the reliquary's crystal glass was broken. Pfeiffer notes that the veil in Manoppello has on its bottom edge, a small piece of glass."[113] It does seem odd that a relic of such great significance to the Church would not even merit a mention in the inventory of objects held by the Vatican if it were still at the Vatican at that time.

While Pfeiffer offers no theory about how the 'stolen' veil wound up at Manoppello, a Capuchin friar by the name of Donato da Bomba, wrote in 1646, "…in 1608, Marzia Leonelli, to ransom her husband from jail, sold Veronica's veil, which she had received as her dowry, for 400 scudi (a form of Italian currency at the time) to Donato Antoinio de Fabritiis. As the relic was not in good condition, after 30 years, de Fabritiis gave it, in 1638, to the Capuchin friars of Manoppello. Friar Remigio da Rapino cut out the veil's contour and fixed it between two panes of glass framed with chestnut wood."[114]

Finally, there is substantial evidence to confirm that the model used by the various artists who painted the image of the Holy Face, was in fact the veil of Manoppello. This will be discussed further in chapter 9.

Perhaps that is why in 1963, after reading *The Face of God*, written by German journalist and historian Paul Badde, which documented his lifelong research on the veil of Manoppello, Pope Benedict XVI was deeply moved. He visited the Capuchin Friars

---

[112] Ibid. Page 3.
[113] Ibid.
[114] Ibid.

shrine at the Basilica of the Holy Veil in Manoppello, Italy, on September 1, 2006, and then proclaimed it the Year of the Great Jubilee of the Divine Countenance Sanctuary in Manoppello. Equally moved at the site of the Holy Face, "Padre Pio had observed that the Holy Veil of Manoppello was "the greatest miracle in our possession."[115]

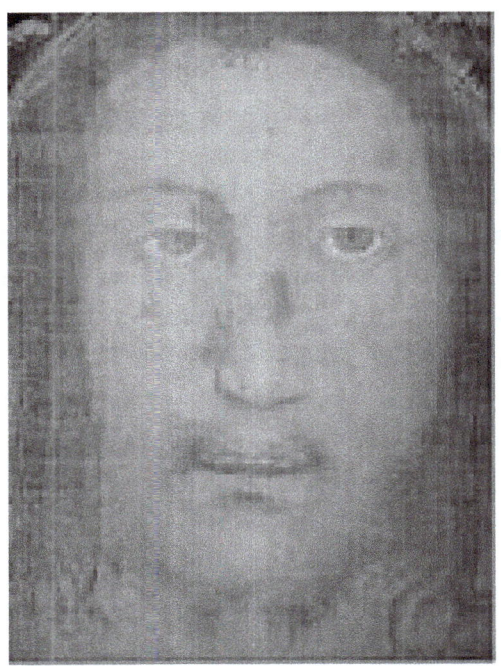

The image of Christ as it appears on the Veil of Manoppello. The preponderance of the evidence suggests that this is the authentic Veil of Veronica. (Wikicommons)

In a homily given in Santo Spirito on January 16, 2016, the Most Reverand Archbishop Georg Ganswein, Prefect of the Papal Household, noted, "Before coming to Rome, the Holy Veil was kept in Constantinople, earlier in Edessa and even before in Jerusalem." Yet, to this very day, the veil of Manoppello remains on display in that same chestnut wood case between those two panes of glass where it

---

115

is venerated every day in the chapel of a Capuchin Friary in Abruzzo, Pescara, near Rome.

The Face Cloth of the Crucified Christ

There is a third theory as to the travel history of Veronica's veil. This hypothesis is similar in many details to the accounts presented previously but varies with regard to its beginning. According to some historians, "the veil has long been acknowledged as the 'sudarium' or the burial face cloth of Jesus, generally referred to as the Sudarium of Oviedo. This theory places the veil in the tomb and alleges that it is the cloth described by the Apostle John in Chapter 20:1-9 of his Gospel. Recall that John's account of the Resurrection reads, "Peter and the other disciple started out for the tomb. They were both running, but the other disciple outran Peter and reached the tomb first. He stooped and looked in and saw the linen wrappings lying there, but he didn't go in. Then Simon Peter arrived and went inside. He also noticed the linen wrappings lying there, while the cloth that had covered Jesus' head was folded up and lying apart from the other wrappings. Then the disciple who had reached the tomb first also went in, and he saw and believed – for until then they still hadn't understood the Scriptures that said Jesus must rise from the dead."[116]

Those who espouse this theory believe that the veil of Manoppollo has long been acknowledged as the sudarium which covered the postmortem face of Jesus as he hung from the cross and remained over His face throughout the burial process. As such, they contend that "together with the Shroud (Sacra Sindone), the Holy Veil (Volto Santo) travelled from Jerusalem to Capadoccia to Edessa where they were kept until the fifth century."[117] In the eighth century

---

[116] Sanctuary of the Holy Face website, Immaculate Conception Church, Nampicuan, Nueva Ecija, Philippines. http://www.holyfacenampicuan.com/. Homepage.
[117] Ibid.

the Holy Veil arrived in Rome where it was kept at St. Peter's Basilica in the Chantry called St. Veronica's Chapel.

There are several references contained in the Vatican records that support the hypothesis that the veil was in Rome. In 753 AD, for example, the records indicated that Pope Stephen II walked "barefoot carrying the imprint of Christ's Countenance. The record also notes that Pope Innocent II in 1208 AD [was] parading the Veil in the Vatican on the first Sunday after Epiphany."[118] Proponents of this theory also note that many famous people through the Middle Ages also attested to the existence of the Veil. They include the writer Dante, the poet Francesco Petrarca and St. Bridget of Sweden. Pope Urban VII actually constructed a "column with the most important vault of the Vatican for 'keeping the True Countenance of Christ.'"[119]

Conclusive historical evidence presented in the next chapter, however, strongly suggest that the cloth of Manoppello is not the sudarium that covered the face of Jesus and was subsequently discovered by Saints Peter and John in the empty tomb of the risen Christ. This verification leaves just two other possibilities. First that the actual veil bearing the image of Christ is held at the Vatican in Rome, or second, that this veil is in the Capuchin Monastery in Manoppello.

Reconciling the Conflicting Accounts

While the Shroud of Turin is known throughout the world, the Veil of Manoppello rests in obscurity to a great number of Christians. The volume of research, however, has been expanding recently and "this cloth seems to point to the material having properties not fully understood."[120] The Basilica Shrine of the Holy Face of Manoppelo

---

[118] Ibid.
[119] Ibid.
[120] Turley, K.V. The Mysterious Holy Veil of Manoppello, Catholic Exchange. https://catholicexchange.com/the-mysterious-holy-veil-of-manoppello/. February 16, 2023. Page 1.

was the site of a Mass celebrated on January 20, 2019, by Archbishop Salvatore Cordileone of San Francisco, California, Cardinal Gerhard Miller and Archbishop Bruno Forte. The occasion was the feast of Omnis Terra. Being in the presence of the Holy Face clearly had a profound impact on Cordileone, as five years later, on January 20, 2024, the Archbishop celebrated the Omnis Terra Mass at the Cathedral of St. Mary of the Assumption in his home diocese of San Francisco. The Mass was celebrated just prior to the Walk for Life West Coast and attracted a great number of the faithful from that region. The Basilica overflowed as the archbishop began to speak about the history of the feast and its relationship to the veil which bore the image of the Holy Face. In his homily, Cordileone provided insight as to why the history of the cloth is less important than its features.

Cordileone noted that the relationship between the cloth and the feast "recalls a bit of Church history that underscores why Jesus came into the world. The story is told that in pre-Christian Rome the Emperor decided to have all Roman residents originally from other places take soil from their homeland and deposit it in a designated place close to the Vatican Hill, less than a quarter of a mile away. There he built a temple to honor the pagan Roman gods, as it contained soil from all the earth, "omnis terra."

After Rome became Christian, the Pope built a church over that spot, which we know as the church of the Holy Spirit, and every year on that Sunday, "Omnis Terra" Sunday, he would process from St. Peter's Basilica to the church of the Holy Spirit with a veil bearing the face of Jesus. The veil in question was preserved from antiquity as one of the burial cloths that covered Jesus' face and was believed to be such an accurate representation of his face that it was called "the true icon of Rome," in Latin, vera icona Romana: "vera icona," whence the name, "Veronica." This is how the story circulated later in the Middle Ages of a woman by that name who wiped our Lord's face as he carried his Cross to Calvary.

There are many truly remarkable, even miraculous, features about this cloth that point to its authenticity, but that is a subject for another discourse," Cordileone said. "The point for us here today is that that procession instituted in the Middle Ages was to claim Jesus Christ as the one Savior of all the world, the Second Person of the Most Holy Trinity, the one, true God to whom all the earth owes worship and allegiance. This is the spiritual lesson of the ritual that developed around that veil.

The story of Veronica, though, also bears for us a spiritual message. As Pope St. John Paul II reflected in his meditation on the sixth Station of the Cross, every act of charity done in the name of Jesus Christ, with the spirit of His love, leaves the imprint of His image. This is how we translate the universality of the salvation Jesus won for us into language people can understand in our own time and place. The love of Christ is truly a universal language, understood everywhere and in every culture, leaving His image and thus changing both persons involved in that encounter of authentic Christian charity."[121]

---

[121] Blogspot, Holy Face of Manoppello, "In San Francisco Archbishop Cordileone Calls Attention to the Feast of Omnis Terra and the Veil Bearing the Holy Face of Jesus. January 26, 2024. http://holyfaceofmanoppello.blogspot.com/.
*Tradition used to claim 33 AD as the year of the death of Jesus, but this year does not reconcile with the timing of the death of Herod the Great, which is historically known, placing the death of Jesus in 30 AD instead of 33 AD. This also means the birth of Christ was in the year 4 BC, unlike the former assumption that placed His birth in 1 AD. The dates in this chapter, therefore, have been adjusted from the original text to reflect the death of Jesus in the year 30 AD. Adding 3 years to the date will provide the year provided in the documents from which this information was gleaned.

CHAPTER IV

THE SHROUD OF TURIN

The First Century
Discovery in the Empty Tomb - 30 AD*

When John the Evangelist entered to tomb of Jesus "He bent down to look in and saw the linen wrappings lying there, but he did not go in. Then Simon Peter came, following him, and went into the tomb. He saw the linen wrappings lying there..."[122] The linen wrappings refer to the larger cloth which wrapped the body of Jesus "for some thirty-six to forty-two hours,"[123] and is believed to be the Shroud of Turin. The scientific evidence that

---

[122] Holy Bible, The – New Testament, The Word on Fire Bible, The Gospels. New Revised Standard Version. John 20:1-10. Brandon Vogt, General Editor. Word on Fire, Park Ridge, IL. 2020. John 20:5-6. Page 574.

[123] Hynek, R.W. MD, Science and the Holy Shroud: An Examination Into the Sacred Passion and the Direct Cause of Christ's Death. Freely translated from the Czech by Dom Augustine Studney, O.S.B. Benedictine Press, Pilsen Station, Chicago, IL. 1936. Page 17.

*See footnote 9 on page 4.

links the Shroud of Turin to the body of Jesus will be the subject of another chapter. This chapter, however, will trace the provenance showing how the burial cloth went from the tomb to the City of Turin, Italy.

An Apostle Brings the Shroud to Edessa

Information pertaining to the whereabouts of the Shroud in the years prior to the mid-fourteenth century is scant at best. There is a Syrian text written in the year 325 AD that associates this cloth with a miraculous cure of King Abgar V, who ruled Edessa from the first century BC until his death in 50 AD. Today this area is known as Urfa and lies in the southeastern region of Turkey.

According to the fourth century text, which Eusebius, bishop of Caesarea, translated almost verbatim, King Abgar suffered from a leprosy-like disease. "Having heard about the healing powers of Jesus, he sent a certain Ananias around the year 29-30 AD. with a letter to Jesus requesting that He come and heal him. Jesus replied that He was unable to go but promised to send one of His disciples. It was not until after His death and Resurrection that one of the seventy-two disciples, Thaddeus, brought a cloth to Abgar bearing an image of the face of Jesus. Upon seeing the cloth, Abgar was cured, and the Christian Faith was established in the city."[124] It is interesting to note that the Syrian text referenced the cloth, but in the translation offered by Eusebius, a cloth is not mentioned. According to the Eusebian translation, "Immediately on his entrance there appeared to Abgar a great vision on the face of the Apostle Thaddeus. When Abgar saw this, he did reverence to Thaddeus, and wonder seized all who stood about, for they themselves did not see the vision, which appeared to Abgar alone."[125]

---

[124] Guerrera, Vittorio, Fr. The Shroud of Turin: A Case for Authenticity. Tan Books and Publishers, Inc. Rockford, Il. 2001. Pages 1-2.
[125] Ibid. Page 2.

Despite the reference to Thaddeus being one of the seventy-two, it is commonly believed that the person who visited Abgar is St. Jude Thaddeus, the cousin and apostle of Jesus. This belief is supported by a sixth century painting. "One of the earliest Byzantine icons to depict Thaddeus holding the image of Edessa was painted in the year 550 AD. and is located at St. Catherine Monastery on Mount Sinai."[126] According to Ian Wilson, a British historian, the face of Jesus witnessed by Abgar is the face as it appears on the Shroud, which was folded in such a way as to make only the face visible. In fact, The Acts of Thaddeus, a text written in the sixth century, "refers to such an image as a *tetradiplon*, a Greek word which literally means "doubled in four", or, put another way, folded in eight layers".[127] Dr. John Jackson, a physicist who worked on the Shroud of Turin Research Project in 1978*, discovered that "doubling the cloth in four did indeed expose the face area."[128]

Following his healing, Abgar V converted to Christianity and honored that religion in Edessa. Upon his death, however, his son Man'nu, a pagan, began to persecute Christians. The cloth disappeared at that time, probably hidden away by the faithful to avoid its destruction.

The Fifth Century

Helena, the mother of Emperor Constantine was most zealous in her memorial of the Passion of Jesus. She is credited with having located and excavated the true cross and, according to Byzantine historian, Nicephorus Callistus, the "Empress Pulcheria deposited the sepulchral linens, which she had obtained from Empress Eudoxia, in the newly erected basilica of Our Lady of Blachernes at

---

[126] Ibid.
[127] Ibid. Pages 2-3.
[128] Ibid. Page 3.
*The 1978 Shroud of Turin Research Project will be discussed in much greater detail in part 2 of this book.

Constantinople."[129] Saint Braulion, Bishop of Saragossa verified this in his seventh century writings as did Saint John Chrysostom in the eighth century and William, Bishop of Tyre, in the twelfth century.

The Sixth Century

In the year 525 AD, Edessa was nearly destroyed by raging floods. In addition to the destruction of almost every building, about one third of the population was killed. Future emperor Justinian responded by sending engineers to rebuild the city. "According to popular tradition, the cloth was found in a niche above Edessa's west gate during the reconstruction of a wall."[130] The historical silence about the reemergence of the Shroud is attributed to the fact that in 525 AD, Edessa was predominantly Monophysite which means they believed only in the divine nature of Jesus. As such they opposed any physical representation of Christ. It is unlikely, therefore, that these people would welcome the discovery of a relic that would tend to confuse their beliefs.

After its rediscovery, the Shroud was placed in a reliquary and housed in the chapel of the new Cathedral of Hagia Sophia. It remained there until 544 AD when the city came under siege by the Persians. The Syrian historian Evagrius wrote that the people of Edessa took the image out of the reliquary and displayed it until the attackers retreated. In his writings, Evagrius referred to the cloth as "acheiropoietos", which means, not made by human hands.

---

[129] Hynek, R.W. MD, Science and the Holy Shroud: An Examination Into the Sacred Passion and the Direct Cause of Christ's Death. Freely translated from the Czech by Dom Augustine Studney, O.S.B. Benedictine Press, Pilsen Station, Chicago, IL. 1936. Page 17.

[130] Guerrera, Vittorio, Fr. The Shroud of Turin: A Case for Authenticity. Tan Books and Publishers, Inc. Rockford, Il. 2001. Page 3.

The Tenth Century

In 943 AD, the Byzantine Emperor Romanus Lecapenus requested the cloth as a means to protect his city from invasion. He dispatched John Curcuas, one of his generals, to Edessa with a proposition that the Muslim leader could not refuse. Lecapenus would pay twelve thousand pieces of silver, release two hundred Muslim prisoners, and promise that Edessa would be spared attack, in exchange for the Shroud. Thus, in the year 943 AD, the Shroud was moved to Constantinople.

Constantinople
References to the Shroud as the Mandylion

In the tenth century, a Byzantine author wrote about the arrival of the "Mandylion" in Constantinople. "Emperor Romanus Lecapenus, his two sons and future son-in-law Constantine, who was a young boy at the time, had a private showing of the image. According to Constantine, the image was 'moist secretion without colors or the art of a painting.'"[131] Symeon Magister, another author of the same period, said that "the emperor's sons were disappointed after viewing the cloth. Rather than a vibrant image like that of a painting, the boys could distinguish only a faint image of a face.

In 1986, Dr. Gino Zaninotto discovered a Greek manuscript of a sermon that was given by Gregory, archdeacon and administrator of Hagia Sophia Cathedral in 944 AD. The document notes that on August 16, the Mandylion was placed by Ecumenical Patriarch Theophylartos for veneration by the faithful. It was positioned on the emperor's throne and adorned with the imperial crown to show the sovereignty of Christ as the omnipotent lord of the universe, the almighty ruler, Pantocrator. In his sermon, Gregory urges: "The splendor – and may everyone be inspired by this description – was

---

[131] Ibid. Page 5.

impressed during agony only by the drops of sweat that poured forth from the face, which is the source of life, dropping down like drops of blood, as from the finger of God. These are really the beauties that have produced the coloration of the imprint of Christ, which was further embellished by the drops of blood that issued of His own side."[132] This writing further emphasizes that the Mandylion was a cloth that bore more than the image of the face of Christ. It was actually the Shroud doubled in four or folded in eight layers.

This mid-17th century Russian icon of the Mandylion was painted by Simon Ushakov.

Skeptics Argue that the Mandylion is Not the Shroud

There are those who believe that the Mandylion and the Shroud are two separate cloths. They contend that the mandylion

---

[132] Ibid.

depicts the face of Jesus when he was alive, whereas the Shroud depicts Him in death. Early Christians, however, were reluctant to portray Jesus in death, so the Shroud was rarely unfolded to reveal the rest of the body. Consequently, when many early artists copied the Holy Face from the Mandylion, they painted Christ with His eyes wide open. "… As early as the sixth century, many facial features found on the Shroud are reproduced in paintings. Artists often depicted the face in a frame surrounded by an ornamental trellis. If the Mandylion were indeed the Shroud folded in such a way so that only the face was exposed, it would be natural to depict Jesus alive with His eyes open."[133] Pioneer Shroud historian, Fr. Edward Wuenschel C.Ss.R., noted that "realistic representations of the crucifixion did not become common until the thirteenth century, and even then, mainly in the Western Church."[134]

Boucoleon Palace – 945 AD

Following its solemn exposition in 944, the Mandylion was relocated to Boucoleon Palace in Constantinople, and placed in the Pharos Chapel where it was rarely exposed. In 945 AD, Byzantine Emperor Constantine Porphyrogenitos commissioned the composition of a hymn that would recount the "history of the Mandylion, and established August 16, the anniversary of the solemn exposition of the cloth, as the feast of the Holy Mandylion in the Orthodox Church."[135]

The Twelfth Century
Could A Mandylion Replica
Be One of the Veils of Veronica?

In 1104 AD, a replica was made of the Mandylion and sent to Rome. It was received by Pope Sergius IV who had an altar

---

[133] Ibid.
[134] Ibid. Page 6.
[135] Ibid.

consecrated for it within the Vatican chapel of Pope John VII. There, it became known as the Veil of Veronica, referencing the cloth commemorated in the sixth station of the cross.

By the year 1080, Alexis I of Comnenus asked Emperor Henry IV and Robert of Flanders for help in "defending 'the linens found in the tomb after the Resurrection.'"[136] Historical documents note that many other dignitaries had the opportunity to view the Mandylion. These include King Louis VII of France in 1147, Bishop William of Tyre, and King Amaury of Jerusalem in 1171.

The Thirteenth Century

In 1201 AD, while still in the Pharos Chapel, the Mandylion was in the custodial care of Nicholas Mesarites who described how he had to defend the relic in a palace uprising. "In this chapel," he wrote, "Christ rises again, and the sindon with the burial linens is the clear proof....The burial sindon of Christ: this is of linen, of cheap and easily obtainable material, still smelling fragrant of myrrh, defying decay, because it wrapped the mysterious, naked body after the Passion..."[137]

In 1202, Knight Robert de Clary, from Picardy, reported seeing the Holy Shroud at Constantinople. "There was another of the churches which they called My Lady St. Mary of Blachernae," de Clary wrote, "where was kept the sydoine in which Our Lord had been wrapped, which stood up straight every Friday so that the figure of Our Lord could be plainly seen there."[138] Two years later, however, on April 12, 1204, the city was conquered by the Crusaders during the fourth Crusade, "and in the division of spoils the Holy Shroud fell to the lot of Otto de la Roche, commander of the army of Marquis of Monteferrat. He sent it to his father, who in about the year 1206,

---

[136] Ibid. Page 7.
[137] Ibid.
[138] Ibid. Page 8.

entrusted it to the care of Amedee de Tramelay, Archibishop of Besancon," where it was frequently venerated in exposition.

Did the Knights Templar Take Possession of the Shroud?

There is speculation, however, that the cloth was being held by a religious order known as the Knight Templars, an organization founded in the year 1118 under the name, the Poor knights of Christ of the Temple of Solomon. The Knights took vows of poverty, chastity and obedience and were charged with defending sacred sites in the Holy Land. They were present in the second through the tenth Crusades between 1095 and 1291.

There is some tangible evidence that the Knights were in possession of the Shroud. In 1944, a painting of the Holy Face dating to the year 1280 was discovered on a wooden panel in the village of Templecombe, England, a village that the Knight's Templars owned from about 1185. Shroud scholar Rex Morgan believes that "the wooden panel may actually have been a lid to a wooden box which contained the Shroud when it was transferred from France to England during the suppression of the Templars. The Templecombe panel has one hundred and twenty-five points of congruence with the Shroud face...the fleur-de-lis decoration of the painting strongly suggests French influence and the quatrefoil design is recurrent in Templar...decorative motifs."[139] Despite the plausibility of this theory, the Templars never admitted to having the Shroud in their possession.

The Fourteenth Century The Shroud in France and Greece

Though the Knights Templar's never acknowledged possession of the Shroud, the French city of Besancon does claim to

---

[139] Ibid. Page 9.

have possessed the Shroud from 1208 to 1329. The theory is that the cloth became part of the recompense of a Bergundian Knight by the name of Othon de la Roche, the Duke of Athens and Sparta. There is actually some evidence that the Shroud was in Athens. Theodore of Epirus attested to that fact in a letter dated August 1, 1205, and Nicholas of Otranto, the abbot of the monastery of Casole provides indirect evidence as well. Othon then sent the cloth to his father, Ponce de la Roche. He, in turn, gave it to the Bishop of Besancon who placed it in the Cathedral of St. Etienne where it was venerated in an exposition that took place on Easter Sunday of each year until 1349 AD. In that year, a fire destroyed that Cathedral, but the Shroud sustained only minimal damage. It did, however, disappear once again.

Possession of the Shroud is Taken by the de Charny Family, Geoffrey I de Charny 1349 AD to 1356 AD

One account, written in the sixteenth century, suggests that the Shroud was given to King Philip VI, who then gave it to Geoffrey I de Charny, but he was taken prisoner by the English after the Battle of Calais in 1349. It is speculated that he hid the Shroud in Templecombe before his capture. King John II of France paid for his release in 1351 and in June 1353, the King granted de Charny permission to build a collegiate church in Lirey. Henri de Poitiers, Bishop of Troyes, sent a letter to de Charny dated May 28, 1356. The letter is currently in the archive of Aube, Lirey and is the only genuine act of that bishop that can be authenticated. While the letter doesn't mention the Shroud by name, it suggests that the precious relic was kept in Lirey at that time.

Jeanne (de Vergy) de Charny - 1356 AD to 1397 AD

When de Charny was killed in battle on September 19, 1356, possession of the Shroud was given to his widow, Jeanne de Vergy, who happened to be the great-great-great-great granddaughter of

Othon de la Roach. In 1357, without the support of her husband, Jeanne began to exhibit the Shroud to raise money for the church. For reasons unknown, however, it would not be exhibited again for about thirty years.

In 1389, Jeanne remarried Aymon of Geneva, who was uncle to the anti-pope, Clement VII who reigned in Avignon during the Western schism. The exhibition of the Shroud in April of that year caused such a furor that the bishop appealed to Pope Clement VII to stop the exhibition. Instead, the Pope reaffirmed permission and ordered the bishop to be silent. In an act of disobedience, the bishop appealed all the way to King Charles VI, who also refused to stop the exhibition.

The Fifteenth Century
Margaret de Charny – 1398 AD to 1443 AD

The relic then passed to the hands of Geoffrey II de Charny, but when he died on May 22, 1398, his daughter, Margaret de Charny became the owner of the Shroud. In 1400, she married Jean de Baufremont, but in 1415 he was killed in the Battle of Agincourt leaving behind no children. Three years later, Margaret remarried. Her new husband Humbert de Villerexel, Hyppolytus Duke de la Roach, the Lord of Lirey. That turned out to be quite fortuitous, because when war broke out near the chapel, the clergy asked him to protect the Shroud in his castle of Montfort near Montbard. In a letter dated July 6, 1418, de Villerexel wrote: "…we have received from our kind chaplains, the dean and chapter of Our Lady of Lirey, the jewels and relics of the aforesaid church, namely the things which follow: first a cloth, on which is the figure or representation of the Shroud of our Lord Jesus Christ, which is in a casket emblazoned with the de Charny crest…"[140]

---

[140] Ibid. Page 16.

Despite de Villerexel assurances that the objects would be returned to the clergy after the war, his death in 1438, prior to the war's end, prevented the return. Margaret was very vigilant about protecting the relic during the balance of the war years and took it with her even when she travelled. On May 8, 1443, after the war had ended, the clergy at Lirey, feeling that the relics should have been returned, made a formal request of Margaret for their return, but she refused to return the Shroud even in the face of threats of excommunication. It is unclear if she returned the other relics.

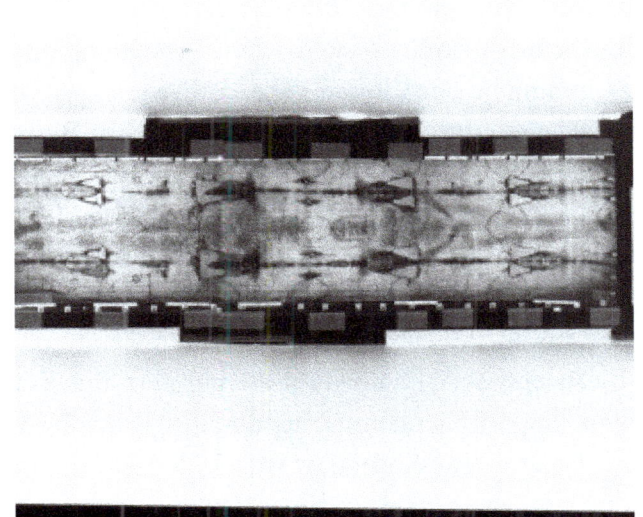

Photograph of the Shroud of Turin.
"© Vernon Miller, 1978. No unauthorized reproduction of Material on other Websites is allowed without prior written permission from the shroudphotos.com copyright holder. Original photos are available for free at www.shroudphotos.com".

de Charny Cousin Anna, Wife of Duke Louis I of Savoy 1453 AD to 1460 AD

On March 22, 1453, Margaret gave the Shroud to her cousin Anna, who was the wife of Duke Louis I of Savoy and the daughter of the King of Cyprus. Seven years later, on October 7, 1460,

Margaret died. Meanwhile, the Duke oversaw construction of an ornate chapel in Chambery, a town approximately fifty miles east of Lyons. As a means of compensating the clerics of Lirey for the Shroud, the Duke gave them fifty francs.

The Sixteenth Century
Amadeus IX – 1471 AD to 1577 AD

Amadeus IX succeeded Duke Louis I, upon his death and in 1471, while still only sixteen years of age, Amadeus IX enlarged the chapel which was inaugurated on June 11, 1502, by Duke Philbert II. "The Shroud was placed in a silver reliquary above the high altar, closed by an iron grate and locked with four keys."[141]

After being locked away for over one hundred years, the Shroud was exhibited once again. The date was April 14, 1503 -- Good Friday. The exhibition took place in the city of Bour-en-Bresse and was in honor of the safe return from Spain of Archduke Philip. Antoine de Lalaing, secretary to Philip, "tells of how one of the three bishops holding the Shroud for veneration solemnly announced: 'Here, my brothers, among holy things, is the most holy and contemplative on all the earth. It is the precious and noble 'sindon' purchased by Joseph of Arimathea for the burial of the divine Master, when, with the help of Nicodemus, he took him down from the cross. To prove if it was the true Shroud, it was boiled in oil, tossed in fire, laundered different and numerous times. But one could not efface nor remove these imprints and marks of our sweet Lord."[142] Of course, there is no direct evidence that any of these things actually happened, though it was, after all, during medieval times that they were alleged to have taken place.

---

[141] Ibid. Page 17.
[142] Ibid.

Fire Nearly Destroys the Shroud – 1532 AD

Despite the seemingly excessive measures undertaken by Amadeus IX to safeguard the Shroud from wars and villains, he couldn't have imagined the events of December 4, 1532. On that night, a fire broke out in the sacristy of the church and quickly spread to the chapel in which the Shroud was secured. The heat was so intense that it melted the silver reliquary that housed the sacred relic causing molten silver to drip from the cover. The igneous silver penetrated the folded Shroud. If not for the quick action of two Franciscan friars, Francesco Lambert and Guglielmo Pessod, who penetrated the flames to pour water on the reliquary, the precious Shroud may have been destroyed. Despite their heroics in extinguishing the fire, the dripping silver created eight symmetrical burn marks that are visible the entire length of the Shroud. "This was the second test by fire, and the first by water, which the holy relic underwent."[143] The Poor Clare nuns of Chambery worked for two weeks to repair the cloth the best they could, by sewing triangular patches to those areas burned in the tragic fire.

In 1537, the Shroud was taken to Vercelli and then to Nice to protect it from invading French troops. From Nice it was taken back to Vercelli, but when the French sacked that city on November 18, 1553, the cloth was hidden in the home of a canon, Antoine Claude Costa. It was returned to Chambery on June 3, 1561, and exhibited for the first time on August 15 of that year. "The author of the French atlas of the year 1560, who personally saw the Holy Shroud, writing of Chambery, remarks that 'they keep there the sacred linen on which can be seen a human figure formed by blood stains.'"[144]

---

[143] Hynek, R.W. MD, Science and the Holy Shroud: An Examination Into the Sacred Passion and the Direct Cause of Christ's Death. Freely translated from the Czech by Dom Augustine Studney, O.S.B. Benedictine Press, Pilsen Station, Chicago, IL. 1936. Pages 23-24.
[144] Ibid. Page 24.

In some troublesome wartimes that followed, the Shroud traveled up and down the countries of France even finding refuge in Belgium for a short time. While there, it was copied by Albrecht Durer, of Nuremberg. It returned to Nizza, Italy for a time.

Turin, Italy – 1578 AD

On September 14, 1578, Emmanuel Philibert, the Duke of Savoy, brought the Shroud to Turin, Italy to provide future saint Charles Borromeo an opportunity to venerate the relic. It was kept in the chapel of the ducal palace. Borromeo was archbishop of Milan and had promised to venerate the Shroud in return for Milan's escape from the ravages of the plague that had devastated northern Italy. Though relatively young, Borromeo was not in good health and the Duke had tried to spare him the travel that a pilgrimage to Chambery would have required. The Duke's motives for bringing the Shroud to Turin were not strictly virtuous, however, as he had plans to relocate the capital to that city.

On October 10, 1578, Borromeo arrived in the city of Turin and, for the next eight days, venerated the sacred relic. Borromeo died in 1584, but not before making two additional pilgrimages to Turin to venerate the Shroud.

The Holy Shroud now had a permanent home in the City of Turin "and was exposed for veneration each year on the 4th of May in front of the Palazzo Madama."[145] Over the course of the next fifty or more years, many future saints would make the same pilgrimage in an effort to venerate the Holy Shroud. They included Saint Francis de Sales and Saint Frances de Chantal.

---

[145] Guerrera, Vittorio, Fr. The Shroud of Turin: A Case for Authenticity. Tan Books and Publishers, Inc. Rockford, Il. 2001. Page 19.

The Seventeenth to the Twenty First Century

On June 1, 1694, the Shroud found a new home in the Cathedral of St. John the Baptist, "a magnificent chapel built by Guarini in the royal palace."[146] With the exception of a brief period during World War II, it has been there ever since. Cardinal Maurilio Fossati, the Archbishop of Turin, clandestinely relocated the Shroud in 1939 amidst fears of destruction during the war. From that date until 1946, it was hidden in the Benedictine Abbey of Montevergine in Avellino, about 140 miles south of Rome. With the end of World War II, it was returned to Turin in 1946.

The First Photographs of the Shroud

When King Umberto II, the last Duke of Savoy died on March 19, 1983, he "bequeathed the Shroud to the Holy See, but the Pope left the relic in the custodial care of the Archbishop of Turin."[147] At that location, it has been on public display twenty-three times. During one such exposition in 1858, lawyer and amateur photographer, Secondo Pia, was given permission to take photographs of the Shroud. He did so over the course of four days, from May 25-28, 1898. His discovery of a positive image on the negative plates changed everything. Secondo described the moment this way:

> "Shut up in my darkroom all intent on my work, I experienced a very strong emotion when, during the development, I saw for the first time the Holy Face appear on the plate, with such clarity that I was

---

[146] Hynek, R.W. MD, Science and the Holy Shroud: An Examination Into the Sacred Passion and the Direct Cause of Christ's Death. Freely translated from the Czech by Dom Augustine Studney, O.S.B. Benedictine Press, Pilsen Station, Chicago, IL. 1936. Page 24.

[147] Guerrera, Vittorio, Fr. The Shroud of Turin: A Case for Authenticity. Tan Books and Publishers, Inc. Rockford, IL. 2001. Page 20.

dumbfounded by it. It was a great glory, and I was seized by trepidation at what I had seen."[148]

The Shroud was allowed to be photographed a second time when it was on public display from May 2 to May 23, 1931, in honor of the marriage of Prince Humbert of Piedmont to Marie Josephine, the daughter of King Albert of Belgium. Armed with more sophisticated equipment than that used by Secondo, photographer Giuseppe Enrie took new photographs of the Shroud at the request of Cardinal Fossati. The new images were clearer than those taken by Secondo and were quickly circulated throughout the world.

"Historical analysis has revealed that there is reasonable evidence for the route of the Shroud to have led from Jerusalem to Turin,"[149] according to Gerard Verschuuren. Further, the Catholic Church has "never made a pronouncement adverse to the authenticity of the Holy Shroud of Turin. As a matter of fact,…three popes, Leo XIII, Pius X and Pius XI, have approved its veneration by the faithful by the grants of many favors."[150] To date, despite belief in the Shroud not being a matter of Church dogma, over twenty five popes have spoken favorably of the Shroud's authenticity.

Still, there are those who argue that because the Shroud of Turin has a broken chain of custody, with many years unaccounted for in its provenance, that it cannot be authenticated as the cloth that wrapped the body of Jesus. Despite the cynicism, "It really doesn't matter what the history of the Shroud has been," notes Richard Bernanchi, professor of engineering and founder of Faith-Based Communications. "We could have discovered it fifty years ago and

---

[148] Ibid. Page 22.
[149] Ibid. Page 152.
[150] Hynek, R.W. MD, Science and the Holy Shroud: An Examination Into the Sacred Passion and the Direct Cause of Christ's Death. Freely translated from the Czech by Dom Augustine Studney, O.S.B. Benedictine Press, Pilsen Station, Chicago, IL. 1936. Pages 25 – 26.

done the scientific study that we've done in the last few decades, and it would not change anything."[151]

The simple truth is that many artifacts have been discovered and perhaps rediscovered over the centuries with a determination being made as to what the artifact is without question about the provenance. Upon the object's unearthing, research authenticates the discovery with or without a thorough knowledge of where the object has been since its origin.

---

[151] YouTube Video, Richard Bernanchi, Who Do You Say I Am? A Shroud of Turin Documentary Blending Science and Faith, Patchwork Heart Ministry, https://video.search.yahoo.com/yhs/search?fr=yhs-tro-freshy&ei=UTF-8&hsimp=yhs-freshy&hspart=tro&p=youtube+video+who+do+you+say+I+am%3F+A+shroud+of+turin+documentary+blending...&type=Y219_F163_204671_102220#id=2&vid=cc7eba355eb83531d5687df304132472&action=click. December 2023.

CHAPTER V

THE SUDARIUM OF OVIEDO

Why the Face of Jesus Was Covered

As noted earlier, first century Jewish law required the preservation and burial of blood with the body in anticipation of the ultimate resurrection. In the case of traumatic death resulting in severe blood loss, the law compelled the use of a sudarium, or facecloth, to cover the victims face, thereby preserving any blood that might flow after death. Blood was considered as much a part of the body as the flesh, and Jews of the time would even dig up blood-soaked earth and inter blood-stained clothes.

After the violent death of Jesus, his face was covered for about an hour while the body still hung on the cross. Once permission was granted to bury the Lord's remains, the lifeless body of Jesus was removed from the cross, but the sudarium remained wrapped around his head until he was laid in the tomb. At that point, the sudarium was removed, and the body was quickly and crudely anointed with aloe and myrrh provided by Joseph of Arimathea. Finally, the sudarium was more than likely rewrapped and knotted at the top, "as documented in a fifth-century paraphrase of John's Gospel."

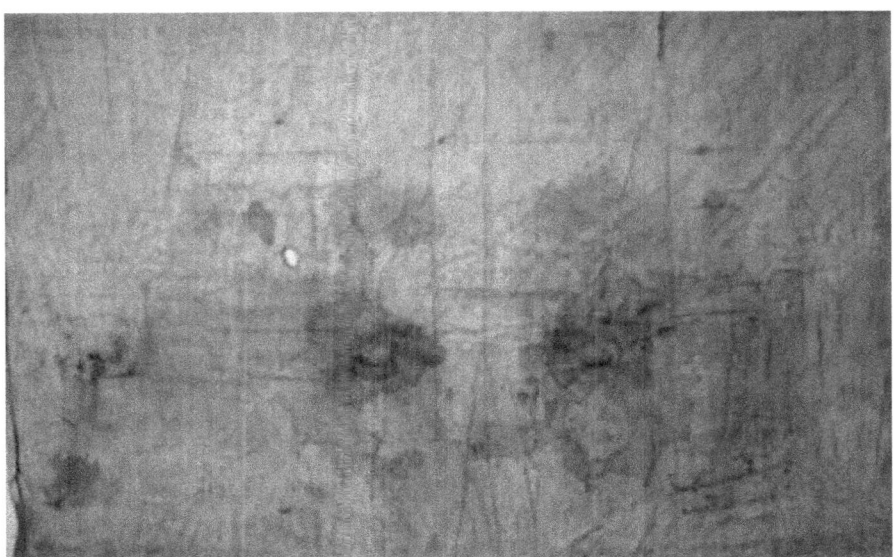

The Sudarium of Oviedo, a blood-stained cloth or 'napkin' was used to cover the postmortem face of Jesus as He hung on the cross and as he was carried to the tomb. (WikiCommons)

[152] In that document, written by Nonnus of Panopolis in Egypt in the first half of the fifth century, a few "revealing details to the evangelical account of John 20:6-7" are added. Nonnus wrote, "When Simon Peter arrived after him, he immediately went into the tomb. He saw the linens there together on the empty floor, and the cloth that covered his head, with a knot toward the upper back of the part that had covered the hair. In the native language of Syria it is called sudarium. It was not with the funerary linens, but was rolled up, twisted in a separate place."[153] When the cloth was later set apart in

---

[152] Bennett, Janice, Sacred Blood, Sacred Image: The Sudarium of Oviedo – New Evidence for the Authenticity of The Shroud of Turin. Ignatius Press, San Francisco, CA. 2001. Page 22.
[153] Ibid.

the tomb for burial, this knot would have given it the twisted or rolled-up appearance described by John."[154]

A manuscript known as the San Antonino Martir recalls a 570 AD pilgrimage from Piacenza, Italy to the Holy Land by an anonymous pilgrim. The document "mentions the existence of a cave close to the Monastery of St. Mark, on the other side of the River Jordan, in which lived seven nuns in seven cells – according to what they told him, they 'looked after the sudarium of Christ.'"[155]

There are also two historical sources that "affirm" that charge of the sudarium was taken by Peter the apostle. The first reference is revealed in the life of Santa Nino of Georgia. Nino died in 338 AD and his autobiography, probably written in that year, notes that the apostle hid the cloth, and the hiding place is not known. The second reference is attributed to Isodad of Merv who penned the Commentaries on the Gospels in the Syriac language in about 850 AD. Bennett notes that this Nestorian bishop collected early Eastern traditions. Regarding the Gospel of John, Isodad said, "…but they gave the burial linens to Joseph the senator [Joseph of Arimathea], and it was right that they be returned to him for safekeeping as he was the owner of the tomb, as it was he who brought them for the honor of Jesus. But Simon [Peter] took the sudarium, and it was for him a crown on his head. And every time that he laid his hands on someone, he put it on his head. He obtained much and frequent aid from it, in the same way that even today the leaders and the bishops of the Church put turbans on their heads and around the neck in place of that sudarium."[156]

---

[154] Bennett, Janice, Simply Catholic, Face Cloth of Jesus' Burial: The Sudarium of Oviedo. Scott Richert, publisher. https://www.simplycatholic.com/about-us/. Page 3.
[155] Bennett, Janice, Sacred Blood, Sacred Image: The Sudarium of Oviedo – New Evidence for the Authenticity of The Shroud of Turin. Ignatius Press, San Francisco, CA. 2001. Page 22-23.
[156] Ibid. Pages 23-24.

There is only one other mention of the sudarium in the New Testament. According to Acts 19:11-12, Paul carried the cloth, which measures thirty-four inches long by 21 inches wide, to Ephesus and used it in the performance of many miracles. "And God did extraordinary miracles by the hands of Paul, so that handkerchiefs or aprons were carried away from his body to the sick, and diseases left them, and the evil spirits came out of them."[157]

Following the Sudarium Through History from Jerusalem to Spain

Owing to "the destruction of important manuscripts, the remoteness of the times in which the cloth was brought to Spain, and the fact that no one has undertaken"[158] the task of studying the cloth until the very last years of the 1900s, the provenance of the sudarium is a bit spotty. From the time of St. Paul's use of the cloth in Ephesus, until its appearance in Oviedo, Spain, approximately one thousand years later, there is very little historical mention of the sudarium. And "these references are often confusing because as Latin had no word of its own for the Greek 'sindon' of the synoptic gospels (i.e. the Shroud), the word 'sudarium' was often used to mean this larger cloth that covered the whole body. Janice Bennett, author of *Sacred Blood, Sacred Image: The Sudarium of Oviedo*, attributes this confusion, at least in part, to the fact that the function of the sudarium is not clear in the biblical passages and, artistically speaking, "the 'Descent from the Cross' is never portrayed with a sudarium covering the head of the Lord."[159] Further, Bennett notes, "the majority of books written about

---

[157] The Holy Bible - New Testament, Acts 19:11-12, The Great Adventure Bible, Revised Standard Version, Second Catholic Edition, Ascension Press, West Chester, PA. 2006. Page 1,444.

[158] Bennett, Janice, Sacred Blood, Sacred Image: The Sudarium of Oviedo – New Evidence for the Authenticity of The Shroud of Turin. Ignatius Press, San Francisco, CA. 2001. Page 20.

[159] Ibid.

the Shroud hardly mention the existence of the head cloth. If they do, its usage is purely conjecture and often contradictory."[160] In the Vulgate, the official Latin translation of the Bible, the sudarium that John speaks of is clearly that face cloth, whereas for the linen cloths or wrappings the neuter plural 'linteamina' is used."[161] Bennett notes that the Evangelist John never left the foot of the cross during the crucifixion and "most probably accompanied the procession with the body to the sepulcher."[162] He, the only one of the apostles to be an eyewitness to the events of Friday, April 7, 30 AD, knows the exact purpose of the sudarium and clearly identifies it on his visit to the empty tomb on Sunday morning. "The position of the burial cloths was extremely important to him and has great significance because it is what brought him to faith in the Resurrection."[163]

One such reference is made in a seventh century letter written by San Braulio de Zaragoza, the bishop of Zaragoza. It is one of forty surviving letters written by the bishop and provides historically relevant information about the Visigoth kingdom in Spain. In this particular letter, dated in the year 631 AD, Braulio wrote, "…but in those times, it is known that many things occurred that are not written, as for example the linens and the sudarium in which the body of the Lord was wrapped. We read that it was found, but we do not read that it was preserved. Nevertheless, I do not believe that the relics would have been disregarded, but preserved for future times."[164]

It is not Braulio, however, but rather Pelayo, a local historian and bishop of Oviedo, who provides the best accounting of how the sudarium came to rest in Oviedo. Pelayo wrote two books in which

---

[160] Ibid.
[161] Guscin, Mark, The Oviedo Cloth. The Lutterworth Press, Cambridge, Britain. 1998. Page 11.
[162] Bennett, Janice, Sacred Blood, Sacred Image: The Sudarium of Oviedo – New Evidence for the Authenticity of The Shroud of Turin. Ignatius Press, San Francisco, CA. 2001. Page 21.
[163] Ibid.
[164] Ibid. Pages 33-34.

he chronicles the events that took place during the years 986 AD and 1109 AD. In short, the Christians took the sudarium from Jerusalem, through the north of Africa, and to Toledo, Spain, when they fled the Persian invasion in the seventh century. When the Muslims invaded Spain in the eighth century, however, the Christians carried the cloth further north to the only part of Spain not impacted by the invasion, Oviedo.

Though not always the most accurate of historians, this particular story, as written by Pelayo, coincides perfectly with the historical record, which notes that Chosroes II* was the king of Persia from 590 AD to 628 AD. After the death of his father, Chosroes had to fight the usurper Bahram VI. This required an alliance with the Byzantine emperor Mauritius. That alliance was short lived though, as in the year 602 AD, when Mauritius was dethroned by Phocas, Chosroes declared war on the Byzantines. "He attacked and occupied Damascus, Antioch and Jerusalem in 614, and Alexandria in 616. Phocas was succeeded by Heraclius, who restored the strength of Byzantium, and Chosroes was defeated at Nineveh in 628."[165] There he was imprisoned and assassinated.

So, like the chronicles of Braulin, history places the sudarium in "Jerusalem, or at least Palestine, from the death of Jesus until this time, and was taken away shortly before Chosroes attacked the area"[166] in the year 614 AD. That small cloth, stained with the blood of Jesus, was so critical a relic to the early Christians that they surreptitiously carried it away to safety. It was first taken to Alexandria, in the north of Africa, by the presbyter, Philip, but when it became apparent that Chosroes was leading the Persians in the same direction, the Christians removed the cloth from Alexandria which was conquered two years later in 616 AD. The sudarium was taken

---

[165] Guscin, Mark, The Oviedo Cloth. The Lutterworth Press, Cambridge, Britain. 1998. Page 14.
[166] Ibid.
* Chosroes II is also spelled Khosrow II in various places.

through the north of Africa before arriving in Spain "entering the Iberian peninsula at Cartagena in the company of people who were fleeing from the Persians. The bishop of Ecija, Saint Fulgentius, welcomed the refugees and the relics, and surrendered the oaken chest or ark, in which the sudarium was kept, to Saint Leandro, who was bishop at Seville."[167] Leandro carried the ark to Seville, where it remained for many years.

The Arrival of the Sudarium in Oviedo

Fulgentius was succeeded as bishop by Saint Isidore, but when Isadore was appointed the bishop of Toledo in 657 AD, he took the ark with him where it remained until 718 AD. The unabated Muslim invasion of Spain occurred at the beginning of the eighth century at which time the ark was secretly taken to northern Spain where the relics were hidden in a cave in an area which is now known as Monsacro, located just ten kilometers from Oviedo. The sudarium remained in the cave until King Alfonso II built a special place for it in the year 840 AD. That place is in the 'Camara Santa' in the cathedral. Other historical accounts differ slightly in the details, but essentially support this timeline.

According to Bennett, the kings of this period never knew the contents of the chest, "since, in order to avoid any possible profanity, people were made to believe that he who tried to open it would be struck down."[168] Bishop Ponce, according to a historical reference from 1075 AD, tried to open the chest in 1030 AD in order to discover its contents. "One day the bishop brought together in the Holy Chamber dignitaries of the Chapter of the Cathedral, relatives, and close friends, and proceeded to open the reliquary coffer. With the lid barely raised, a 'cutting and blinding whiteness' escaped from it,

---

[167] Ibid.
[168] Bennett, Janice, Sacred Blood, Sacred Image: The Sudarium of Oviedo – New Evidence for the Authenticity of The Shroud of Turin. Ignatius Press, San Francisco, CA. 2001. Page 40.

which frightened all those present and blinded several people, including the bishop; some of them never regained their sight."[169] This event was popularized in the 1981 blockbuster fictional movie, *Raiders of the Lost Ark*.

On March 14, 1075, the fourth Friday in lent, the ark containing the sudarium was opened. King Alfonso VI and his sister had traveled from Toledo to Oviedo, and a number of bishops were present for the occasion. To avoid a repeat of events that took place in San Salvador some forty-five years earlier, the king "ordered the celebration of services, extraordinary fasts, and songs, with censors that impregnated every corner with the fragrance of incense. The gathering was amazed to find within the ark an incredible treasure that included relics "of the Passion of Jesus, of the wood of the Cross, of the Sacred Blood and of His Sudarium, as well as innumerable remains of the Holy Saints, Prophets, Martyrs, Confessors, and Virgins."[170] The ceremony was recorded as an official act, and a copy of it is maintained in the Capitular Archives of the cathedral in Oviedo. "This document states that even in the year 1075, the chest had been in the church for a long time."[171]

This wooden ark, called the Arca Santa, which Alfonso VI had plated with silver in about the year 1113 AD, portrays the images of the twelve apostles, the four evangelists and Jesus. The ark also contains inscriptions in Latin and Arabic, and both have Christian origins. "The Latin inscription invites all Catholics to venerate this relic that contains the holy blood."[172] Also inscribed in the silver plating is a list of all that is contained in the ark. One of the items listed "is clearly registered as 'el Santo Sudario de N.S.J.C.' These

---

[169] Ibid. Page 41
[170] Ibid.
[171] Guscin, Mark, The Oviedo C oth. The Lutterworth Press, Cambridge, Britain. 1998. Page 18.
[172] Ibid.

letters stand for 'Nuestro Senor Jesucristo', and the inscription means, 'The Sacred Sudarium of Our Lord Jesus Christ.'"[173]

Bennett emphasizes the significance of the fact that all of the early references to the sudarium tend to confirm the traditional belief that the cloth was in Jerusalem for almost six hundred years and most likely used by the apostles and disciples of Christ in their acts of healing. Later, the cloth was protected from invaders by being hidden away in a cave.

The Veneration of Relics

The veneration of relics, particularly the remains of saints and martyrs, has been a popular practice since the Middle Ages, and the sudarium became intimately associated with Oviedo since the arrival of the 'Arca Santa' early in the eighth century.

While there are many reasons why pilgrims come to venerate the relics of the ark, this one is particularly noteworthy. It is mentioned in many manuscripts dating to the end of the twelfth, and the beginning of the thirteenth centuries, and because of the vivid detail, it is believed to have been written by an eyewitness to the events.

It seems that "a woman, who was impregnated against her will, cursed her offspring at the moment of conception and commended the child to the devil. She cared for her daughter for seven months after birth, when the infant was carried off by the devil, and given a life of riches, servants, and attention. At the age of sixteen, the girl, although quite thin, was strong and able to speak many languages. At seventeen she was taken to an abbey of Benedictine monks in Jaca, in Aragon, where Santiago appeared to her, imprinting the sign of the cross on her finger. The devil returned, and speaking through her in terrible voices, said that he would leave her only if San Salvador or Santiago ordered it. The girl was therefore sent on a pilgrimage to the Cathedral

---

[173] Ibid.

of San Salvador where she knelt before the Holy Chest of relics. At that moment the devil once again entered her body, and began to speak. The clergy ordered the devil to leave, but he refused, explaining that he had raised the child and instructed her in all of his arts. When the archdeacon brought before the young woman the Cross of the Angels, the devil was forced to leave; the following day, however, when the girl returned to the church, the devil once again entered her. The canon, who feared that, because of the sins of the people, God might allow the devil to demolish the church, ordered that the relics be brought to him. The devil immediately left. On the third day, the girl was brought before the altar of San Salvador. The devil reentered the body and, raising her above the altar, threw her to the pavement, shouting that he would not let her go. Those in the church tried to subject her, but she was once again raised in the air. The archdeacon ordered everyone in the church to pray, and the girl was again thrown to the floor. The canon then brought the Cross of the Angels, and after a terrible confrontation, the demon finally left never to return, saying that the Savior had sent him as an example for the world. The girl remained in Oviedo for six weeks, was baptized and given the name of Maria; she became an extremely beautiful and charming young woman who spoke to pilgrims about the events that had transpired."[174]

---

[174] Bennett, Janice, Sacred Blood, Sacred Image: The Sudarium of Oviedo – New Evidence for the Authenticity of The Shroud of Turin. Ignatius Press, San Francisco, CA. 2001. Pages 46-47.

CHAPTER VI

THE IMAGE OF DIVINE MERCY

The Visions and Locutions of Helena Kowalska

The year was 1931 and thoughts of the world's bloodiest war still haunted the memories of those who were alive during the first couple of decades of the new century. What they could not have known was that a worst war, one in every way more dreadful than the First World War, was on the horizon. In 1917, the Virgin Mary had warned the three children of Fatima, Portugal, of its potential outbreak, and she told them how it could be avoided. The media informed the world, but the world didn't listen.

Jesus knew of the chastisement that was about to befall creation, however, and He desired to communicate with the world prior to its outbreak. So, on the evening of February 22, 1931, a nineteen-year-old woman named Helena sat in her convent cell and prayed. As she did so, Helena Kowalska, now a young nun who took the name Faustina, received an apparition of her risen Lord.

Helena was born on August 25, 1905, the third of ten children. Her parents were poor peasant farmers in Glogowiec, Poland. She came to the convent with virtually nothing but the clothes on her back. She was mostly uneducated, though her father did teach her to read. Despite her miraculous visions, there was nothing extraordinary about her life. The events about to unfold on the night of February 22, however, would change the life of this simple woman, and impact the entire world.

This was not the first time that Helena had unusual visual contact with Jesus. At the age of seven, Helena began to have locutions, a sort of inner experience, and then visions that would continue for pretty much her entire life. She described it this way: "It was in the seventh year of my life that, for the first time, I heard God's voice in my soul; that is, an invitation to a more perfect life."[175] (Diary, 7) Though she didn't really understand, she continued to feel that calling to a more perfect life throughout her childhood and adolescence. As a teenager, while attending a dance, "…There He was. It was Jesus. He was stripped and bloody, the way he had been when the Roman soldiers tortured Him. His face showed the terrible pain He was suffering. And He turned straight to Helena and asked her, 'How long shall I put up with you and how long will you keep putting Me off?'"[176] (Diary 9)

In Search of God's Will

To Helena, everything else at that moment became invisible and silent. She was alone with Jesus. Then, as suddenly as it began, the vision ended. Helena sank into a chair next to her sisters, unable

---

[175] Mariani, Drew, Divine Mercy. Relevant Radio, P.O. Box 10707, Green Bay, WI, 2021. Page 13.
[176] Ibid. Page 15.

to explain what had just taken place. "I have a headache," is all she told them, but Helena knew that she could no longer ignore the will of God. Helena left the dance, walked a short distance to the Cathedral of St. Stanislaus Kostka, entered through the massive doors and fell to her knees before the Blessed Sacrament. "'What should I do, Lord?' she asked. 'What should I do? Please help me understand.' And then she heard Jesus's voice. 'Go at once to Warsaw,' He said. 'You will enter a convent there.'"[177] (Diary 10)

Helena left almost immediately, praying to the Virgin Mary for guidance along the way. And she received it. "'Go out to this place outside the city,' Mary told her, 'and you'll find a safe place to stay. It happened as Mary said and the next day Helena began her search for a convent that would accept her.

Because Helena was from a poor farming family, she didn't have the dowry that was required for acceptance in a convent. She knocked on the doors of many religious orders, but received an equal number of rejections, until she knocked on the door of the Sisters of Our Lady of Mercy. Mother Superior was ready to turn Helena away when something stopped her. Instead, she decided to appeal to the highest authority telling Helena to go to the chapel and ask Jesus if He would accept her. Helena did as she was asked and received an immediate answer from Jesus.

"I do accept; you are in my heart."[178] Filled with joy, Helena returned to Mother Superior who asked Helena if the Lord had accepted her, to which the young girl responded, "Yes." "If the Lord has accepted, I also will accept,"[179] Mother Superior said. (Diary 14)

---

[177] Ibid.

[178] Kowalska, Saint Maria Faustina, Diary - Divine Mercy in My Soul. Marian Press, Stockbridge, MA. 2016. First published in 1987. From the Original Polish Diary, Zgromadzenie Siosr Matkj Boxej Milosierdzia,ul. Zytnia 3/9, 01-014 Warszawa, Poland. 1981. Page 8. (Diary 14)

[179] Ibid. Page 17.

That summer night in 1925, nineteen-year-old Helena's life was dramatically changed. Certainly, she had to earn enough money for a dowry, but as soon as the convent was able to find a place for her, Helena became Sister Maria Faustina of the Most Blessed Sacrament, "and she began her new life of humble duties and constant prayer."[180]

Sr. Faustina's Vision of Divine Mercy

But something about the night of February 22, 1931, was different. Sr. Faustina recorded in her diary, "I was in my cell, I saw the Lord Jesus clothed in a white garment. One hand [was] raised in the gesture of blessing, the other was touching the garment at the breast. From beneath the garment, slightly drawn aside at the breast, there were emanating two large rays, one red, the other pale. In silence I kept my gaze fixed on the Lord; my soul was struck with awe, but also with great joy. After a while, Jesus said to me, 'Paint an image according to the pattern you see, with the signature: Jesus, I trust in You. I desire that this image be venerated, first in your chapel, and [then] throughout the world.'"[181]

Jesus promised Faustina that any soul that venerates the image would not perish. He also promised "victory over all [its] enemies already here on earth, especially at the hour of death. I Myself will defend it as My own glory,"[182] Jesus told her.

Painting Jesus with Divine Inspiration

Sr. Faustina desperately wanted to please the Lord by carrying out his request, but she was not an artist and knew of no one who was.

---

[180] Mariani, Drew, Divine Mercy. Relevant Radio, P.O. Box 10707, Green Bay, WI, 2021. Page 17.
[181] Kowalska, Saint Maria Faustina, Diary - Divine Mercy in My Soul. Marian Press, Stockbridge, MA. 2016. First published in 1987. From the Original Polish Diary, Zgromadzenie Siosr Matkj Boxej Milosierdzia,ul. Zytnia 3/9, 01-014 Warszawa, Poland. 1981. Page 24. (Diary 47)
[182] Ibid. (Diary 48)

That changed two years later when she was restationed to the town of Vilnius (modern-day Lithuania) and was introduced to Father Michael Sopocko, the priest who would become the humble nun's confessor and spiritual director. He put Sr. Faustina in touch with an artist by the name of Eugeniusz Kazimirowski. Together, the priest and the young nun directed the artist as he attempted to paint the image of Jesus as Sr. Faustina described Him. The visionary, with the permission of her Mother Superior, reported to the artist's studio twice a week to guide the painter as he struggled to recreate the exact image Faustina described. The process dragged on for several months and she was never satisfied, saying that the artist's image was simply not as beautiful as Jesus is. In frustration, the artist threatened to quit, and Faustina became very sad, but refused to allow her emotions to show in public. She did, however, go to the chapel where she cried and prayed, "Lord, who will paint You as beautiful as You are?" That's when she heard Jesus say, "Not in the beauty of the color, nor of the brush is the greatness of the image, but in my grace."[183] She knew then, that the image created by Kazimirowski would suffice.

Kazimirowski completed his painting in 1934, but it wasn't until Good Friday in 1935 that it was dedicated. Sr. Faustina had received further instruction from Jesus that the image should be dedicated on that day and publicly venerated on the Sunday after Easter. It was on that day, Sunday, April 28, 1935, four years before the outbreak of World War II, that the image of Divine Mercy was revealed to the world. A few months later, Jesus visited Sr. Faustina again and revealed to her the Chaplet of Divine Mercy, a prayer to be prayed routinely at 3:00 PM in remembrance of the Lord's Passion.

---

[183] Stackpole, Robert, STD, Why So Many Images? Which One is Best?. https://www.thedivinemercy.org/articles/why-so-many-images-which-one-best. Page 1. And from Kowalska, Saint Maria Faustina, Diary - Divine Mercy in My Soul. Marian Press, Stockbridge, MA. 2016. First published in 1987. From the Original Polish Diary, Zgromadzenie Siosr Matkj Boxej Milosierdzia,ul. Zytnia 3/9, 01-014 Warszawa, Poland. 1981. Page 143, Diary 313.

The Kazimirowski painting of Divine Mercy was unveiled for the first public adoration from April 28, 1935, in the sanctuary of Ostra Brama, Wilno, Poland.

The visions and locutions continued throughout Sr. Faustina's short life. She died of tuberculosis in 1938 at the age of thirty-three, before the horrors of World War II would envelop her beloved Poland and the rest of the world.

Since her death, other artists have tried to recreate the image using Sr. Faustina's description from her Diary and interpretation of Fr. Sopocko. The first to try was Polish artist Adolf Hyla. Though his image was still unable to capture the true essence of Jesus as He appeared to Faustina, the painting "was presented to the Sisters of Our Lady of Mercy in Poland in thanksgiving for the preservation of himself and his family during World War II. The sisters placed it over the tomb of Sister Faustina at their convent in Lagiewniki, and it can still be seen there today."[184]

---

[184] Stackpole, Robert, STD, Why So Many Images? Which One is Best?. https://www.thedivinemercy.org/articles/why-so-many-images-which-one-best. Page 2.

Copies of the Divine Mercy Image

In 1982, artist Robert Skemp tried to recreate an image in closer conformance with Sr. Faustina's description. Though this version is ultra realistic, he too, was unable to paint an image in perfect conformance to the description provided by the visionary. His painting now hangs over the altar at the Divine Mercy Shrine outside Manila in the Philippines.

Though all three images have been approved ecclesiastically for display in churches and for distribution to the faithful, it is the original painting by Kazimirowski that will be considered here, and it still resides in Vilnius, Poland. In addition to these three paintings, there are others that do not enjoy the luxury of ecclesiastical approval. One such image was painted by an American artist by the name of Kathleen Weber. It is a revision of the Hyla version and, with its dark blue background, has become a favorite in America.

The Mystery of Divine Mercy

Daniel DiSilva, founder of the Original Divine Mercy Institute, has spent the greater part of his adult life unraveling the mystery surrounding the Divine Mercy, and while "there are many aspects of Divine Mercy that the painting reveals, DiSilva shared three that are most significant. The first is that, as Jesus told Faustina, His mercy is unfathomable. 'In the painting, clearly, the rays that are emanating from Him are unfathomable, and that simply means they can't be measured,' he said. "When we look at the original painting, and the original only, because the other paintings don't have this, the mercy, which is represented by the rays, no one can see where they start, and no one can see where they end. They're unmeasurable.' Secondly, the painting shows that Divine Mercy is freely given. 'In the original image, Jesus is opening up His alb,' DiSilva explained, 'In the other paintings of Divine Mercy, he's simply pointing, or touching, at best. But in the original image, he's lifting his alb, and he's giving it. That's Divine Mercy. God gives it. It's not taken from

Him. It is a giving. It's a true gift. Third is the downward gaze from Jesus in the image, which is not one of the details that Sr. Faustina gave to Kazimirowski as he was painting the image. That feature came from Jesus Himself. 'She didn't give the direction for the downward gaze, but the downward gaze was there, and she asked Jesus, 'Why, in the painting, are your eyes downward cast?' And Jesus' answer was, 'My gaze in the painting is similar to my gaze from the cross,' DaSilva said. 'Only in the original masterpiece is His gaze downward. Why is it important? Because if He's looking for us, He's looking for us at the foot of the cross. That's where we're supposed to be to receive His mercy. And that's a big deal.'"[185]

In April 2000, Sr. Faustina was canonized by Pope John Paul II and since that time, devotion to the Divine Mercy and the image has increased significantly. Author Benedict Groeschel considered a modest estimate of those following Divine Mercy in the year 2010 to be over one hundred million Catholics.

---

[185] Lambert, Aaron, Jesus, I Trust in You: The History and Mystery of the Divine Mercy Devotion, The Archdiocese of San Francisco, March 28, 2024. https://sfarchdiocese.org/jesus-i-trust-in-you-the-history-and-mystery-of-the-divine-mercy-devotion/. Pages 2-3.

PART II

THE SCIENCE

CHAPTER VII

WHAT SCIENCE REVEALS ABOUT THE SHROUD OF TURIN

The Shroud of Turin is unquestionably the most studied Christian artifact in the world. It can be argued with equal ardor that it has become one of the most controversial objects of the last hundred and twenty years, becoming a source of controversy following presentation of the findings of the very first scientific study in 1902. This should come as no surprise, as the stakes are quite high and pits "the world of faith against the world of rational thought, all under the glare of the media."[186]

---

[186] Moorhead, Joanna, The $1M Challenge: 'If the Turin Shroud is a Forgery, Show How it Was Done', April 17, 2022, https://www.theguardian.com/world/2022/apr/17/the-1m-challenge-if-the-turin-shroud-is-a-forgery-show-how-it-was-done.

If skeptics are right, and the Shroud is a medieval forgery of the risen Christ, then not much really changes in our world. Christianity will remain a very popular religion across the globe. That is because Christianity is based upon the passion, death and resurrection of Jesus, and none of those events are contingent upon the authenticity of this cloth.

If however, the Shroud is proven to be authentic, then what we essentially have is a first century photograph of Jesus, the Son of God, and that photograph provides proof of how he suffered and died, and then rose from the dead, just as proclaimed in the Gospels, and that is a thought that terrifies any non-believer.

So, what is the evidence that the Turin Shroud is the authentic burial cloth of Jesus, bearing the image of the crucified Christ at the moment of His resurrection?

The Most Studied Cloth in the World
1901 - 1902

The first scientific study of the Shroud was conducted by Paul Vignon, working on behalf of the Institute Catholique. In the early 1900s, Vignon heard about the photographs taken by Secondo Pio at the end of the nineteenth century and was convinced that the image on the cloth was not a painting. This steadfast Catholic worked side by side with Ynes Delage, an agnostic who was a professor of anatomy at the Sorbonne. After studying the photographs, Delage concurred that the image was anatomically correct and could not be the work of an artist.

Vignon then conducted a series of experiments to try to determine how such an image might have come to be imprinted on the Shroud. He obtained pieces of old linen with a weave and thickness similar to that of the Shroud and painted them with oils and watercolors. Once dry, he rolled the cloth and took note of how the paint cracked and peeled off. To him, this evidence signified that the image was not a painting.

Perhaps the image was "made with a light dye that diffused into the fibrils of the linen cloth,"[187] he hypothesized. But the liquid did not leave vein-like patterns spreading across the threads of the fabric. Neither could such dyes have been affected by the chemical changes required to produce a negative image.

Vignon also studied the wound marks, and "based on the shape of the wounds as well as how the blood clotted on the linen cloth,"[188] he was even more convinced that the image was not a forgery. The blood stains were realistic, and that is neither how medieval artists, nor artists of previous periods of time, portrayed blood in their artistic works.

Satisfied that he had adequately proven that the image was not a painting, Vignon focused on showing how the image might have been made. Donning a false beard, he covered himself in red chalk and lay on an operating table. His colleagues covered him with a linen cloth "coated with albumen that acted as 'lint tape' to which the chalk would adhere. The experiment failed to produce the vivid details of the Shroud. Naturally, the parts of the cloth not touched by the body did not pick up anything. Furthermore, the images that were picked up were distorted."[189]

In an effort to show that the image may have been produced by vaporization, Vignon and Rene Colson, an associate, studied Jewish burial customs. Their research indicated that the myrrh and aloes were often mixed with olive oil "to make an unguent which was applied to the body or the cloth or both. Aloe contains two chemical principles, namely, aloin and aloetine. When aloin is added to water it gives a yellow tone. Aloetine, on the other hand, which oxidizes quickly with alkalies, would turn brown. Vignon and Colson knew that vaporized ammonia could produce images. Ammonia is the by-

---

[187] Guerrera, Vittorio, Fr. The Shroud of Turin: A Case for Authenticity. Tan Books and Publishers, Inc. Rockford, Il. 2001. Page 51.
[188] Ibid. Page 52.
[189] Ibid.

product of fermented urea which is largely excreted by the body in urine and in small amounts through perspiration. A body which has undergone severe torture can emit what is known as morbid sweat. Once fermented, urea becomes a carbonate of ammonia, and this would produce alkaline vapors that could stain the spices and olive oil on the Shroud."[190]

Delage presented the findings in a lecture before the Paris Academy of Sciences. His paper was entitled *'The Image of Christ Visible on the Holy Shroud of Turin.'* In it he explained how his study demonstrated without question that the image was not a forgery. The "presentation caused such controversy that the Secretary of the Academy refused to print in the Academy's journal, *Comptes Rendus*, any section of Delage's paper that indicated the image on the Shroud was that of Jesus Christ."[191]

Delage was so shaken by the reaction to the presentation that he discontinued the study of the Shroud, choosing instead to focus on other studies of interest. His abandonment of the project, however, did not impact Vignon who continued his study of the relic but was unable to duplicate the vaporograph process in a lab.

1933

Dr. Pierre Barbet had an opportunity to see the Shroud in 1933 and he was instantly intrigued by the icon. Barbet was the surgeon general of St. Joseph Hospital in Paris and subsequently conducted one of the most comprehensive anatomical studies of the image. He worked primarily with Enrie's photographs and conducted several tests using cadavers, amputated limbs and living volunteers. He concluded that the image on the Shroud was of a man who had been tortured and crucified.

---

[190] Ibid. Pages 52-53.
[191] Ibid. Page 53.

1950s

Dr. Hermann Moedder, conducted similar research in the 1950s. A German radiologist working at St. Francis Hospital in Cologne, Moedder suspended volunteers, primarily university students, from crosses in a successful effort to determine the physical effects of crucifixion.

1960s

Dr. David Willis, an English physician who followed the work of Dr. Moedder, compiled a summary of all the medical studies of the Shroud that were available at that time.

In 1969, unbeknownst to much of the general public, Michele Cardinal Pellegrino of Turin, Italy, appointed a commission, to examine the Shroud. Monsignor Pietro Caramello was named chairman and Monsignor Jose Cottino, vice chairman. Others included Monsignor Sergio Baldi, secretary; Professor Silvio Curto, curator of the Egyptian Museum of Turin; Professor Enzo DeLorenzi, head of radiology at Mauriziano Hospital in Turin; Professor Giorgio Frache, from the Institute of Forensic Medicine at the University of Modena; Dr. Noemi Gabrielli, retired director of the art galleries of Piemonte; and Dr. Giovanni Battista Judica Cordiglia, photographer and lecturer in Forensic Medicine at the University of Milan. Three other professors, Camillo Lenti, Enrico Medi and Luigi Gedda, rounded out the commission, sometimes referred to as "the secret commission."

This team examined the Shroud on June 16 and June 17, 1969, taking note of its good condition and offering precautionary measures that needed to be taken to preserve the Shroud from deterioration. They also suggested proposals for the continuation of scientific research. Thread samples from the linen were examined revealing that it was a mixture of cotton, an interesting revelation since cotton doesn't grow in Europe. The cotton in the linen, however, was of "a Middle Eastern variety known as G. herbaceum. According to Mosaic law, there was a prohibition against combining linen and wool (cf. Lev. 19:19; Deut. 22:11). However, it was licit to combine cotton and wool. That being the case, it would not have been considered unlawful for a weaver to use the same loom to weave cotton and linen."[192]

1970s

Following a very rare, televised exposition of the Shroud, there was a renewed interest in the cloth and calls for new studies intensified. Consequently, a new study team was assembled, and it included several members who served on the 'Secret Commission' of the 1960s. Those returning were Dr. Cordiglia; Professor Curto; Professor Gabreilli, Professor DeLorenzi, and Dr. Frache. In addition to those study veterans, several new professionals joined the team, including: Dr. Cesare Codegone, director of the department of technological physics at the Polytechnic of Turin; Professor Guido Filogamo from the Institute of Human Anatomy at the University of Turin; and his colleague, Alberto Zina. In addition, the newcomers included Professor Mario Milone, director of the Institute of Chemistry at the University of Turin; Dr. Max Frei, a Swiss criminologist and botanist; and Professor Gilbert Raes, Belgian textile expert from the Ghent Institute of Textile Technology; and two of Dr. Frache's colleagues, Dr. Eugenia Mari Rizzati and Dr. Emilio Mari.

Unlike the previous commission, these scientists were actually granted permission to remove from the cloth seventeen sample threads for analysis. No official 'commission' report was issued, but in January 1976, individual findings resulting from those analysis were published as follows:

- Doctor Frache and his colleagues, after an examination of five of the seventeen threads from the bloodstained areas of the Shroud, would not concede that the stains were blood. They

---

[192] Ibid. Pages 55-56.

did however, acknowledge that after examination of the fibers of the frontal image, the "body image appeared on the upper surface of the cloth and was composed of yellow fibrils that did not penetrate the linen"[193] and though they substantially affected the majority of fibers, they were not found in the spaces between the fibers.
- In a dissertation published by Doctor Codegone, he said it was inadvisable to perform a carbon-14 dating test on the Shroud "because such a test would be unreliable."[194]
- Professor DeLorenzi went a step further, finding that even a less invasive radiological test would be meaningless. Radiographs performed on works of art, he said, provide results because of the use of pigments containing heavy metals and these are absent in the Shroud.
- Professor Gabrielli found that while there is no evidence of pigment or dye on the Shroud, the image is never the less the work of an artist and suggested a couple of ways that an artist may have accomplished it.
- Professors Zino and Filogamo studied two threads under a microscope to determine the presence of blood. While they did find evidence of plant fibers within the threads, their quest for evidence of blood proved inconclusive.
- Professor Raes studied the weave and found it to contain fibers of cotton and linen "spun in a 'Z' twist pattern and woven in a three-to-one twill, meaning that the horizontal (weft) thread passes alternately over three and under one of the vertical (warp) threads."[195] Additionally, there are twenty-four threads in each square centimeter in the weft and thirty-six in the warp.

---

[193] Ibid. Page 57.
[194] Ibid. Page 56.
[195] Ibid. Pages 58 – 59.

Essentially, the results of the testing were largely inconclusive primarily due to the lack of coordination among team members. Each worked independently on a specific aspect of the study and there was no collaboration of effort. Despite the uncertainties resulting from the study, it did leave open a path for additional scientific inquiry.

1978
The STURP Study

Anastasio Ballestrero, the newly appointed Archbishop of Turin, hoped to make the 400th anniversary of the transference of the Shroud from Chambery to Turin a memorable occasion. The planned ceremonies began with the public exposition of the sacred relic from August 27 to October 8, and culminated with the most comprehensive scientific examination of the cloth in history. Over forty scientists from Italy and America were allowed to carry out non-destructive tests on the Shroud for one hundred and twenty hours over a period of five days.

The American scientists, numbering just over thirty, became known as the Shroud of Turin Research Project (STURP) and was led by Doctors John Jackson and Eric Jumper, two US Air Force captains and physicists. Armed with seventy-two crates of equipment, "the group was composed of specialists from different disciplines: Donald Lynn headed a group from the Jet Propulsion Laboratory of Pasadena that included Jean Lorre, and Donald Devan from the Oceanographic Services, Inc. of Santa Barbara. Bill Mottern, from the Sandia Laboratories, led the team of specialists who carried out a series of radiography exams of the Shroud with the following group from Los Alamos National Scientific Laboratories: Robert Dinegar, Donald and Joan Janney, Larry Schwalbe, Diane Soran, Ron London, Roger Morris, and Ray Rogers, who took various sticky tape samples of dust particles from the surface of the Shroud. Joseph Accetta from

Lockheed Corporation coordinated the group that inspected the Shroud with infrared rays. Roger and Marion Gilbert from the Oriel Corporation of Connecticut examined the light spectrum emitted by fluorescence beneath ultraviolet lighting.

Also participating in the examination of the Shroud were Steven Baumgard and John German from the US Air Force Weapons Laboratories; Robert Bucklin, medical examiner; Joseph Gambescia, chairman of medicine at St. Agnes Medical Center in Philadelphia; Rudoph Dichtl from the University of Colorado; Ken Stevenson from IBM; Thomas D'Muhala from the Nuclear Technology Corporation; and Thomas Haverty from Rocky Mountain Thermograph. Photographers included the following: Ernest Brooks, Vernon Miller and Mark Evans from the Brooks Institute of Photography in Santa Barbara, CA; Barrie Schwortz; and Sam Pellicori, an optical physicist from the Santa Barbara Research Center. Dr. Max Frei, the Swiss botanist and criminologist who had taken pollen samples back in 1973, attended as well." Finally, some nuns from the Sisters of St. Joseph attended and assisted in the unstitching of a portion of the protective cloth which had been added to the Shroud in 1534, enabling a mini vacuum to extract some dust particles. They also extracted some sample threads from the cloth. [196]

Working around the clock, the team conducted extensive tests including:

micro and macroscopic observations; Thirty-two sticky tape samples; X-ray fluorescence spectrometry; photomacrographs; low energy X-radiography; infra-red; visible and ultra-violet reflectance spectra; photographic images of wavelength regions, including thermal emission images; and electron microscopy and microprobe. The team also took over thirty thousand photographs and conducted additional tests when they returned to the United States.

---

[196] Ibid. Pages 60 – 61.

In addition to the hours spent viewing and testing the Shroud, just about a quarter million hours were spent in the analysis of the data collected. Unfortunately, like those of the secret commission, the findings were not published in a single book or report. Rather, they were presented in individual professional and scientific journals making them very difficult for the public to access. The essence of the findings are summarized as follows: "the image is not formed by paint, there is evidence of human blood on the cloth, and the image formation must be caused by some cellulose oxidation/dehydration process. Ray Rogers declared: 'I am forced to conclude that the image was formed by a burst of radiant energy – light if you like.'"[197]

The Result of Decades of Study
The Textile Analysis

The Shroud measures fourteen feet, three inches by three feet, eight inches and is woven in an intricate three-over-one herringbone pattern. The STURP Study provided conclusive evidence that it is a high-quality linen consisting of fibers made of "hand-spun flax, a strong fiber, finer and more textured than cotton, with the linen thread coming from the stems of the flax plant."[198] Flax is botanically connected to two plants, *Linum usitatissimum* and *Gossypium haerbaceum*, both of which grow in the region that extends from the eastern Mediterranean to India. With a documented use history of five thousand years, it is unmistakably one of the oldest fiber crops in the world.

The Z-shaped twist to the weave of the Shroud tends to be a bit counterintuitive as it requires a clockwise spin rather than a more traditional counterclockwise spin that produces an S-shaped twist and has been used for centuries. "The resulting cloth is very fine, with a

---

[197] Guerrera, Vittorio, Fr. The Shroud of Turin: A Case for Authenticity. Tan Books and Publishers, Inc. Rockford, Il. 2001. Page 66.
[198] Verschuuren, Gerard, A Catholic Scientist Champions the Shroud of Turin. Sophia Institute Press, Manchester, NH. 2021. Page 73.

density of 35 threads per centimeter, or about 89 threads per inch. To give some perspective, the finest surviving Egyptian mummy fabrics are 30 threads per centimeter (75 threads per inch)."[199]

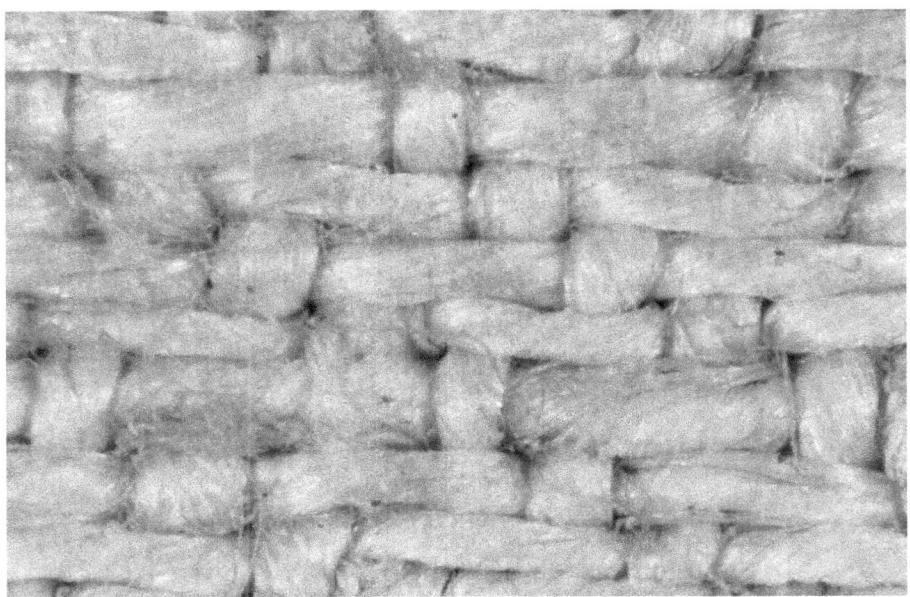

Enlarged area of the Shroud showing the herringbone pattern weave. "© Vernon Miller, 1978. No unauthorized reproduction of Material on other Websites is allowed without prior written permission from the shroudphotos.com copyright holder. Original photos are available for free at www.shroudphotos.com".

The fibers themselves measure thirteen micrometers in diameter, falling squarely within the flax plant fibers average range of between twelve to sixteen micrometers. The textile analysis indicated that the linen of the Shroud is indeed finely made, a fact supported by the biblical texts. All four Gospels of the New Testament note that it was Joseph of Arimathea who assumed responsibility for the burial of Jesus. He approached Pontius Pilate for permission to remove the body from the cross, he provided the tomb, which he had hewn from

---

[199] Downing, Ray, The Fabric of the Shroud of Turin, March 30, 2017.
https://www.raydowning.com/blog/2017/2/23/the-fabric-of-the-shroud-of-turin.

rock for his own personal use, and he tended to the anointment of the body with aloes and myrrh. The Gospel of Matthew describes Joseph as a "rich man"[200]. As such, he presumably could have afforded the finest linen. The Gospel of Mark tells of how Joseph, after receiving permission from Pilate to remove the body of Jesus from the cross, immediately "brought a linen shroud, and taking him down, wrapped him in the linen shroud."[201]

The STURP Committee measured the thickness of the Shroud so that it could address the possibility that the image was formed by heat penetration. It was determined that the cloth was 345 microns thick which translates into a thickness of about one hundredth of an inch. Producing a heat-induced image so faint would require the application of heat for less than one second. Because the image is imprinted on only the uppermost fibers of the Shroud, it is most improbable that it could have been produced by a hot object in that short a period of time. For purposes of this experiment, Fr. Vittorio Guerrera noted that "a thread is composed of one hundred or more fibers. Each thread is about one-seventh of a millimeter wide. When fiber is separated, it is called a fibril; each fibril is fifteen microns in diameter."[202]

The STURP study also noted that the coloration penetrated the cloth to a depth of only one or two fibers and that the fibers were not stuck together, confirming the results of prior studies that the image was not painted. Further, the image was found to be monochromatic, "meaning that the yellow discoloration of the fibers is the same

---

[200] Holy Bible, The – New Testament, The Word on Fire Bible, The Gospels. New Revised Standard Version. John 20:1-10. Brandon Vogt, General Editor. Word on Fire, Park Ridge, IL. 2020. Matthew 27:57.

[201] Holy Bible, The – New Testament, The Word on Fire Bible, The Gospels. New Revised Standard Version. John 20:1-10. Brandon Vogt, General Editor. Word on Fire, Park Ridge, IL. 2020. Mark 15:46.

[202] Guerrera, Vittorio, Fr. The Shroud of Turin: A Case for Authenticity. Tan Books and Publishers, Inc. Rockford, Il. 2001. Page 62.

throughout the image [and that] any variations in color scheme are due to the number of fibers that are discolored."[203]

That the image does not penetrate the fibrils was confirmed by the fact that the image disappears when viewing the cloth with light directed from behind.

Unfortunately, the Cloth also showed the destruction that fire had caused to it. Not only the December 4, 1532, fire in Sainte-Chapelle, Chambery, but damage caused by a previous fire were also discovered during ultraviolet fluorescence testing. The damage from the Chambery fire displayed with a reddish fluorescence, an indication that the Shroud "smoldered in an encased environment of low oxygen."[204] These burns were clearly caused by the Chambery fire during the time that the cloth was kept in the silver reliquary. The additional damage, however, was caused by a fire that must have taken place prior to 1516. That is known because in that year a smaller replica of the Shroud was painted. On that replica, which is kept in Saint Gommaire Church in Lier, Belgium, the artist depicted only four of the burn marks that are visible today, indicating that the previous fire damage must have occurred prior to that date. In fact, the "Pray Codex, dated to the early 1190s, also displays a shroud with four clear L-shaped holes. These holes must be the marks of the fire that had damaged the Shroud at some date prior to 1190."[205]

The exact dates that fire damaged the Shroud, mattered little to the Poor Clares of Chambery, the nuns who worked painstakingly to patch the burn marks. Textile analysis determined that they used dyed cotton fibers to repair the flax-fiber cloth. Further, they "reinforced the ancient cloth by attaching the linen to new material that dates to Europe between 1532 and 1534. This practice of affixing

---

[203] Ibid.
[204] Verschuuren, Gerard, A Catholic Scientist Champions the Shroud of Turin. Sophia Institute Press, Manchester, NH. 2021. Page 76.
[205] Ibid. Page 77

older cloth to newer was not unusual – the support cloth is known as the 'Holland cloth' or 'Dutch cloth.'"[206]

The repairs made by the Poor Clares were not the only preservations made to the Shroud. Additional restoration work was undertaken in 1694 by Sebastian Valfre of the Oratory of St. Philip Neri, and in 1868 by Princess Clotilde of the House of Savoy (who possessed the Shroud at the time) each in an effort to improve its ability to withstand public display and veneration.

The difference in cloth fibers was confirmed by Gilbert Raes from the Ghent Institute of Textile Technology in Belgium. He concluded that "the original linens were an ancient Near Eastern variety of Gossypium herbaceum, which grows typically in the Middle East. He based his report on the distance between reversals in the tape-shaped flax fibers (about eight per centimeter). This discovery made it extremely likely that the cloth had been made in the Middle East."[207]

Of course, while the textile evidence suggests that the Shroud could have been produced in first century Jerusalem, it does not provide scientific proof that the cloth is from that time period.

The Mysterious Side Strip

As if the Shroud itself isn't mysterious enough, a linen strip measuring fourteen feet, three inches by three inches, runs along the left side (when looking at it upright) of the Shroud. Commonly referred to as the "side strip," this cloth is affixed to the Shroud with but a single seam, and a substantial portion of it - five and a half inches from the bottom and fourteen inches from the top left corner - appears to be missing. This strip "is made from the same piece of linen as the Shroud. They both have a twill herringbone weave, with the same textile irregularities. They also both showcase the same threading. The thread in the side seam imitates that of the Shroud in identical

---

[206] Ibid.
[207] Ibid. Page 78.

fiber thickness and weaving pattern, strongly suggesting that the two pieces were made of the same fabric."[208]

The analysis of the side strip reveals no information as to whether the strip was attached to or detached from the Shroud itself. Alan Adler and his team performed a chemical analysis of the strip and determined that it certainly predates the 1534 repairs made to the Shroud suggesting that the strip and the Shroud were made at the same time. Textile expert Flury-Lemberg later discovered that there is "a peculiar stitching pattern in the seam of one long side of the Shroud, where a three-inch-wide strip of the same original fabric was sewn onto a larger segment."[209] She had encountered this 'essentially identical' type of stitching situation only one other time in her long career in the tombs just outside of Masada, Israel, an area that "contains the ruins of Jewish fortress sacked by the Romans at the end of the First Jewish-Roman War, between 66AD and 73 AD. That cloth dated to the time of the burial of Jesus."[210] Flury-Lemberg noted the astounding similarities between the Masada sample and the Shroud, commenting that this kind of stitch has never been found on cloths originating from Medieval times in Europe.

She speculated that the strip was one of the cloths (plural) in the tomb and referred to by the apostles who entered on that Easter Sunday morning. It is likely that someone sewed the side strip to the main cloth as a means of keeping them together. Catholic tradition teaches that it was Jesus' mother Mary who did so prior to her nephew Thaddeus bringing the Shroud to Edessa. It may have also provided a useful means of protecting the Shroud from damage during its many public displays. It is quite possible that pieces of the Shroud were gifted to dignitaries over the centuries accounting for the missing pieces of the side strip at the top and bottom of the cloth.

---

[208] Ibid. Pages 78-79.
[209] Ibid. Page 79.
[210] Ibid. Pages 79-80.

The Crown of Thorns

As has been noted earlier, the Romans executed thousands of people by crucifixion. Typically, that particular form of execution followed a prescribed script. The condemned person was flogged, forced to carry his own patibula, and nailed or tied to a cross made in a variety of shapes. Apparently, only one historically recorded crucifixion, that of Jesus the Christ, involved the condemned person being forced to wear a crown of thorns. Over the approximately twenty centuries that have passed since the torturous death of Jesus, many artists have portrayed His crucifixion in paintings, sculptures and religious articles, from Rosary beads to statues, and almost all of them feature the crucified Christ wearing a crown of thorns that encircled his head.

The Shroud, however, provides evidence of something quite different. It shows that the body covered by the fabric actually wore a 'cap' of thorns, one that encased the entire head, not just encircled it. Consequently, in addition to providing more evidence that the Shroud might be the actual burial cloth of Jesus, the blood evidence of the Shroud shatters the common assumption that the crown of thorns simply encircled the head of Jesus.

The blood pattern depicted on the Shroud resulting from the crown of thorns even made it possible for scientists to determine the thorns used to plate the head of Jesus. Columbia University professor of pathology, Frederick Zugibe, the chief medical examiner of Rockland County, New York, said, "the tortuous flows on the forehead and the significant amount of blood on the head region had to have been the result of penetration of the skin by sharp thorns from plants like those of *Ziziphus spina* or *Ziziphus paliuris*, both of the Buckthorn family (Rhamnaceae). Using forensic analysis, he also notes that '*Ziziphus spina Christi* (Syrian Christ thorn) or *Ziziphus paliuris Christi* (Christ's thorn) would cause puncture-type wounds with significant bleeding when struck with the reed…accounting for the blood flows and accumulations of blood in the head region of the

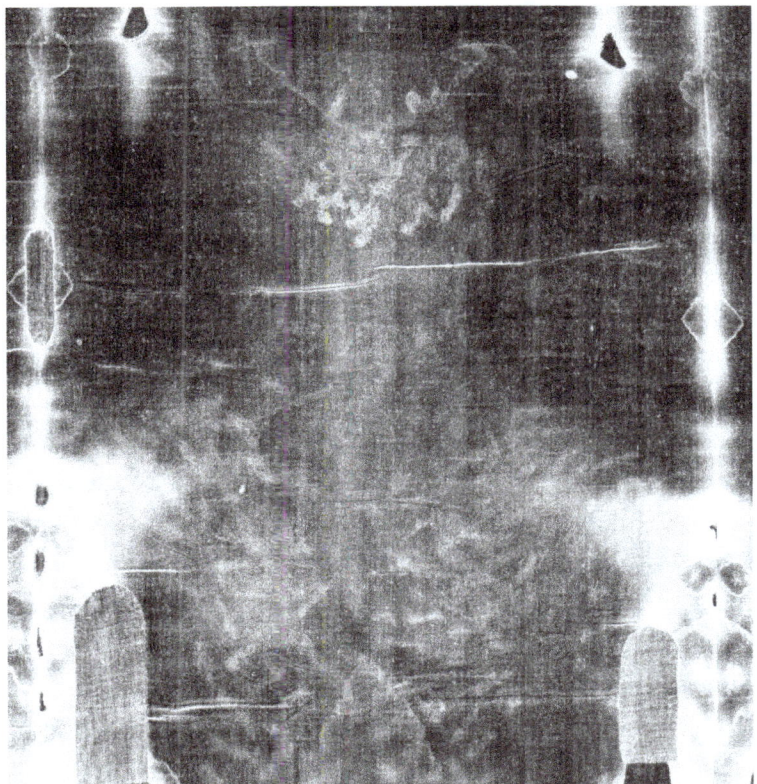

This image of the Shroud shows the back of the head and back. The blood stains on the head provide evidence that the thorns crowned the entire head of Jesus. "© Vernon Miller, 1978. No unauthorized reproduction of Material on other Websites is allowed without prior written permission from the shroudphotos.com copyright holder. Original photos are available for free at <u>www.shroudphotos.com</u>".

Shroud.'"[211] Either one of those varieties can be easily plaited into a cap of thorns, and a cap (as opposed to a circular crown) would have provided far more head surface area to penetrate with thorns.

According to Michael Evanari, a professor of Botany at the University of Jerusalem, Ziziphus spina can indeed be found at the southern border of Israel and, to a lesser degree, in Sumaria, but it cannot be found today in Jerusalem, making it unlikely, but not impossible, that it grew there during the time of Jesus. However, a

---

[211] Ibid. Page 92.

different species of thorns that is found in Jerusalem in abundance is *Acacia nilotica*. Incredibly, a crown of thorns made from the Acacia nilotica was found by Robin Hewitt, a archaeologist who unearthed a sarcophagus dating to the year 1189.

Finally, Hebrew University professor, Avinoam Danis, a highly respected Israeli botanist, believes that the cap of thorns may have been made from *Gundelia tournefortii*, a thorny tumbleweed in the thistle family. Danis suggested this as a possibility after finding significant amounts of pollen from that plant on the Shroud of Turin. Critics are quick to point out, however, that the Gundelia tournefortii can be described more as prickly than thorny and may not have thorns large enough to produce the head wounds revealed on the Shroud.

The evidence left on the Shroud by the thorny cap worn by the man who was covered by the cloth suggests that it may have come from first century Jerusalem, but once again, scientific analysis cannot confirm that based solely upon this evidence. Gerard Verschuuren, author of *A Catholic Scientist Champions the Shroud of Turin*, is quick to note that "science cannot prove anything with absolute certainty – at best it can confirm its conclusions to a higher degree."[212]

Pollen Analysis

Pollen consists of a mass of microspores in seed plants and generally appears as a fine dust. Each pollen grain is a microscopic body that varies widely in shape and structure depending on its plant of origin. It is formed in the male structures of seed-bearing plants and is transported by insects, wind, water, etc., to the female structures of plants allowing for fertilization to take place. Each plant variety contains its own very distinctive pollen structure providing for science a straightforward form of plant identification.

---

[212] Ibid. Page 89.

Swiss forensic scientist, Max Frei-Sulzer, microscopically examined dust and pollen samples extracted from the Shroud with sticky tape. He hoped to apply a crime solving method he had developed in the course of his career to the analysis of the dust and pollen taken from the surface of the Shroud. Using this method, Frei-Sulzer was able to identify pollen grains from fifty-eight species of plants. Seventeen of those plants, were indigenous to Europe, including the regions of Lirey and Chambery. The balance of the species identified, however, forty-one in all, were plants indigenous to the area of the Dead Sea and Turkey. These included *Hyoscyamus aureus, Artemisia herba-alba,* and *Onosma syriacum*. One of the grains identified was from a species called *Zygophyllum dumosum*, a specie exclusive to Israel.*

Suspicious of the findings, the cloth was subjected to further examination. But rather than discrediting Frei-Sulzer's findings, Avinoam Danis discovered not one, but twenty-eight species unique to Jerusalem. In a report published in 2010, Danin wrote, "March-April is the time of year when the whole assemblage of some ten of the plants identified on the Shroud are in bloom."[213] If these pollen grains were attached to the cloth from its first use, then this information confirms not only the Shroud's appearance in Jerusalem, but also its use during the very month of Jesus' burial.

While providing the Shroud another link to the region of Jerusalem, the pollen analysis does not, in and of itself, prove that the Shroud was in Jerusalem at the time that the body of Jesus was laid in the tomb.

Paint Analysis

Many who refuse to believe that the Shroud might be the actual burial cloth of Jesus, also believe that the image on the cloth is

---

*Some pollen grains can be traced only to the level of genus (IE. *Zygophyllum*) and may not be traceable to the specific level of species (IE. *Dumosum*).
[213] Ibid. Page 87.

the work of an artist. Naturally, before trying to show that the image is that of Jesus, it is prudent to explore the possibility that it is an elaborate work of art.

If the Shroud is the work of art, however, the artist would have had to have created it prior to 1355, the year of its first public exhibition. That rules out such artistic behemoths as Leonardo daVinci, Raphael, Michelangelo, Donatello, Lorenzo Ghiberti, Jan van Eyck, Giovanni Bellini, and other masters, none of whom were even born by the year 1355.

To provide evidence needed to respond to the 'artistic forgery' speculation, several scientists inspected the Shroud using some of the most sophisticated tools available to science at the time. These tools included "visible and ultraviolet spectrometry, infrared spectrometry, X-ray fluorescence spectrometry, and thermography. Fiber observations were made by pyrolysis-mass-spectometry, Raman lasermicroprobe analysis, and microchemical testing."[214] The result of all of these tests was unambiguous and unanimous. The Shroud contains absolutely no evidence of paint or pigments of any kind!

The 1978 STURP Research Group included technical photographer Barrie Schwortz, a non-practicing Jew who believed that the Shroud was a fake, a medieval painting. By his own admission, it took Schwortz only ten minutes to discover that it was not a painting, as it contained no paint or brush strokes. There are several identifying factors that every painting would be expected to contain. None of them are present in the Shroud.

- The first of these telltale signs is that a painting would likely have an outline on the image. There is no outline on the Shroud.
- Second, paint or pigment would cause the fibers of the fabric to stick together. This did not happen on the Shroud.

---

[214] Ibid. Page 111.

- Third, the stains on the Shroud are superficial and do not extend completely through the thread of the cloth which are only a few fibers deep. Paint would penetrate the fibers of the cloth.
- Fourth, a painting can reflect only the information known by the artist. The detail of the image on the Shroud could not have been known by anyone in medieval times.
- Fifth, paint cracks when subjected to heat with the intensity of the fire of 1532. There is no cracking present on the Shroud.
- Sixth, the wounds of the man on the Shroud, when exposed to ultraviolet light, "display chemical particularities such as serum clots, that can be found only in real blood. It is nearly impossible that a medieval artist would have a microscopic knowledge of the qualities of human blood."[215]
- Seventh, an artist could not have painted with human blood because real blood would have clotted too fast.
- Eighth, it would have been very difficult at best for a forger to cut and later stitch the two parts of the Shroud.
- Ninth, the raw, unprepared linen of the Shroud would repel water. There is no known paint that could be applied to such a cloth and produce the same optical effect seen on the Shroud.
- Tenth, the image is a perfect photographic negative. With the advent of photography still hundreds of years into the future, no artist of the time could have the knowledge necessary to create that. Further, the blood on the Shroud is real and precedes the appearance of image. There is, in fact, no image beneath the blood stains.
- Eleventh, and perhaps most significantly, there is a direct correlation between the intensity of the image and the distance of the skin of the man in the image to the cloth. In essence,

---

[215] Ibid. Page 112.

"the closer the body is to the cloth, the darker the body image."[216] Consequently, "the image of the man on the Shroud can be read by 3D imaging technology, but paintings fail this test."[217] Typically, paintings are only two dimensional. The three-dimensional concept was first demonstrated in 1976 as a result of testing performed by John Jackson and Eric Jumper, working with Bill Mottern of Sandia Laboratory in Albuquerque. The team used a VP-8 Image Analyzer with "black and white photos of the Shroud taken by Enrie in 1931. For Jackson, this is a 'confirmation that the Shroud covered a body shape at the time of image formation.'"[218]

- Finally, the Shroud was also found to be stable both thermally and chemically. This means that neither the fire of 1532, nor the water used to extinguish it, affected the image. This would not be the case if nonorganic pigments had been used to create the image. In fact, the image is most likely "caused by an alteration of the microfibrils of the cellulose structure of the cloth caused by oxidation, dehydration and conjugation of long-chain sugar molecules that make up the microfibrils."[219] This essentially means the when the image was formed, the chemical makeup of the fiber in the cloth was changed.

Based on this analysis, the STURP Committee concluded that the fact that "no pigments, paints, dyes or stains…found on the fibrils, and microchemistry on the fibrils, preclude the possibility of paint

---

[216] Guerrera, Vittorio, Fr. The Shroud of Turin: A Case for Authenticity. Tan Books and Publishers, Inc. Rockford, Il. 2001. Pages 64-65.
[217] Verschuuren, Gerard, A Catholic Scientist Champions the Shroud of Turin. Sophia Institute Press, Manchester, NH. 2021. Page 76.
[218] Guerrera, Vittorio, Fr. The Shroud of Turin: A Case for Authenticity. Tan Books and Publishers, Inc. Rockford, Il. 2001. Page 65.
[219] Ibid. Page 66.

being used as a method for creating the image."[220] This finding is further supported by the fact that no brush marks were detected on the Shroud.

The Presence of Blood on the Shroud

Typically, the presence of blood is determined by conducting a chemical test that involves a reaction with the ring structure of the

An enlarged portion of the Shroud stained with the blood of the man it covered. "© Vernon Miller, 1978. No unauthorized reproduction of Material on other Websites is allowed without prior written permission from the shroudphotos.com copyright holder. Original photos are available for free at www.shroudphotos.com".

blood protein hemoglobin. When this test was applied to the Shroud, the result showed the presence of both blood and serum albumin, a protein of the blood made by the liver. Additionally, microchemical testing performed on the Shroud revealed the presence of proteins in the areas of the cloth containing blood stains but proved negative for proteins in the part of the cloth not containing blood stains.

---

[220] Verschuuren, Gerard, A Catholic Scientist Champions the Shroud of Turin. Sophia Institute Press, Manchester, NH. 2021. Page 115.

The STURP study had gathered blood flecks on some of the sticky-tape samples taken from the Shroud. These flecks were examined by chemist Alan Adler, from Western Connecticut State University, and physician John Heller, from the New England Institute, who compared the samples with the spectra of blood spots, using a technique that can accurately demonstrate the presence of ten-thousand-year-old blood.[221] Their microspectrophotometry testing found that the Shroud contained "serum, [which could be detected with ultraviolet fluorescence], blood proteins, hemoglobin, blood clots, porphyrin and bilirubin."[222] Their conclusion: the stains that appear on the Shroud are human blood.

The discovery of high levels of bilirubin is significant of two very substantial findings. The first is that the body had been subjected to a tremendous amount of trauma which causes the presence of bilirubin in the blood. According to Fr. Vittorio Guerrera, bilirubin is present in the blood "When blood begins to break down, particularly after someone has suffered a severe trauma."[223] Second, the effect of significant trauma will prevent the aging blood from appearing brown in color, but rather will cause it to remain bright red even after hundreds of years have passed. In addition, the blood stains on the Shroud had clearly marked edges which "reproduce the shape of the

---

[221] According to Fr. Vittorio Guerrera, the twelve specific tests performed by Heller and Adler included: High Iron in blood areas by X-ray fluorescence; Indicative reflection spectra; Indicative microspectrophotometric transmission spectra; Chemical generation of characteristic porphyrin fluorescence; Positive hemochromagen tests; Positive cyanmethemoglobin tests; Positie detection of bile pigments; Positive demonstration of protein; Positive indication of albumin specifically; Protease tests, leaving no residues; Microscopic appearance as compared with appropriate controls; and Forensic judgment of the appearance of the various wound and blood marks. (Page 64 of A Catholic Scientist Champions the Shroud of Turin).

[222] Guerrera, Vittorio, Fr. The Shroud of Turin: A Case for Authenticity. Tan Books and Publishers, Inc. Rockford, Il. 2001. Page 63.

[223] Ibid. Page 64.

clots as they were formed naturally on the skin."[224] Generally speaking, "It takes only three out of twelve blood tests to prove the presence of whole blood in a court of law. On the Shroud there are four times that number."[225] Finally, the Guilio Fanti team found that the bloodstains on the cloth appeared to be covered with nanoparticles of irregular size, shape and distribution, containing creatinine and ferritin. Since high levels of creatinine and ferritin suggests that the blood is from a patient suffering from strong polytrauma, such as torture, it can be logically suggested that the man wrapped in the Shroud of Turin suffered a violent death.

In addition to revealing the type of death the man of the Shroud suffered, the blood on the cloth was also chemically tested for antigens and antibodies necessary in determining the blood type of the victim. Without getting into the scientific details of blood typing, suffice it to say that, while there are some twenty-blood antibody-antigen groupings available, the one most frequently used is the ABO system. Within that system, four main blood types are distinguished. They are type A (which indicates the presence of A molecules); type B (which indicates the presence of B molecules); type AB (indicating that both type A and type B molecules are present); and type O (which notes the absence of both A and B molecules). In addition, more advanced testing, developed in 2010, was applied to determine if the blood on the Shroud was of human origin or if it originated from some other animal.

In the 1980s, Pier Luigi Baima Bollone, an Italian scientist working with a team of scientists, determined that the blood from the Shroud is type AB, a rare blood type shared by only about three percent of the world population, but very prevalent in the area of Palestine. Once again, science could not state that fact with absolute

---

[224] Verschuuren, Gerard, A Catholic Scientist Champions the Shroud of Turin. Sophia Institute Press, Manchester, NH. 2021. Page 116.
[225] Guerrera, Vittorio, Fr. The Shroud of Turin: A Case for Authenticity. Tan Books and Publishers, Inc. Rockford, Il. 2001. Page 64.

certainty, because as blood ages it loses antibodies, meaning there is a higher probability that the blood type will present as AB. Bollone was able to determine that the blood contained both the N and S antigens. Since the S antigen is absent in primates and other animals, he was able to conclude, with a much higher degree of certainty, that the blood was of human origin.

Details of the Wounds Evident on the Image of the Man on the Shroud

After the STURP Committee concluded its work as a group, several members of the committee continued to work individually or in smaller groups to assess the information gleaned from the committee's research. Included among them are three pathologists: Dr. Bucklin, Los Angeles County deputy medical examiner; Dr. Frederick T. Zugibe, M.D., Ph.D., New York's Rockland County, chief medical examiner; and Dr. Joseph Gambescia, chairman of medicine at St. Agnes Medical Center in Philadelphia. The three worked independently and arrived at very similar conclusions. Of the three, only Doctors Bucklin and Gambescia were part of the STURP committee. Their findings follow:

Wounds Evidenced on the Shroud

In his over fifty years of practice as a forensic pathologist, Dr. Bucklin performed over twenty-five thousand autopsies. He certainly has more than a cursory understanding of forensics as it relates to a corpse. While not dealing with an actual body, the image of the man on the Shroud is so detailed that forensic science is easily applicable to its study. During his examination of the body image, Dr. Bucklin noted five major categories of wounds.

Wounds of the Back

The first set of wounds examined are on the back and spread from the top of the shoulders to the calf. They are double puncture wounds that "appear to go from lateral downward, indicating that an instrument was used in a flickering manner which tore the skin."[226] This corresponds to a 1978 discovery of a minute muscle fragment on the back of image on the Shroud that was located in an area of the

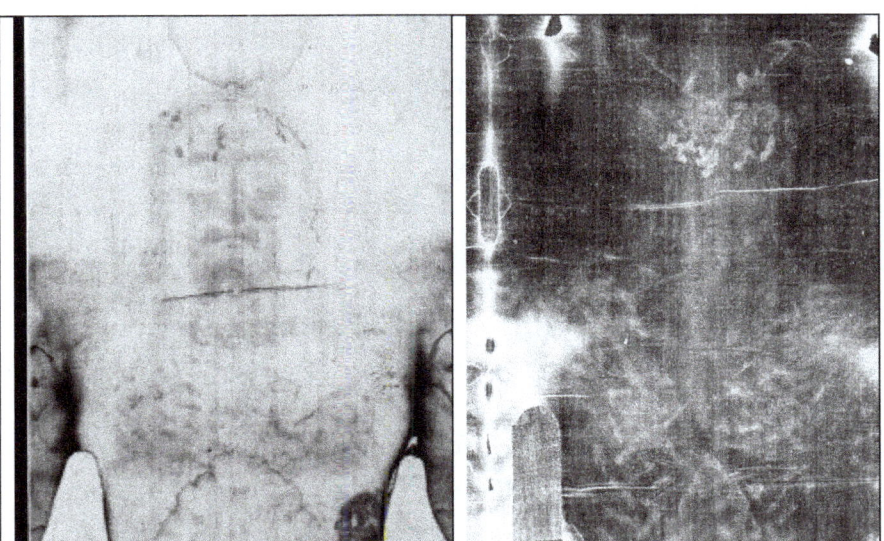

The two images of the Shroud showing the scourge marks on both the front of the man (L) and on his back (R). the image on the left also clearly shows the blood on His head trickling down from the cap of thorns. "© Vernon Miller, 1978. No unauthorized reproduction of Material on other Websites is allowed without prior written permission from the shroudphotos.com copyright holder. Original photos are available for free at www.shroudphotos.com".

image designated 3BB. Dr. Eugenia Nitowski made the notation that was supported by other scientists working with her. The body image on the Shroud is marked with over 120 similar strokes made by a "whip having either two or three dumbbell-shaped weights made of metal or bone."[227] The positioning of these whip strokes on the body image suggests that there were two men scourging the victim and that one of them was shorter than the other. The taller one, it seems,

---

[226] Ibid. Page 80.
[227] Ibid. Page 81.

focused on thrashing the victim's legs. So much information was gleaned from the forensic science that Dr. Zugibe was able to recreate the following scene:

The victim "was bent over and tied to a low pillar when he was flogged across the back, chest, and legs with a multifaceted flagrum with bits of metal on the ends. Over and over again the metal tips dug deep into the flesh, ripping small vessels, nerves, muscles, and skin.... His mouth was dry, and his tongue stuck to the roof of his mouth. Unfortunately, the scourging was initiated by the Romans so that the Deuteronomic limit of forty lashes less one was not followed."[228]

Wounds of the Face and the Head

The second group of injuries are found about the face and head. The scalp and forehead are marked by a series of blood stains that were caused by something with sharp points such as could have been made by a cap of large thorns. The forehead displays one median and two lateral flows of blood. The former, when viewed on the negative photo, is in the shape of the number three. When viewed on the positive photo it takes on the characteristics of the Greek letter epsilon. When the positive image is turned on its side, it forms the Greek letter omega in the lower-case.

Wounds of the Hands

The wounds found on the wrist and forearm comprise the third group of wounds. Dr. Barbet concluded that the wound is that of a large nail that was "driven between the bones of the Space of Destot, the space between the bones of the wrist."[229] Such placement allows the nail to separate the four wrist bones (Capitate, Semilunar, Triquetral and Hamate) without shattering them. This, however,

---

[228] Ibid.
[229] Ibid. Page 82.

causes injury to the median nerve, the nerve responsible for flexing the thumbs. This would cause the thumbs to contract. Such an injury explains why both hands, as viewed on the Shroud, show only the four fingers, as the two thumbs are concealed in the palms of the hands.

Dr. Zugibe and other contemporary researchers dissented from the findings of Dr. Barbet. They noted that the thumb naturally turns itself inward in both the living and the dead. Further, Dr. Zugibe noted that the four bones that make up the Space of Destot are located on the side of the wrist opposite the thumb, making it impossible for

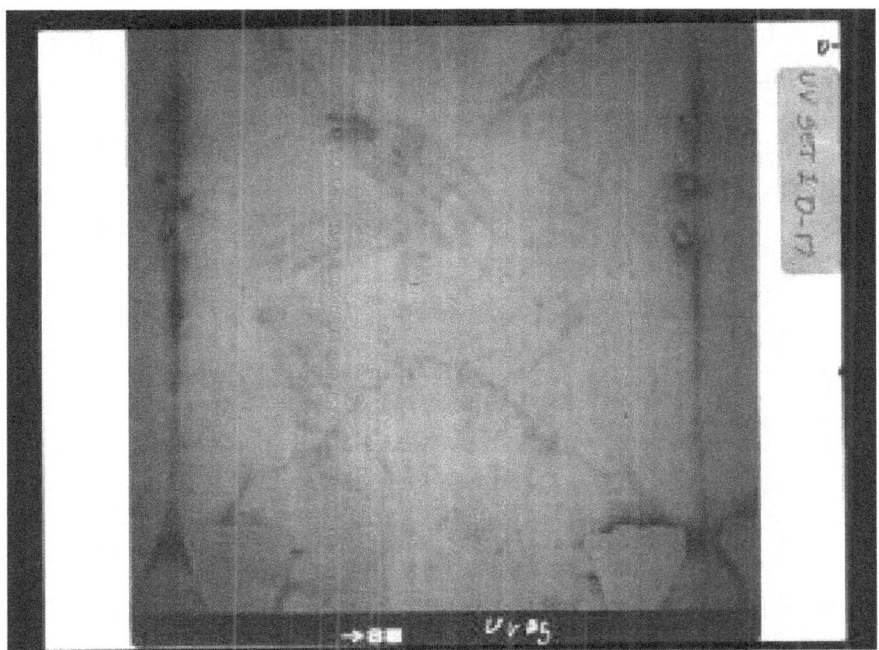

Shroud Image showing the nail mark of the right hand. The wound on the left hand is covered by the right hand. "© Vernon Miller, 1978. No unauthorized reproduction of Material on other Websites is allowed without prior written permission from the shroudphotos.com copyright holder. Original photos are available for free at www.shroudphotos.com".

a nail inserted in that location to sever the radial nerve which is not located in this area. Renowned hand surgeon, Dr. Ernest Lamp, wrote that even with the severance of the median nerve, "there is inability to flex the thumb, index and middle fingers."[230] The Shroud does not allow one to see where the nail entered the body, rather only where it exits the flesh and enters the wood of the cross. Based on his hypothesis drawn from the Shroud evidence, Dr. Zugibe reasons that there are two places where a single nail might have "penetrated the hand: the radial side of the wrist, or at an angle through the thenar furrow located at the base of the thumb, that is, through the upper palm, slanted toward the wrist. The upper part of the palm could easily have supported the weight of the body."[231]

The forensic pathologists also noted that the left forearm looks shorter than the right. In fact, when measured from the tip of the middle finger to the tip of the elbow, the left forearm is three inches shorter than the right forearm. This, however, is an optical illusion created by the left wrist being bent forward over the right with the fingers curled.

Wounds of the Feet
Varying Theories

The wounds of the feet comprise the fourth group identified by Dr. Zugibe and his associates. As with the other wounds of the victim, the damage to the feet is easily identified. The heel of the left foot is raised a bit higher than the heel of the right foot, which is rather well defined, suggesting that the left foot may have retracted during the process of rigor mortis. Further, both heels show evidence of fingerprints, presumably made by the person who carried the body to the tomb. Monsignor Ricci noted, "The little finger, and the ring and middle fingers of the left hand, in contact with the heel, were surrounded by the blood running down from the hole in the left foot. The same thing happened with the right hand on the right heel, though

---

[230] Zugibe, Frederick T. M.D., Ph.D., Pierre Barbet Revisited, Sindon, No. 8, December 1995, Page 110.
[231] Guerrera, Vittorio, Fr. The Shroud of Turin: A Case for Authenticity. Tan Books and Publishers, Inc. Rockford, Il. 2001. Page 82.

the imprint is less clear. When the image is viewed from the dorsal side, there is a complete imprint of the right foot that was likely pressed against the cross. This foot shows a bloodstain in the middle, whereas only the top heel of the left foot is visible over the right with a bloodstain visible on the outer portion."[232] The image clearly shows that the nail penetrated at the base of the right foot between the metatarsal bones. As a result of the aforementioned, Doctors Gambescia and Zugibe believe that a separate and distinct nail was used to attach each foot to the stipe. In this way, their assessment differs from that of Doctors Jackson and Bucklin who agree with Dr. Barbet, that a single nail penetrated both feet. In defense of his position, Dr. Zugibe wrote, "It is logical to assume that both feet were

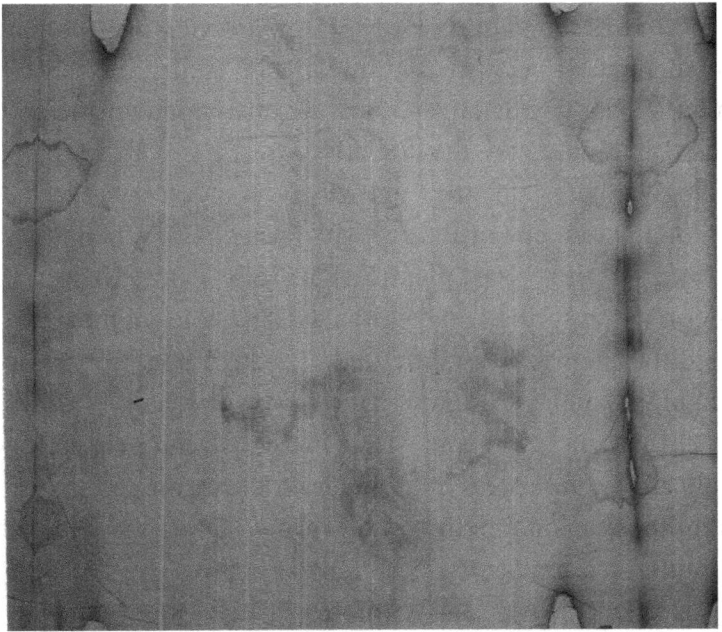

Transparency of the Shroud showing the foot wound. "© Vernon Miller, 1978. No unauthorized reproduction of Material on other Websites is allowed without prior written permission from the shroudphotos.com copyright holder. Original photos are available for free at www.shroudphotos.com".

---

[232] Ibid. Page 84.

nailed separately and flush to the cross without being placed one on top of the other because to do this is easier to execute, no bones are broken, and it would correspond to the earliest Christian references."[233]

Barbet's theory, however, holds that the nail entered through a single hole that pierced both feet which were crossed one over the other, passing through the second intermetatarsal spaces. The Shroud evidence shows that the right foot was against the cross while the left foot was on top of the right.

In yet another description, Dr. Jackson maintains that it is more likely that the left foot was "placed sideways over the right in such a way that the nail penetrated the heel of the top foot through the bottom without breaking any bones."[234]

Remains found during a 1968 construction project in northern Jerusalem tend to support the single nail theory, however. In the Giv'at ha'Mivtar site discovery workers uncovered an ancient Jewish cemetery that dates to the 70 AD Jewish revolt against Rome. Archeologists subsequently unearthed at least twelve ossuaries containing the remains of the Jewish victims. The remains of at least one of the victims was identified as, his name, Jehohanan ben Ha'galgol, was inscribed on the ossuary. The holes in the man's hands indicated that he had been crucified. The heel bone of the right foot still contained the bent fragment of a seven-inch nail.

Orthopedic surgeon, Dr. Pierre Merat, speaking at a November 27, 1988 press conference in Paris, opined that the "nail wound of the man on the Shroud of Turin did not enter the metatarsal space, but rather, the tarsus. 'If a transparency of the skeleton [X-ray photo] is placed over the contour of the foot and these two transparencies are placed over the bloodstain of the cloth, the point where the nail emerges through the sole is evident. It is the little dark

---

[233] Ibid.
[234] Ibid.

stain, surrounded by a clear halo, from which the blood ran down towards the ball of the foot.'"[235]

Wound of the Side

The fifth group of injuries suffered by the crucified man, as identified by Dr. Bucklin, is the wound that appears on the right side of the man on the Shroud. The blood stain associated with this wound is two and a quarter inches wide and spreads about six inches in a downward direction. Barbet described the wound as follows:

"The greatest axis of this wound is just under two inches in length, while it has a height of about two-thirds of an inch…The inner end of the wound is about four inches below and a little to the outside of the nipples, on a horizontal line running just under four inches below it."[236]

The side injury is an oval-shaped wound which has a direct correspondence to the shape of a Roman lance. The lance entered the body between the fifth and sixth ribs and while it entered on the right side of the body, it extended to the right auricle of the heart and perforated the pericardium. The right auricle of a lifeless body, unlike either of the ventricles, still contains blood which, as evidenced by the stains, trickled out. "In addition to the blood, a watery substance, probably from the pleural cavity, also flowed out and can be seen on the lower back of the image."[237] Of these findings, Bucklin is certain.

Wounds on the Knee

The man whose image is on the Shroud also suffered significant lacerations tied to contusions to his left knee. Evidence of dirt was found on one knee as well as on the tip of the nose. These injuries are consistent with those that might be sustained from a fall,

---

[235] Ibid. Page 85.
[236] Ibid. Page 88.
[237] Ibid.

particularly one in which the victim cannot break the fall with his hands or arms. This, of course, would be the case for someone about to be crucified, as his arms would have been tied to the patibulum.

The dirt particles were analyzed by "Joseph Kohlbek at the Hercules Aerospace Laboratory in Salt Lake City, Utah. He determined the particles to be travertine aragonite, which is a rare kind of calcite found in Jerusalem."[238] The samples were also sent to Enrico Fermi Laboratory at the University of Chicago where Dr. Ricardo Levi Setti confirmed Kohlbek's findings.

The Position of the Man on the Shroud
Proof of the Resurrection

In the 1930s the results of Dr. Barbet's investigation of the blood on the Shroud led to the unchallenged conclusion that the man represented there died in the upright position of someone crucified. The chief evidence supporting this conclusion is the directionality of the blood stains, which can be seen flowing in a downward position on the body. The blood from the cap of thorns flowed downward toward the eyes. The blood from the hands flowed downward as did the blood from the side wound and the feet.

In 1986, Dr. Gilbert Lavoi became aware of an off-the-body-image blood mark located at the left elbow that confirms this finding.

Lavoi was at a loss to explain how the off-image blood mark was on the Shroud as it didn't seem to comport to any of the body wounds. It wasn't until Lavoi placed a replica of the Shroud over his own reclining body that he realized the blood mark lined up perfectly, and touched, the back of his upper arm.

Lavoi continued his experiment, "working on a full-size tracing of the left arm off-image blood mark. In going through the process of making the tracing," Lavoi said, "I followed the blood line from the forearm to where it ends its course at the off-image round

---

[238] Ibid. Page 65.

HISTORY'S GREATEST MYSTERY

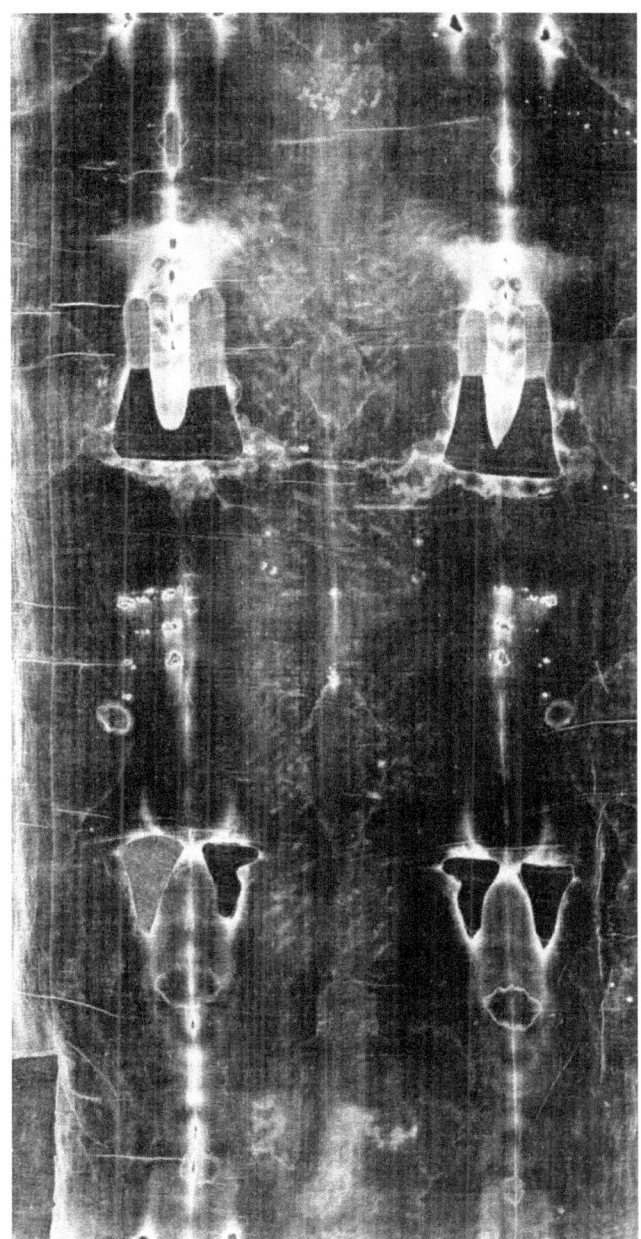

The wounds to the back of Christ as seen on the Shroud. "© Vernon Miller, 1978. No unauthorized reproduction of Material on other Websites is allowed without prior written permission from the shroudphotos.com copyright holder. Original photos are available for free at www.shroudphotos.com".

blood mark. Never once is the continuity of this line broken. Once the tracing was completed, I then turned it over and laid it over a volunteer in the same way that I felt the Shroud cloth had been laid upon a body. From this direct frontal view of the volunteer, I noted that the off-image blood mark was not visible. What I saw through my camera was similar to what I saw on the Shroud; an image with no sides. The Shroud image is, therefore, similar to a direct frontal photograph of a man. On the side view of the same subject, the paper tracing drapes over the side of the body, simulating a cloth drape. From this information, it becomes obvious that the off-image blood mark was caused by the cloth touching the clot on the back of the upper arm as the cloth draped over the side of the body."[239]

Oddly, this experiment also confirms the three-dimensional nature of the image on the Shroud. "The other blood marks on the image translate into two-dimensional information, corresponding to the man's height and width. However, the off-image blood mark is graphic evidence pointing to yet a third dimension – depth. It was evidence that a three-dimensional figure had been under the cloth."[240]

Because the victim's body lay in a horizontal position, it is reasonable that his hair would have fallen back away from his face. The image, however, "shows bloodstains on the hair on each side of the face, which means that the image formation did not occur when the cloth first made contact with the body. The only way this could occur was if the body were in an upright position, with the cloth stretched, at the time that the image was made.

Dr. Lavoi noted three salient points in this regard: "1. The blood demonstrates a pattern that is consistent with that of a cloth having been draped over a supine body; 2. the direction of the blood flows illustrates that the body had previously been in a vertical

---

[239] Lavoi, Gilbert, Dr. The Shroud of Jesus and the Sign John Ingeniously Concealed. Sophia Institute Press, NH. 2023. Pages 72-73.
[240] Ibid.

position; 3. these blood marks are consistent in demonstrating that one process formed the blood marks and that another completely different process created the image."[241]

Professor Nicolo Cinquemani, a specialist in neurosurgery in Rome, further noted that during the time when the body was upright, the man's head was downward by just under four inches and turned at a thirty-degree angle to the corporeal axis. This, Cinquemani argues, is evidence that the 'figure 3' bloodstain visible on the forehead of the man on the Shroud was originally a bloodstain on the face that was the result of a dislocation of the nasal cartilage, IE. A broken nose. The broken nose that is evident in the image of the Shroud most likely occurred during a fall just a few minutes before crucifixion, a fall that also would have caused a wound to the right zygoma. After burial, when the man on the Shroud moved, and the cloth stretched, the 'figure 3' stain was transferred to the forehead. As Dr. Lavois stated, "In the sepulcher the blood from the left naris had traced the '3' on the cloth and the drop that appears under the '3' on the left eyebrow...The last drop had also soaked the corpse's left part of the moustache...The arrow-head shaped clot visible on the hair to the top right, lowered on the vertical by ten centimeters, appears with the tip corresponding to the zygomatic bone."[242]

In conducting his blood-flow experiments, Dr. Lavoi accidentally uncovered another amazing discovery that is now known as the 'double image formation theory'. This is the finding that the bloodstained image occurred prior to the body image, a theory that is also supported by the studies of Cinquemani. Quite simply, these findings mean that the body of the man whose image appears on the Shroud of Turin, was in an upright position after his death. This is strong evidence in support of the occurrence of a resurrection-like

---

[241] Guerrera, Vittorio, Fr. The Shroud of Turin: A Case for Authenticity. Tan Books and Publishers, Inc. Rockford, Il. 2001. Page 90.
[242] Ibid. Pages 90-91.

event. And, if a resurrection took place, that is evidence that the Shroud did indeed cover Jesus, the one man in history believed to have resurrected.

The finding happened by accident when Dr. Lavoi reviewed two photo negatives, one taken of the experimental subject's face while in a supine position and the other of the subject's face while sitting upright. He compared those negatives with the negative image on the Shroud and found that the negative image of the subject sitting upright was almost identical, in terms of shadows of light and dark, with the negative image of the Shroud. Dr. Lavoi explained, "after trial and error, the conclusions were simple enough, and they were easily reproducible. If light is from above, as it usually is in daily life, and a person is upright, there are shadows (light areas on the negative) around the eyes, under the nose, and at the lips. If an individual is supine and the light source is from above, there are virtually no shadows."[243]

The continuation of experimentation on this accidental discovery led Lavoi to study the hair of the victim. "The hair flows down on both sides of the face to the shoulders following the force of gravity....totally consistent with that of an upright man....It is simple enough. Long hair responds to gravitational force and takes on a typical appearance that is familiar to everyone. The hair of the man of the Shroud is that of a man who is upright...but not standing. The image of the man of the Shroud shows that his left foot is on top of his right foot. His feet are crossed. He is upright but he is not in the position of standing on the ground....the image is not that of a man who has been laid out on his back but is that of an upright man whose hair falls to his shoulders and whose feet do not touch the ground." Lavoi continued, "I must admit that I was overwhelmed with the discovery of the upright man. It caused me to back out of the room in

---

[243] Lavoi, Gilbert, Dr. The Shroud of Jesus and the Sign John Ingeniously Concealed. Sophia Institute Press, NH. 2023. Pages 89-90.

awe and respect for what the image of the man of the Shroud was visually telling me. My first thought was that indeed this image is a reflection of the moment of His resurrection."[244]

The Coins Covering the Eyes of the Man on the Shroud

One of the most disputed questions about the Shroud is the presence of coins covering eyelids. It is, at the same time, one of the most interesting discoveries in recent years.

In 1977, Dr. Jackson and Dr. Jumper obtained three-dimensional photographs of the Shroud of Turin. Upon close examination of the photos, the doctors "detected small objects, like buttons, in the eye sockets of the face of the Shroud." Professor Tamburelli confirmed those findings in 1978, and in the following year, Loyola University theologian, mathematician and physicist, Fr. Francis Filas, S.J., studied enlargements of those images. The enlargement enabled him to identify what appeared to be a coin over the right eyelid. In the first century, coins were often used to cover the eyes before burial as a means of keeping the eyes closed. The coin measured fifteen millimeters in diameter, identical to the diameter of the coins struck under the reign of Pontius Pilate.

Depicted on the coin, around the astrologer's curved staff, an emblem frequently used by Pilate, were the letters YCAI. These four letters formed part of the Greek inscription: TIBERIO(Y), KAICAPOC which translates, 'Of Tiberius Caesar.' Some would argue that because the coin contains those spelling errors, it must be a fake. However, "Sometimes in transliteration, the letter 'C' would be substituted for 'K' and the letter 'Y' for 'U' which is actually the

---

[244] Lavoi, Gilbert, Dr. The Shroud of Jesus and the Sign John Ingeniously Concealed. Sophia Institute Press, NH. 2023. Pages 95-96

Greek letter upsilon with a tail."[245] There is also a possibility that the vertical bar of the Greek letter kappa (K) was detached when the

Close up of the type of coin that may have covered the eyes of the man of the Shroud. Photo from Wikipedia - https://aleteia.org/2017/04/26/shroud-of-turin-coins-may-finally-have-been-identified.

image was transferred to the Shroud. Research indicates, however, that spelling mistakes on coins were also common due to the hand casting of coins. Not knowing about the letter substitution concept, Fr. Filas was concerned and subsequently searched out first century coins in the hope of resolving the dilemma. Sure enough, he found another coin with a similar misspelling.

In 1983, armed with what he thought was a new discovery, Fr. Filas contacted Dr. Robert Haralick, the Director of the Spatial Data

---

[245] Guerrera, Vittorio, Fr. The Shroud of Turin: A Case for Authenticity. Tan Books and Publishers, Inc. Rockford, Il. 2001. Page 98.

Analysis Laboratory of Virginia Polytechnic Institute, asking if he would review the photos and the coin that he had acquired. Fr. Filas died in 1985, but his pioneer research of the coin image on the Shroud was confirmed by others.

Italian numismatist, Mario Moroni, noted that what Fr. Filas thought was the letter 'C' on the coin was, in reality, part of an astrologer's staff. Later still, Dr. Alan Whanger, a surgeon, and his wife Mary, both internationally renowned Shroud researchers, reviewed photographs of the coin that Fr. Filas had obtained and, using their polarized image overlay technique, compared them with the eyes on the enlarged photos of the Shroud. They noted, "comparing the same area on the 1931 and 1978 photographs, this technique shows that the cloth is not in exactly the same position and drape for the two photographs and that threads over the eye area might have been stretched or rotated. This accounts for some apparent distortion of the letters and images in the 1978 photographs, indeed making it more difficult to see them on these photographs." [246]

The Whangers were able to identify the coin obtained by Fr. Filas through numismatics books. It was verified as a coin that was struck during the reign of Tiberius in the year 29 AD. Confirming their discovery, the Whangers wrote, "We identified three tiny letters: L (signifies that the letters following have numerical value), I (number value of ten), and a letter called Stigma that looks something like a rounded number five that was at that time becoming obsolete (number value of six). Thus, the coin was dated to the sixteenth year of the reign of Tiberius Caesar, which is A.D. 29."[247]

The Whangers also determined that the object covering the right eye of the man on the Shroud had two hundred and eleven points of congruence with the coin, and eighty-six points of discordance.

---

[246] Ibid.
[247] Ibid.

The features of the coin covering the left eye of the man on the Shroud, though not as pronounced as that of the coin over the right eye, was nonetheless identifiable. It is the Julia lepton, a coin equivalent to a 'widow mite.' The Julia lepton was also struck in the year 29 A.D. in honor of Julia, the mother of Tiberius Ceasar. This coin had seventy-three points of congruence with the object covering the left eye of the man on the Shroud.

The presence of coins over the eyes was again confirmed in 1996, this time by Professor Bollone and computer expert, Professor Nello Balossino, both from the University of Turin. They also noted that, probably due to the facial swelling of the man on the Shroud, the coin covering that eye was higher. They further noted that traces of that coin are identical with the features of a coin held at the British Museum and minted during the reign of Tiberius Ceasar. Bollone called this "intrinsic proof clearly stamped, as it were, upon the Shroud itself,"[248] adding that they no longer needed to rely on tests or calculations. He is certain that no medieval forger could possibly have accomplished this, saying that "In my opinion, this latest research is just about 100% proof that the Shroud of Turin truly held the body of the crucified and buried Christ."[249] Dr. Adler added to Dr. Whanger's analysis of the coin-covered eyes hypothesizing that the superimposition of the coins to the cloth was achieved by a high energy phenomenon associated with corona discharge.

Despite the evidence and the certainty of the conclusions expressed by the aforementioned researchers, skeptics abound, some insisting that no Jew would have covered the eyes of a corpse with a pagan coin because of the Talmud's prohibition of images. Even some Shroud experts voice consenting opinions with regard to the coin evidence.

---

[248] Ibid. Page 99.
[249] Ibid.

How Jesus May Have Looked

If the image on the Shroud is the image of Jesus, then the Shroud provides a pretty accurate description of what Jesus may have looked like. The scriptures themselves do not provide such a description, nor do the other early Christians, as they were more preoccupied with the message of Jesus than with his appearance. In fact, according to Fr. Vittorio Guerrera, many of the early representations of Jesus depicted him with short hair and no beard. In the sixth century, however, images of Jesus as he is pictured today began to surface. Those images show Him with long hair, a mustache, and a forked beard and were very likely inspired by the image on the Shroud.

This transformation was first identified by Paul Vignon in the 1930s and his observations were followed by those of Fr. Edward Wuenschel, C.Ss.R., the 1919 founder of The American Catholic Historical Association. The pair identified some twenty unusual details that appear both on the Shroud and in representations of Jesus beginning in the sixth century. These oddities include:

- two strands of hair at the top of the forehead,
- the wisps of hair pointing to the right,
- a three-sided square between the brows that may have been caused by a phylactery (small black leather cube-shaped cases that held parchments of scriptural texts and were worn by Jewish men around the forehead),
- a "V"-shape at the bridge of the nose,
- an enlarged left nostril,
- a transverse line across the throat (which may have been a fold-crease in the Shroud,
- uneven eyebrows, with one being higher than the other,
- a forked beard,
- and long hair.

The Whangers compared the image of the face on the Shroud with the image of Jesus on two coins, the first coinage bearing his image. They are highly pure gold solidus coins minted in the reign of Justinian II between the years 692 and 695 A.D. After photographing the coins and the face on the Shroud on transparencies and in the same proportions, the Whangers overlayed the images. The first coin produced one hundred and forty-five points of congruence including wrinkles, bloodstains and other minute details. The second coin produced one hundred and five points of congruence. This is remarkable, since in an American court of law, "only fourteen points of congruence are needed to establish the same fingerprint and between forty-five and sixty points of congruence are sufficient to determine the same face."[250] This finding was confirmed by subsequent research as well.

The Age of the Shroud as Determined by Textile and Methods of Analysis Other Than Carbon Dating

Based on just the analysis of the textile, it is more than speculative that the cloth dates to at least the 1190s, the approximate date listed in the *Pray Codex* as the date of the first fire in which the Shroud was damaged. The weave pattern and the stitching of the side seam, both of which are consistent with first century Jewish burial practices indicate that the cloth dates to first century Israel. The lack of animal hair in the Shroud further supports the hypothesis that the cloth could be from the first century as the Laws of Moses followed at the time prescribed that animal by-products, such as wool, could not be mixed with linens.

Even the odd size of the Shroud, one hundred and seventy-two inches by forty-four inches, dates the cloth to the first century, because when converted to cubits, the unit of measure in the time of Jesus, the

---

[250] Ibid. Page 102.

"Assyrian sizing of the Shroud exactly aligns with the dimensions dictated by Jewish burial practices"[251] of that era.

Additional confirmation of the Shroud as an ancient fabric is provided by chemical tests developed by Raymond Rogers from the Los Alamos National Laboratory. Rogers is the chemist who identified the presence of vanillin, "a product of a chemical compound found in flax. As the compound breaks down over time, vanillin is released, but as more time passes, the vanillin levels decline."[252]

Rogers determined that it takes more than thirteen hundred years for the fibers in the Shroud to lose ninety-five percent of their vanillin at a consistent seventy-seven degrees Fahrenheit. At seventy-three degrees Fahrenheit it would take eighteen hundred years and at sixty-eight degrees Fahrenheit, it would take more than three thousand years. The Shroud, like the Dead Sea Scrolls, contains no vanillin. Because it is known that the Dead Sea Scrolls date between 300 BC and 300 AD, they provide a means of date comparison for the Shroud. That comparison makes it clear that the Shroud could easily be from the first century.

Finally, other date-testing methods for ancient materials were developed by Giulio Fanti, a professor at the University of Padua's Engineering Faculty. These methods include compressibility tests and break-strength tests. The application of these techniques on the Shroud determined with a ninety-five percent confidence level, that the origin of the cloth was around 400 AD with a plus or minus range of four hundred years. The Shroud, therefore, with a possible date-range from 1 AD to 800 AD, could easily date the to the time of Jesus' burial.

At a 1990 forum held in Cagliari, Italy, "Silvio Diana, from the Central institute of Restoration in Rome, spoke about a method of

---

[251] Ibid. Page 82.
[252] Ibid.

dating woven textiles such as the Shroud. This method measures the state of the cellulose in the material, which gets worse as the fabric gets older. The first part of the method consists of counting the cellulose units and observing the double joints in the polymers. If these joints are not broken, the fiber must be recent. The analysis requires a sample of 50 milligrams, which is destroyed in the process. In order to do a correct analysis, samples should be taken from all areas of the cloth, not just one as in the case of carbon dating. The second part of the experiment measures the decomposition of the protoplasm, which also decomposes at a fixed rate and is quantifiable. The conclusion reached from this was that the Shroud cannot be medieval."[253]

In 2022, Italian scientist Liberato De Caro discussed a technique he utilized based on an X-ray method of research used to determine the age of the Shroud's fibers. His peer-reviewed findings show the Shroud of Turin "to be much older than some scientists have stated, and that it does in fact coincide with Christian tradition by dating back to around the time of Christ's death and resurrection."[254]

De Caro, of Italy's Institute of Crystallography of the National Research Council in Bari, worked with a team of other researchers to conduct his experiments using a *"Wide-angle X-ray Scattering* method to examine the natural aging of cellulose that constitutes a sample of the famous linen cloth."[255] Their research indicated that the Shroud is "compatible with the hypothesis that it is…around 2,000 years old."[256]

---

[253] Guscin, Mark, The Oviedo Cloth. The Lutterworth Press, Cambridge, Great Britain. 1998. Page 55.
[254] Pentin, Edward, New Scientific Technique Dates Shroud of Turin to Around the Time of Christ's Death and Resurrection. National Catholic Register, 2022. https://www.ncregister.com/interview/new-scientific-technique-dates-shroud-of-turin-to-around-the-time-of-christ-s-death-and-resurrection. Page 1.
[255] Ibid. Pages 1-2.
[256] Ibid. Page 2.

De Caro verified in a 2022 interview with National Catholic Register that, for about thirty-years, he has been "using investigative techniques on the scale of atoms, in particular through X-rays." It was only about three years ago, however, that he developed a "new method for dating samples taken from linen fabrics."[257] De Caro explained that "a macroscopic example of a fabric microfiber is like that of a bundle of spaghetti: at first they all have the same length, but if you subject the bundle to accidental shocks, the more the shocks increase, the more the spaghetti breaks. As the number of shocks increases, always of the same intensity, the average length of the spaghetti decreases over time, until it reaches a minimum length. A similar thing happens to the polymer chains of cellulose which, like spaghetti but with a section on the scale of a billionth of a meter, gradually break over the centuries due to the combined effect of temperature, humidity, light and the action of chemical agents in the environment in which they are found. Natural aging depends only on ambient temperature and relative humidity. We have therefore developed a method to measure the natural aging of flax cellulose using X-rays and then convert it into time elapsed since fabrication."[258]

De Caro began his research in 2019. His team's findings were published in Heritage, an international journal, and the work was peer reviewed by three other independent experts and the journal's editor. The work has also been highlighted on the website of the Consiglio Nazionale delle Ricerche, Italy's National Research Council.

Dating the Shroud with the Sudarium of Oviedo

In October 1994, Oviedo, Spain was the venue of an international congress to discuss the Sudarium of Oviedo. During that congress, the Shroud of Turin was mentioned and was the subject of

---

[257] Ibid.
[258] Ibid.

one of the papers read and discussed. The Shroud was tied to the Sudarium of Oviedo in a number of ways suggesting that the two cloths were inextricably linked. This connection obviously means that if the Sudarium is the cloth found in the tomb of Jesus in 30 A.D., it is then impossible for the Shroud to be a medieval forgery. In the words of Mark Guscin, Author of *The Oviedo Cloth*, "All of the studies on the Sudarium point to its having covered the face as the Shroud did, and we know that the Sudarium was in Oviedo in 1075. On the other hand, the carbon dating specialists have said that the Shroud dates from 1260 to 1390. Either the Sudarium has nothing to do with the Shroud, or the carbon dating was wrong – there is no middle way, no compromise."[259]

In all, during the Oviedo conference, twenty-six papers were read and later published in Spanish by the Centre for Sindonology. These papers reviewed all the medical and historical connections between the Sudarium and the Shroud. The conclusions link the two cloths together in terms of the stains, the type AB blood, and the DNA found on both the Shroud and the Sudarium.

Dating the Shroud with the Veil of Manoppello

In 1989, Andreas Resch presented a paper to the *International Symposium La Sindone e le Icone* in Bologna, Italy, comparing the images on the Shroud of Turin and the Veil of Manoppello to early artistic portrayals of the face of Christ. "Amazingly, it turned out that even with the image of the Good Shepherd (200–250 AD) in the Priscilla Catacomb the proportions are almost perfect. The image of the Good Shepherd, portrayed as a Cynic philosopher in the hypogeum of the Aurelians (before 270), shows a significant degree of correspondence, too.

---

[259] Guscin, Mark, The Oviedo Cloth. The Lutterworth Press, Cambridge, Great Britain. 1998. Page 64.

Dating the Shroud with Early Frescos and Catacomb Paintings

The fresco, *Christ with disciples* 'in the Domitilla Catacomb, dates back to between 330 and 340 AD. The image of the young Christ on the chair in the center of the fresco takes more than a quarter of the painting and proves an impressive degree of correspondence with the face on the Shroud and on the Veil. Particularly impressive is the correspondence of the sketch with the first portrayal of Christ, i.e. *Christ Enthroned*, in the catacomb of Peter and Marcellinus, Via Labicana, Rome. Again, the correspondence of the sketch is like the one on the original face on the Shroud. The imposing painted ceiling showing Christ between the apostles Peter and Paul dates back to 375. Also, the splendid image of Christ in the Comodilla Catacomb (375 AD) shows a significant correspondence with the original face on the Shroud, and thus, with the reverse side of the face on the Veil of Manoppello."[260]

Resch concludes that "since the face on the Veil of Manoppello seems to be congruent with the face on the Shroud of Turin, it may be concluded that both faces refer to one and the same person. The correspondence of Justin II, with the face of Christ on the Cross showing the characteristic tuft of hair, is a very convincing proof that the face on the Veil served as a model. "This detail is so significant that any counterargument becomes superfluous, because the correspondence described above is also important as far as the dating of the Shroud is concerned. That the person on the Shroud of Turin might be Jesus Christ can only be deduced from the correspondence of the Gospels with the specific features of the body image on the Shroud."[261]

---

[260] Resch, Andreas, The Face on the Shroud of Turin and on the Veil of Manoppellp, Proceedings of the International Workshop on the Scientific Approach to the Acheiropoietos Images, ENEA Frascati, Italy, May 4-6, 2010. http://www.acheiropoietos.info/proceedings/ReschWeb.pdf. Page 4.
[261] Ibid. Page 7.

The Resch research made clear that "if the face on the Veil of Manoppello dates back to Jesus Christ – the impregnation is likely to have occurred between flagellation and the crucifixion, because the image is that of a tortured but living and self-assured man."[262]

It is clear that a preponderance of the evidence presented makes it entirely possible that the Shroud dates to the time of Jesus burial in the first century AD, that evidence would normally be sufficient to convince most observers that the Shroud might be the authentic burial cloth of Jesus. One test however, cast that conclusion into serious doubt and many who deny the cloth's authenticity latch onto that singular test as conclusive evidence that the Shroud is a Medieval forgery. That test is discussed below.

Radiocarbon Dating Analysis

Radiocarbon testing may be the test singularly relied upon by traditional science to determine the age of an object. Because Carbon testing is invasive and requires the removal of pieces of the object being tested, the Vatican made a decision to allow the test to be conducted on only a small piece of the Shroud.

Franco Testore, professor of textile technology at the Turin Polytechnic, and Gabriel Vial, curator of the Ancient Textile Museum in Lyon, France, were chosen to undertake the study, and they selected a small corner of the Shroud to sample. The samples were sent to three labs which were located in Oxford, Zurich, and Tucson, Arizona. All three labs dated the Shroud, with ninety-five percent confidence, to 1260-1390 AD. The results shocked the faithful, satisfied the doubting, and sparked a debate that rages to this day.

Radiocarbon testing was developed in the 1940s by Willard Libby and is based on the use of isotopes. Some isotopes, because of the number of protons in the nucleus of an atom, are unstable or radioactive and undergo radioactive decay that follows a particular

---

[262] Ibid.

pattern. That means that after a certain period of time, the number of radioactive isotopes will be reduced by one half. After the passing of another period of time of the same duration, it will again be reduced by half. This interval of time is commonly referred to as the half-life of the isotope.

For carbon, that half-life is approximately 5,730 years, give or take forty-years. Consequently, after 11,460 years, only a quarter is left while after 17,190 years only an eighth remains. The testing is effective on plants or animals and is applicable to the Shroud because it is comprised of linens from the flax plant. So, carbon dating in terms of the Shroud, was used to determine the approximate date that the flax plant from which the cloth was made, died.

William Meacham, an archaeologist with the University of Hong Kong, has considerable experience in the radiocarbon dating of ancient artifacts. In March of 1986, two years before the carbon 14 tests were conducted on the Shroud, Meacham presented at a symposium in Hong Kong. At the symposium, Meacham presented his concerns in performing such a test on the Shroud of Turin. The paper, titled, *Radiocarbon Measurement and the age of the Turin Shroud: Possibilities and Uncertainties*, was little noticed, but suggested that contamination could easily skew the results. "It should be abundantly clear," Meacham wrote, "that neither Raes pieces nor the charred portions of the Shroud can be relied upon for carbon-dating the relic. The charred linen has, since 1532, constituted a different system from the rest of the cloth, with larger surface areas and higher absorbency, thus being more subject to post-fire contamination. The charred areas are also subject to possible contamination by direct transfer of cellulose pyrolysis products contemporary with the 1532 fire, by carbonized substances present in the cloth at the time of the fire and by the introduction of more recent carbon through isotopic exchange during the fire."[263]

To test the Shroud in 1988, the cloth was "separated from the backing cloth along its bottom left-hand edge, and a strip was cut from just above the place where a sample was previously removed in 1973 for examination," according to Paul Damon, a geoscientist of the University of Arizona who was also a member of the testing team. The carbon testing showed, with ninety-five percent certainty, that the Shroud dated from between 1260 and 1390. Because the cloth could not be dated earlier than 1260, there could be only one conclusion - the Shroud is a medieval forgery.

As with some of the other tests related to the Shroud, there was a problem with the carbon testing. It was later discovered that the "scientists had tested a piece of the cloth that had been added to the Shroud later."[264] Because it is known that the patches were added to the cloth following the Chambery fire in 1532, it is very possible that the sample taken by Damon and the team for carbon testing was taken from one of the many patched areas. Consequently, the carbon test is essentially useless in determining the age of the original portion of the cloth but does tend to support the history of the Shroud as it pertains to the repair of the fire damage.

Raymond N. Rogers, retired Fellow of the Los Alamos National Laboratory, published a peer reviewed scientific paper on January 20, 2005. It appeared in an issue of *Journal Thermochimica Acta*, Volume 425, Issues 1-2, Pages 189-194 and was titled, *Studies on the Radiocarbon Sample from the Shroud of Turin*. As a result of his extensive research Rogers concludes, "As unlikely as it seems, the

---

[263] Meacham, William, Archeologist, Radiocarbon Measurement and the Age of the Turin Shroud: Possibilities and Uncertainties. From the Proceedings of the Symposium "Turin Shroud – Image of Christ?"" Hong Kong, March 1986. https://www.shroud.com/meacham.htm.

[264] Guerrera, Vittorio, Fr. The Shroud of Turin: A Case for Authenticity. Tan Books and Publishers, Inc. Rockford, Il. 2001. Page 154.

sample used to test the age of the Shroud of Turin in 1988 was taken from a rewoven area of the Shroud. Pyrolysis-mass spectrometry results from the sample area coupled with microscopic and microchemical observations prove that the radiocarbon sample was not part of the original cloth of the Shroud of Turin. The radiocarbon date was thus not valid for determining the true age of the Shroud."[265]

Rogers, who led the STURP chemistry group, confirmed that the "radiocarbon sample is totally different in composition from the main part of the Shroud of Turin and was cut from a medieval reweaving of the cloth. Rogers' statement has profound implications, since it was his team that "performed the first in-depth scientific examination of the Shroud in 1978."[266]

In response to Rogers' findings, the Centro Internazionale in Turin said in part, "the Shroud samples taken in 1973 by Professor G. Raes, when compared to those contiguous samples taken in 1988 for radiocarbon testing, present anomalies in their composition. According to Brown, "on the cloth there are 'plant gums' with a polysaccharide structure and colored compounds deriving from interactions with Madder (alizarine) and aluminum ions. These colored additives were apparently used after a reconstructive restoration of the cloth to make the color of the new fibers the same as those of the Shroud."[267] The Center concludes that "Dr. Rogers' observations are very interesting and certainly provide a basis for further investigation and studies on the chemical characteristics of the cloth and its possible lack of homogeneity."[268]

A 2005 paper presented by John L. Brown, Principal Research Scientist (retired) with the Georgia Tech Research Institute, titled, *Microscopical Investigation of Selected Raes Threads From the*

---

[265] Rogers, Ray, Carbon 14 Dating Invalidated. BSTS Newsletter No. 61- Part 6 – n61Part6.pdf. https://www.shroud.com/pdfs/n61part6.pdf. Page1.
[266] Ibid. Page 2.
[267] Ibid. Page 3.
[268] Ibid.

Shroud of Turin, supports the studies claiming that the 1988 carbon testing results are invalid.

Because of the controversy surrounding the result of the 1988 carbon testing, several other symposiums or congresses were held to address the dating issues. One such meeting took place in Cagliari, Italy in 1990 on April 28 and 29. The conclusion reached at this meeting was that the result of the 1988 carbon test was unacceptable.

During the session, "Dr. Sebastian Rodante from Sicily, and Dr. Virginio Gagliardi, from the University of Rome, read papers on the alteration of the level of carbon 14 in the Shroud. Such alterations would annul the results of the carbon dating. Others doubted the whole process of the experiment, accusing those involved of deliberately changing samples and falsifying results. Such were the conclusions of Bruno Bonnet Eymard and Dr. Werner Bulst."[269]

It might also be of interest to the discussion of the carbon dating issue that an invitation to the Cagliari meeting was extended to Oxford Professor Edward Hall. Hall's Research Laboratory for Archaeology and the History of Art laboratory in Keble Road, Oxford was one of the three used for the Shroud radiocarbon dating in 1988. He declined the invitation citing his unwillingness to be questioned about the carbon testing analysis he performed suggesting that those results were incontrovertible.

Conclusions Resulting from Many Decades of Testing

As noted earlier, the Shroud is perhaps the most tested piece of fabric in history. It has been subjected to virtually every non-invasive test available. It has also been exposed to many non-destructive, invasive tests. All of this testing has been undertaken in an effort to determine if the Shroud of Turin might be the actual burial cloth of Jesus of Nazareth.

---

[269] Guscin, Mark, The Oviedo Cloth. The Lutterworth Press, Cambridge, Great Britain. 1998. Page 40.

What then, is to be gleaned from all the scientific attention paid to the Shroud? While science has been unable to, and could never, conclude with certainty that the Shroud is the genuine burial cloth of Jesus, it has also been unable to prove that it is a forgery. Science was, however, able to determine many things with a high degree of certainty: Decades of scientific research, conducted by Catholics, non-Catholics, atheists, agnostics, clergy, laymen, scientists, engineers, photographers, doctors and other medical professionals, university and college professors, and many others, have produced voluminous conclusions that were reviewed in this chapter. The following summarizes what science has been able to determine with a high degree of certainty:

1. The Shroud measures fourteen feet, three inches by three feet, eight inches. Though an odd size when measured in inches, it is the exact size of a first century Jewish burial cloth when measured in cubits.
2. The cloth is a fabric made from linen and a mixture of a Middle Eastern variety of cotton known as G. herbaceum.
3. The cloth conforms to the Mosaic law which was strictly adhered to in the burial practices undertaken by Jews of the first century.
4. The linen is of high quality consisting of fibers made of hand-spun flax, a strong fiber, finer and more textured than cotton, with the linen thread coming from the stems of the flax plant. Flax is botanically connected to two plants, *Linum usitatissimum* and *Gossypium haerbaceum*, both of which were available in Jerusalem in the first century.
5. The linen and cotton fibers were spun in a 'Z' twist pattern and woven in a three-to-one twill, meaning that the horizontal (weft) thread passes alternately over three and under one of the vertical (warp) threads. This weave is an intricate three-over-one herringbone pattern. The cloth is very fine with a

density of thirty-five threads per centimeter or about eighty-nine threads per inch. The cloth would have been very expensive and something that people such as Joseph of Arimathea might have been able to afford.
6. There is clear evidence of fire damage on the Shroud emanating from two distinct fire-related events. The burn areas were patched in Medieval times.
7. There is water damage evident on the cloth, probably from attempts to extinguish either, or both, of the known fires to which the Shroud was exposed.
8. The Shroud contains a side strip that is affixed with a single seam to the main cloth on the left side. Five and a half inches of the strip are missing from the top, and fourteen inches are missing from the bottom. The strip is made from the same piece of linen as is the Shroud, and is presumed to have been part of the Shroud before being cut, perhaps for use in wrapping the Sudarium to the face of Jesus. The single seam is a peculiar stitch that was found only one other time, and that cloth dated back to the time of the burial of Jesus.
9. The Shroud contains no paints, dyes, stains, or other pigments. There are no brush strokes. There is no outline used, though outlines are generally used by artists before painting. The fact is, that of the many items found in paintings that identify them as a painting, none are present on the Shroud.
10. The image of the man on the Shroud is a perfect photographic negative. That negative produces a perfect photographic positive image on the negative plate used by photographers. The image was made many hundreds of years before the advent of photography and photographic principles, meaning that no one would have had the knowledge of photography needed to create such an image.
11. The image of the man on the Shroud is anatomically correct in every detail. The image depicts the body of a bearded man,

who was 5'11" tall, had shoulder-length hair, and suffered significant trauma to the body.
12. The man whose image appears on the cloth was a man who had been tortured, scourged, and crucified using three nails that were driven into the wrists and feet. The Shroud shows evidence of 213 scourge marks on the back and 159 on the front for a total of 372 marks. The scourge marks match a Roman flagrum unearthed in 1704 AD in the city of Pompei that was destroyed by a volcano. The flagrum was dated to 79 AD and the marks on the image are an EXACT match to that flagrum.
13. The man whose image appears on the Shroud wore a cap of thorns that not only encircled the forehead of the man, but encased the entire head like a cap. The forensic and pathologic evidence of the cap of thorns suggests that the thorns were sharp and caused significant bleeding. Evidence suggests that the thorns may have been from a variety of plants that date to first century Jerusalem.
14. The Shroud shows evidence that the man's right side was pierced with a lance. The wound measures 4 centimeters (1.57 inches) in length, which is an exact match to the width of a first century Roman lance.
15. Pollen from fifty-eight species of plants were identified on the Shroud. Seventeen are indigenous to Europe and forty-one are indigenous to the area of the Dead Sea and Turkey, including one specie that is exclusive only to Israel. Oddly, these plants bloom between March and April, the exact time of the crucifixion of Jesus.
16. There is a significant amount of human blood present on the Shroud emanating from the various wounds of torture. The blood contains high levels of bilirubin signifying that the man was subjected to significant amounts of trauma prior to his death.

17. The blood contains significant amounts of creatinine and ferritin, suggesting that the victim was tortured.
18. The blood is bright red in color and has not turned brown with age. Trauma prevents aging blood from appearing brown in color. Rather, trauma will cause blood to remain bright red even after hundreds of years.
19. The blood stains on the Shroud have clearly marked edges which reproduce the shape of the clots as they were formed naturally on the skin. The blood type is AB, which is present in only about three percent to the world's population but is prevalent in the area of Palestine.
20. The Shroud shows evidence of a coin placed in each of the eyes of the man whose image appears there. The coin was numismatically dated to the sixteenth year of the reign of Tiberius Caesar, which is A.D. 29.
21. Scientists, doctors, and other researchers have been unable to duplicate the image in a lab, even when using the most sophisticated twentieth-century equipment available to them.
22. The Shroud has three-dimensional qualities that cannot be duplicated with paints, dyes, or other pigments.
23. Evidence on the Shroud suggests that the man was crucified with a seven-inch nail that penetrated the hand at the palm and was either driven straight through the palm exiting at the front of the hand or was driven into the palm at an angle and exited at the wrist.
24. Age testing based on a textile analysis of the Shroud, including the stitching of the side seam, and the lack of animal fibers in the cloth, suggest that the cloth dates to the first century.
25. The lack of vanillin present on the Shroud suggests that it is from the same time period as the Dead Sea Scrolls, which also contained no vanillin. That date range, 300 BC to 300 AD, places the possibility of the Shroud dating squarely within the first century.

26. The evidence on the Shroud suggests that the man was in an upright position when he died (IE. hanging on the cross) and was also in an upright position at the time that the image was made on the Shroud (IE. sitting up from the waist). It is also clear from all the evidence that the image was produced post-mortem and post burial.
27. The Shroud contains no evidence of decomposition, meaning that the body remained wrapped in the Shroud for only a short period of time.
28. Testing revealed that radiological testing and carbon-14 testing would be unreliable because their accuracy relies on the presence of heavy metals in the pigments and there is no evidence of the presence of paints, dyes, or other pigments on the cloth.
29. Carbon-14 testing was faulty. It indicated that the Shroud dates from 1260 AD to 1390 AD. The samples taken for testing, however, were taken from the patched area that was applied to repair the damage caused by the Chambery fire of 1532, and is therefore not indicative of the age of the main cloth of the Shroud.
30. The Carbon-14 test results have been refuted in symposiums, forums, research studies and through other scientific testing performed by a plethora of scientists, archaeologists, botanists, chemists and other experts.
31. Those who support the conclusions of the carbon dating tests on the Shroud have no explanation as to why every other scientific test dates the cloth to the first century. Nor are they able to provide any proof or evidence to refute the results of the other scientific tests.

As has been noted many times, science cannot tell, with any degree of certainty, who was covered by the Shroud of Turin. As Gerard Verschuuren points out, "nothing in science is final or definitive. Science is always a work in progress."[270] Science has, however, provided with a high degree of certainty, specific facts about the Shroud and the man it covered. That scientific evidence suggests that the Shroud was made from very expensive cloth which could be from the first century. It covered a man who was scourged by two men with a flagellum commonly used by Roman torturers. The man was forced to wear a cap of thorns that caused significant penetration to the skin and severe bleeding. The man was crucified with three nails that pierced the wrists and feet. The man's right side was pierced with a lance the size of which was used by first century Roman soldiers. The man's blood was type AB and contained bilirubin, a byproduct of torture, that causes it to remain bright red in color. History records the crucifixion of only one person that fits all the details that science has identified in the Shroud of Turin, and that crucified person is Jesus of Nazareth. While science cannot yet identify the evidence that can tell with certainty who the man of the Shroud is, the question can, by necessity, be answered only by the preponderance of evidence discovered to date, and of course, by faith.

Guskin notes that "it can hardly be considered rational or scientific to blindly accept what conveniently fits in with one's own personal ideas without even taking into consideration what others say. And after all, carbon dating is just one experimental method compared with dozens of others, and it stands alone in its medieval theory."[271]

Models Created Based On the 3-D Characteristics of the Shroud of Turin Image

Giulio Fanti, a professor of mechanical and thermic measurements at the Department of Industrial Engineering, University of Padua, has studied the Shroud since 1998. He notes in one of his research studies that the cloth is "a linen sheet 4.36 m long

---

[270] Page Guerrera, Vittorio, Fr. The Shroud of Turin: A Case for Authenticity. Tan Books and Publishers, Inc. Rockford, Il. 2001. Page 153.
[271] Guscin, Mark, The Oviedo Cloth. The Lutterworth Press, Cambridge, Great Britain. 1998. Page 64.

and 1.10 m large that wrapped the corpse of a scourged, crowned with thorns and crucified man; from recent probabilistic studies that man was confirmed to be Jesus."[272]

Fanti's study confirmed that the "body image is impressed in a scientifically unexplainable way and contains 3D information related to the body-sheet distance."[273] These 3D characteristics, Fanti notes, provides a cursory understanding of how Jesus was wrapped in the shroud and "the possible radiant mechanism that caused the image," though the "high grade of image damage, due to the various marks,"[274] makes that analysis rather difficult. That is the reason that Fanti produced a computerized reconstruction and cleaning of the body image. A "numeric-anthropomorphous manikin was constructed by computer and wrapped in the digitized front and back images. The front and back images resulted in a figure mutually compatible with a man 175 + or – 2 cm tall, which, due to cadaveric rigidity, remained in the same position (except for the arms) it would have assumed during crucifixion."[275]

Fanti's 3D model became the first hyper-realistic recreation of the body of Christ based on data obtained from the Shroud of Turin. It was on display at the Gaudix Cathedral in Granada, Spain from April to June 2023, after which it toured Europe for the remainder of 2023. The sculpture is made of latex and silicone and weighs about 165 pounds. The posture is of the deceased Christ in rigor mortis.

---

[272] Fanti, Guilio, A Review of 3d Characteristics of the Turin Shroud Body Image, A research study presented to the Workshop Italy-Canada on 3D Digital Imaging and Modeling Applications of: Heritage, Medicine & Land. Padova, April 3-4, 2001. Page 1.
[273] Ibid.
[274] Ibid.
[275] Ibid.

CHAPTER VIII

WHAT SCIENCE REVEALS ABOUT THE SUDARIUM OF OVIEDO

As discussed in Section I, the Sudarium of Oviedo is the bloodstained cloth believed to have covered the face of Jesus as His body hung on the cross postmortem and after it was taken down from the cross and brought to the tomb. Though woven from the same type of thread that is found on the Shroud, this 2'9" by 1'9" cloth contains no image, simply splotches of blood. St. John the Apostle refers to it in his Gospel as a 'napkin' which had been on the head of Jesus. Such a covering was required under Jewish law whenever a person suffered a violent and bloody death.

As has been shown, the Sudarium has a more detailed provenance than does the Shroud of Turin. Saint Leandro, the Bishop of Seville, lived in Constantinople between the years 579 A.D. and

582 A.D. and was entrusted with custody of the Sudarium. He may also have seen the Shroud, making yet another connection between the two cloths. Perhaps one of the most interesting entries regarding the origin of the facecloth and the Shroud is one that appears in the Mozarabic Liturgy for Easter Sunday. The Illatio[276] reads, "Peter ran to the tomb with John and saw the recent imprints of the dead and risen one on the cloths."[277]

There is no need to recreate the history and travel of the Sudarium here as it has been covered in some detail in chapter 5. Suffice it to say that there is substantial evidence connecting the Sudarium and the Shroud and tracing their origin to first century Jerusalem. More important here is to review the scientific studies that have been performed on the cloth as well as the findings of that research.

The Spanish Center for Sindonology or Equipo de Investigacion del Centro Espanol de Sindonologia (EDICES)

The majority of research conducted by scientists took place under the auspices of a research group founded in 1987 by famous Italian Shroud scholar, Monsignor Guilio Ricci. The first time he viewed the Sudarium, he was so impressed by the similarities between the bloodstains on it, and those found on the Shroud, that he organized

---

[276] Pray Tell – Worship, Wit and Wisdom, Hispano-Mozarabic Illationes for Advent: A Euchological Enrichment, Part One. "When in the aftermath of the Second Vatican Council some non-Roman Western rites undertook the task of liturgical revision, Fr. Pinell served as chairman for a committee of experts preparing the so-called "Visigothic," "Mozarabic," or "Old Spanish" Rite for wider usage, especially in the Spanish-speaking world. The fruits of their labor appeared in the 1990s when the *Missale Hispano-Mozarabicum* and the *Liber Commicus* were published under the auspices of the Spanish Episcopal Conference and the Archbishop of Toledo."
[277] Guerrera, Vittorio, Fr. The Shroud of Turin: A Case for Authenticity. Tan Books and Publishers, Inc. Rockford, Il. 2001. Page 42.

Equipo de Investigacion del Centro Espanol de Sindonologia (EDICES), translated the Spanish Center for Sindonology. The Center is a nonprofit association founded for the purpose of studying the Shroud of Turin and any matter directly or indirectly related to it.

At the request of the Archbishop of Oviedo in 1988, Ricci's group began to study the Sudarium in late 1989 and continued their work into 1990. The team included some thirty specialists in language, theology, science, and other related disciplines. The Team "used the same techniques employed in forensic investigations, including many types of photography: infrared reflection, ultraviolet light, transparency, and lateral illumination."[278] It focused on an analysis of several aspects of the cloth and their findings are summarized below.

Cloth Type

The Sudarium is mounted in a silver frame that has no glass or other protective covering. The obverse (front) of the Sudarium is the side that is publicly exposed for veneration[279]. The reverse (back), however, is the side of the cloth that actually touched the face of Jesus. "It is dirtier, and its stains are more intense in color. It is covered with micro-scabs of blood from wounds on the head."[280] Because the linen

---

[278] Bennett, Janice, The Sudarium of Oviedo and its Relationship with the Shroud of Turin, A presentation made at the First International Conference on the Shroud of Turin, Panama City, Panama, June 30 – July 1, 2012. Page 4.

[279] Note – "The belief that this relic was used during Christ's passion and death led to a liturgical rite specific to the Cathedral of Oviedo. Benediction with the Holy Sudarium was first done from a balcony made for that purpose, and it continues to take place from the main altar on three dates every year: Good Friday, and September 14 and 21, the first and last days of the Jubilee of the Holy Cross. Bennett, Janice, The Sudarium of Oviedo and its Relationship with the Shroud of Turin, A presentation made at the First International Conference on the Shroud of Turin, Panama City, Panama, June 30 – July 1, 2012. Page 3.

[280] Bennett, Janice, The Sudarium of Oviedo and its Relationship with the Shroud of Turin, A presentation made at the First International Conference on the Shroud of Turin, Panama City, Panama, June 30 – July 1, 2012. Page 2.

has been sewn to a supporting cloth, it is hidden from view. The cloth has been tautened on a wooden stretcher and is covered with the silver frame. During the scientific study, the Sudarium was separated from its supporting cloth.

Scientists noted that the Sudarium is a linen cloth "with a 'Z' twist, the most common type of weave in the Roman Empire. It has a taffeta texture, the simplest type of weave, and it does not have selvages on any of its edges. Nor does it contain any dye. The linen has a large number of defects, such as loops, loose basting stitches, and the crossing of parallel threads of the wood, indicating that the cloth was made on a vertical loom with weights, and that it is very old, likely from the first century."[281]

Blood and Other Stains

Dr. Villalain Blanco, a Spanish criminologist and forensic physician, was tapped to direct a blood study that would both determine what the stains were and how they were formed on the Sudarium. He performed his work in the laboratories of criminology and forensic biology at the Schools of Forensic Medicine in both Madrid and Valencia.

Dr. Blanco noted that the Sudarium contains an abundance of stains that are spread over a significant area of the cloth. He found that there are three distinct sets of stains "composed of one part blood and six parts of pulmonary oedema fluid. It has also been established that when a person dies by crucifixion, 'his lungs are filled with the fluid from the oedema. If the body is moved or jolted, this fluid can come out through the nostrils.'"[282] In this way, the findings suggest that the person whose face was covered by this 'napkin' suffered a death identical to that which the man on the Shroud suffered.

---

[281] Ibid. Page 4.
[282] Page Guerrera, Vittorio, Fr. The Shroud of Turin: A Case for Authenticity. Tan Books and Publishers, Inc. Rockford, Il. 2001. Page 44.

The cloth was folded allowing the blood to soak through it. This accounts for four-fold identical stains observed on the Sudarium. The fact that those stains are not centered indicate that the cloth was not folded evenly in half. Experiments conducted by the Investigation team from the Spanish Center of Sindonology on the blood stains reveal significant information about the timing of events following the death of Jesus. Liquid stains, such as blood, when mixed with other liquid stains that occur in rapid succession, tend to dry at the same rate of speed. However, if time lapses between the stains, then the liquid from the first stain has time to dry before the fluid forming the second liquid stains the cloth. The Sudarium, however, clearly shows a differentiation in staining, making it certain that time elapsed between the forming of those stains. It is clear from those experiments that "the body was left on the cross for about one hour before being taken down. It was then laid on the ground a further forty-five minutes

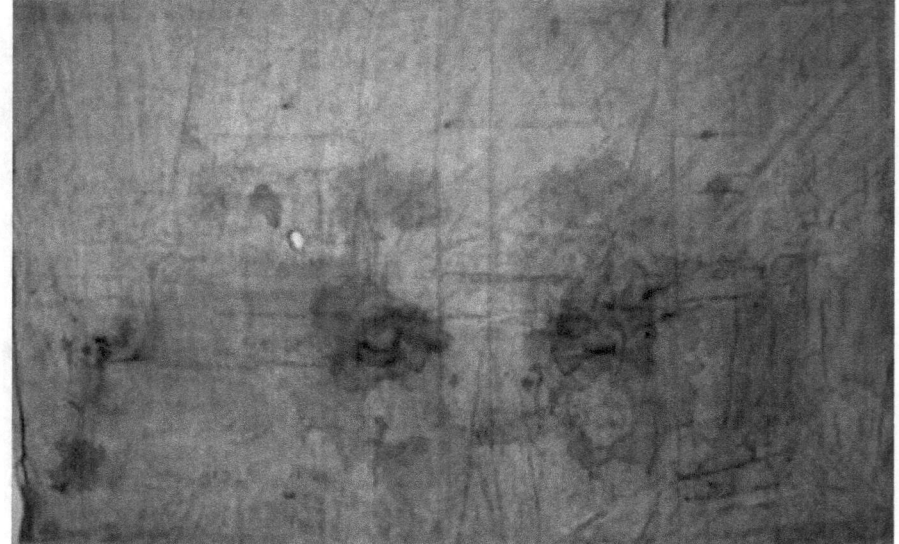

The Sudarium of Oviedo, the cloth that covered the postmortem face of Jesus from the time He hung on the cross to when He was laid in the tomb. (Wikicommons)

before being carried to the tomb."[283] It is quite possible that the body was removed from the cross, but not taken to the tomb until permission to bury the body was granted by Pontius Pilate.

Perhaps more astounding, the bloodstains found on the Sudarium are an exact match to the facial features found on the man whose image appears on the Shroud. The comparison between the stains on the Sudarium and the image on the Shroud of Turin was made by Dr. Alan Whanger and his wife Mary, who developed the polarized image overlay technique used in the process. The pair used polarized filters to superimpose the two images and found "over seventy-five congruent blood stains on the facial portion of the two cloths and fifty-five congruent blood stains on the back of the head and neck."[284]

This provides reasonable evidence that the two cloths were in contact with the same person. In fact, Dr. Whanger believes that the evidence provided by one hundred and thirty points of congruence is overwhelming, especially in light of the fact that only forty-five to sixty points are needed to establish facial identity in an American court of law.

The researchers also discovered that the facial characteristics found on the Shroud and the overlapping blood stains of the Sudarium "both exhibit typical Jewish features: a prominent nose measuring eight centimeters or a little over three inches, and high cheek bones."[285] Even the beard as depicted on the Shroud and the Sudarium are an exact match. The similarities don't end there, however. Researchers found a high concentration of dust on the Sudarium in the area of the nose which is an indication that the man whose face

---

[283] Guscin, Mark, The Oviedo Cloth. The Lutterworth Press, Cambridge, Great Britain. 1998. Page 38.
[284] Guerrera, Vittorio, Fr. The Shroud of Turin: A Case for Authenticity. Tan Books and Publishers, Inc. Rockford, IL. 2001. Page 50.
[285] Ibid.

was covered by it may have hit his face on the ground during a hard, unbroken fall.

The blood found on the Sudarium was not coagulated, but rather fresh, suggesting that the Sudarium covered the man's face for only a short time. It is known that first century Jewish law required a victim's bloody face to be covered after death. Therefore, the face of Jesus would have been covered after his death, resulting in the cloth being stained with fresh, not clotted blood, and until the body was taken to the tomb.

Pier-Luigi Baima Bollone, a professor of Forensic Medicine at the University of Turin and a former Director of the International Center for Sindonology, was asked by Msgr. Ricci to type test the blood. He determined that the blood "found on the Sudarium [belonged] to the group AB. This result was repeated in 1993 by hematologist Carlo Godoni and by the Spanish Center for Sindonology."[286] As was the case with the Shroud, this supports the theory that the Sudarium originated in the Middle East where type AB blood is very common and is not a European fabrication since type AB blood is very rare in Europe.

Dr. Blanco experimented with over six thousand stains that were made using a model of a head with tubes in the nostrils to simulate the expulsion of liquid. From these he was able to calculate that the head of the crucified man was tilted seventy degrees forward and twenty degrees to the right. At this angle the victim's head would have been touching his shoulder making it difficult, if not impossible, to wrap the Sudarium around the entire face. The conclusion, therefore, is that the cloth was wrapped only around the left side of the man's head.

---

[286] Bennett, Janice, The Sudarium of Oviedo and its Relationship with the Shroud of Turin, A presentation made at the First International Conference on the Shroud of Turin, Panama City, Panama, June 30 – July 1, 2012. Page 4.

The hole marks on the Sudarium also support Dr. Whanger's opinion that the cap of thorns may have still been on the victim's head. The cloth even contains the finger marks of the person who held the Sudarium to the head of the victim. "The first time that pressure was applied to the cloth over the dead man's face was by a left hand, with the index, middle, ring and little finger bent inwards, resting on the palm of the hand, and the thumb resting on the knuckle of the index finger."[287] With the hand in this position, it was possible to press the victim's nose with the palm of the hand to stem the blood flow coming from it. That is when the first set of stains was made.

EDICES research also revealed that the postmortem body remained on the cross for about one hour before being taken down. During the process of removing the body from the cross, the hand and the arm came from the other direction (over the head) indicating that the person was behind the head of the deceased. At this point, "the thumb was pressed to the right-hand side of the corpse's nose, and the index finger to its left-hand side. The other three fingers were bent, resting on the cloth over the body's cheek."[288]

Once on the ground, the body would have been placed at the foot of the cross face down with the Sudarium still wrapping the head. In this position, where the body remained for some forty-five minutes, fluids, including blood, would have freely leaked from the nostrils forming a second set of stains. The third and final set of stains would have been made when the body was lifted off the ground. At that point, "both the index and middle fingers were applying pressure to the left-hand side of the man's nose, in another attempt to stem the abundant blood flow. During this whole process, the position of the Sudarium over the face did not change."[289] Finally, the Sudarium provides clues on the distance from the cross to the tomb as the

---

[287] Guerrera, Vittorio, Fr. The Shroud of Turin: A Case for Authenticity. Tan Books and Publishers, Inc. Rockford, IL 2001. Page 48.
[288] Ibid. Pages 48-49.
[289] Ibid. Page 49.

evidence suggests that the body was carried for a period of time no longer than about five minutes.

Pollen and Dust Analysis

During the examination of the Sudarium performed by EDICES, small samples of the cloth were cut off for study. One of the studies undertaken focused on pollen and dust taken from the surface of the Sudarium. Dr. Max Frei is a Swiss botanist and criminologist who was asked by Monsignor Guilio Ricci, to study the pollen and dust particles the Sudarium. Dr. Frei reported that the pollen found on this cloth was from Jerusalem, Oviedo, Toledo and North Africa, all places that the Sudarium is known to have traveled. In all, thirteen types of pollen were identified, and of those thirteen, eight were also found on the Shroud.

In subsequent testing conducted by Dr. Carmen Gomez Ferreras, a University of Complutense biologist, pollen from three genera of plants were found. They were identified as *quercus*, *Pistacia*, and *tamarix*, which are native only to the region of Palestine. In fact, "all the species found on the Sudarium show that it has never been out of the Mediterranean area."[290]

"Professor Avinoam Danin, a botanist from Hebrew University in Jerusalem, and a world authority on the flora of the Near East, said: 'There's no possibility that this cloth in Oviedo and the Shroud would both have the same blood stains, and these pollen grains, unless they were covering the same body.'"[291]

Myrrh and Aloes

In accordance with first century Jewish burial customs, bodies were anointed with myrrh and aloes before burial. In the case of the

---

[290] Guscin, Mark, The Oviedo Cloth. The Lutterworth Press, Cambridge, Great Britain. 1998. Page 55.
[291] Guerrera, Vittorio, Fr. The Shroud of Turin: A Case for Authenticity. Tan Books and Publishers, Inc. Rockford, Il. 2001. Page 47.

burial of Jesus, an anointment process was confirmed in the Gospel of St. John (19:39-40) who wrote, "Nicodemus also, who had at first come to him by night, came bringing a mixture of myrrh and aloes, about a hundred pounds weight. They took the body of Jesus, and bound it in linen cloths with the spices, as is the burial custom of the Jews."[292] Joseph of Arimathea assisted with the 'hasty' anointing of the body so the tomb could be closed before the start of the day of Jewish preparation.

In support of this occurrence, Monsignor Ricci referenced "a statement made by the custodian of the Sudarium, who reassured him that a chemical examination of the cloth found the presence of aloes and myrrh."[293] Felipe Montero Ortego of Madrid, an expert in working with electronic microscopes, confirmed the presence of those ointments, according to Mark Guscin, author of The Oviedo Cloth. The Sudarium covered the face of Jesus when he was carried into the tomb. It was removed, folded, and placed to the side, however, prior to the body being anointed. It probably remained there the entire time that Jesus' body lay in the tomb. It is likely, however, that "this large quantity of myrrh and aloes in the tomb would have been sufficient to leave some traces on the Sudarium."[294] Guscin further suggests the possibility that "some spices could have been applied to the body before the Sudarium was taken off the face."[295]

Wrinkles and Perforations

One thing which is plentiful on the Sudarium is wrinkles and "scientists sought to answer when and why each wrinkle was

---

[292] Holy Bible, The - New Testament, John 19: 39-40, The Great Adventure Bible, Revised Standard Version, Second Catholic Edition, Ascension Press, West Chester, PA. 2006. Page 1409.
[293] Guerrera, Vittorio, Fr. The Shroud of Turin: A Case for Authenticity. Tan Books and Publishers, Inc. Rockford, Il. 2001. Page 50.
[294] Guscin, Mark, The Oviedo Cloth. The Lutterworth Press, Cambridge, Great Britain. 1998. Page 56.
[295] Ibid.

formed."²⁹⁶ If wrinkles on linen are not ironed out, they could be preserved forever and the wrinkles on the Sudarium provided a plethora of information about how the cloth had been kept throughout history. The information gleaned, including the tilt of the head, the position of the arms, the location of the body, and even how the body was removed from the cross, has been presented in the section of this chapter titled, *Blood and Other Stains*. As noted, those stains even provide information about the length of time Jesus hung on the cross postmortem, how long His body lay on the ground at the foot of the cross, and how long it took to carry the body to the tomb.

The Sudarium also contains a number of perforations, some of which relate to the formation of stains while others are a product of the Sudarium being fastened to the head of Jesus. Pins or some other sharp object held the cloth to the hair and beard. "They have a truncated conical nature, and appear in pairs, indicating the possibility that thorns were used. An oval hole is also seen on the linen, very possibly caused by a candle, because there is evidence of a singe and wax."²⁹⁷

The scientific analysis of the Sudarium proves that it "covered a man with a moustache, beard and long hair…[the man] was tortured, likely crowned with thorns, and then crucified…the victim died with acute pulmonary edema and was buried in a nearby tomb."²⁹⁸ The evidence also shows that it would have been impossible for the man to have survived the ordeal because "the blood that flowed from the nose and mouth made breathing impossible. After dying in a vertical position, the man of the Sudarium was placed in a right lateral prone position."²⁹⁹ A crucifixion timetable can be established based on both

---

[296] Bennett, Janice, The Sudarium of Oviedo and its Relationship with the Shroud of Turin, A presentation made at the First International Conference on the Shroud of Turin, Panama City, Panama, June 30 – July 1, 2012. Page 5.
[297] Ibid.
[298] Ibid. Page 7.
[299] Ibid.

the Sudarium studies and Scripture. Jesus was led out of the Praetorium at about 6:00 A.M. He was crucified at 12:00 Noon and died at 3:00 P.M. At 4:00 P.M., the Sudarium was wrapped around His head. At 5:00 P.M. the body was taken from the cross and while lying horizontally on the ground, the Sudarium was removed, the arms and legs were forced from their crucified position (as rigor mortis had set in), and the body was given a preliminary anointing with aloes and myrrh in preparation for the transfer to the tomb. At 6:00 P.M., the Sudarium was placed over the head once again and the body was carried a short distance to the tomb where it arrived at about 6:10 P.M. Once laid in the tomb, the body was placed on the slab, the Sudarium was removed, and the body was enveloped with the Shroud that completely surrounded it.

The work of the Spanish Center for Sindonology continued for many years and their scientific investigations into the Sudarium of Oviedo have resulted in two international congresses, one held in 1994 and the other in 2007.

CHAPTER IX

What Science and Tradition Reveal About the Veil of Veronica and the Image of Divine Mercy

The Veil of Veronica

As noted previously, there are several cloths that are proclaimed to be the Veil of Veronica, but only two, the one held at the basilica in Manoppello, Italy, and the one held at the Vatican, are likely the real veil. A preponderance of the available research, however, indicates that the true veil might be the one called the Veil of Manoppello. Consequently, that is the cloth that will be discussed in this chapter.

The veil of Manoppello has been subjected to some degree of scientific tests in an attempt to determine its authenticity as the cloth that was used to wipe the face of Jesus during his passion. The purpose of some of the scientific inquiry was to determine exactly how the image of a suffering man was imprinted on the cloth and the answer to that question continues to elude researchers.

In 1977, University of Bari Professor Donato Vittori "examined the veil under ultraviolet light and found that the fibers do not have any type of color."[300] When the cloth was studied under a microscope, no paint was detected. It was also evident that the cloth was not woven with colored fibers. A study that included the use of sophisticated photographic technology, including enhanced digital enlargements, made it possible to see "that the image is identical on both sides of the veil."[301]

When German Jesuit scholar, Fr. Heinrich Pfeiffer, studied the many works of art still in existence that depicted the veil, he found that several details contained in those works confirm that the model used by the various artists was, in fact, the veil of Manoppello. The professor of Christian art history at the Pontifical Gregorian University in Rome noted that these features include "the haircut, the blood traces, the shape of the face, the beard's characteristics and even the folds of the cloth,"[302] all of which are identical to the features found on the Manoppello veil. "When the different details are assembled in one image, it means the image must have been the model for all the others," Pfeiffer argues. "So, we can say that the veil of Manoppello is nothing other than the original Veronica's Veil."[303]

---

[300] Gaspari, Antonio, Has Veronica's Veil Been Found?, Urbi et orbi Communications, November 1999. CatholicCulture.org, Inside the Vatican, Martin de Porres lay Dominican Community, KY. Trinity Communications, 2024. Page 2. https://www.catholicculture.org/culture/library/view.cfm?recnum=2856
[301] Ibid.
[302] Ibid.
[303] Ibid.

Roberto Falcinelli, in a research paper presented to the International Workshop on the Scientific Approach to the Acheiropoietos Images, which took place at the ENEA, Frascati, Italy, from May 4-6, 2010, agreed that the Manoppello image may be the authentic veil of Veronica. In his extensive research, Falcinelli was privileged to examine the original code H3, the unpublished work of Giacomo Grimaldi which is preserved in the Vatican Library. He was also granted special authorization to study the two frames of the relic, including the thirteenth century frame that is kept in the museum of the Treasury of the Vatican Basilica. He studied both the original ciborium for the Volto Santo as well as the new ciborium. Finally, Falcinelli studied the five known copies of Veronica's Veil painted by Pietro Strozzi between 1616 and 1617. His opinion is not to be taken lightly.

In 2018, the veil of Manoppello was subjected to a detailed study conducted by Italian professors Liberato De Caro, Emilio Matricciani and Giulion Fanti. They determined that the veil is a rectangular shaped cloth measuring 240 x 175 mm (approximately 10 x 7 inches). It is semi-transparent so that the face is visible on both the front and the back of the cloth. Oddly they discovered that anatomical detail seems to change with light variations. This phenomenon is explained by analysis of the cloth itself which revealed a plethora of information.

The cloth "is a linen fiber fabric consisting of very thin threads, with a thickness of about 0.1 mm, separated by distances even twice the thickness of the threads, so that about 42% of the Veil is empty space. The fibers of the linen threads have been likely cemented by an organic substance of chemical composition similar to cellulose, presumably starch, therefore eliminating the air between them. Such a structure causes the optical behavior of the medium to be intermediate between that of a translucent medium (cemented linen threads) and that of a transparent one (empty space between the threads). Since the face is deformed due to distortions of the meshes of the Veil, caused by the yielding of the very fine structure of the fabric, first we have tackled the problem of digital image restoration to correct the face deformations which, in some regions of the image, are even about 1 centimeter. Afterwards, we have performed a spectral analysis of the transmitted image. As evidenced in the first study, its thin linen threads are translucent, presumably because it is starched, and light passes through them. As a result, the yellowish color of the ancient linen and starch contribute substantially to the final hues of the face, especially when the Veil is lit from the backside with grazing light. Spectrophotometry measurements show how the fabric absorbs the various chromatic components. Through these quantitative evaluations, the colors of the transmitted face image have been compensated, by subtracting the contribution due to the yellowish coloration of the thin linen threads. Furthermore, the rotational spectrum of the image has been studied after digital restoration.

The linear fit of the power spectrum in bi-logarithmic scale with a power law f P provided a surprising value for the slope parameter $P = -3.49 \pm 0.03$. This result was unexpected because it is typical of photographs of human faces, not of portraits of human faces painted by artists, which instead have statistical properties of fractal type, with slope's values $P = -2.0$."[304]

De Caro, Matricciani and Fanti also wrote about their efforts to chromatically restore the image. That restored image presented shades that more closely reflected the skin color of the human face. When the digital restoration was applied to a larger portion of the image by incorporating the hairs, a more detailed image presented

---

[304] De Caro, Liberato; Matricciani, Emilio; and Fanti, Giulio, A Comparison Between the Face of the Veil of Manoppello and the Face of the Shroud of Turin. Heritage 2019, Received December 2018, Accepted January 22, 2019, Published January 24, 2019. www.mdpi.com/journal/heritage. Pages 339, 340, and 341.

itself to the research team. This enhancement proved useful "to better highlight several wounds, visible on the face as red patches."[305]

The same research team conducted additional tests on the Veil of Manoppello. Their subsequent research paper noted that the yellowing of the threads of the thin linen cloth has caused some changes to occur in the aspect of the original face and in particular in the color of the eyes. "Indeed, as inferred by some experimental evidence, both on a microscopic and a macroscopic scale, the eyes were probably originally blue."[306] The authors note that blue is the color that is affected the most by the introduction of the yellowing of the fibers.

The team members found that the optical characteristics presented on the Manoppello Veil "are unique in the world, as it can be evinced by the most complete archive in the world dedicated to the Veronica's Veil and Veil of Manoppello."[307]

It was also determined that the presence of insects and mites on the Veil, as confirmed by a microscopic analysis with polarized light, means that the fibers of the Veil of Manoppello are made of flax and those fibers change color over the centuries.

As noted, and perhaps most shockingly, the research paper suggests that the original eye color of the image on the Manoppello Veil was blue, and that color was altered to reflect a brown hue which is more common among the people of the Mediterranean.

Finally, the authors conclude that the "chromatic retouch of the eyes was done before the time the Veil started to be shown to the public…. If the above conjecture were fully established, then, at the beginning of the year 1200, the Veil of Manoppello had reached 95%

---

[305] Ibid.
[306] De Caro, Liberato; Matricciani, Emilio; and Fanti, Giulio, Yellowing of Ancient Linen and Its Effects on the Colours of the Holy Face of Manoppello. Heritage 2019, Received November 2019, Accepted December 20, 2019, Published December 23, 2019. www.mdpi.com/journal/heritage. Page 1.
[307] Ibid. Page 3.

of the maximum normalized yellowing index (NYI). As ten centuries are needed to reach 95% of the maximum NYI, this would imply that the Veil of Manoppello would be a fabric of the Roman epoch. The minimum time interval to reach 95% of the maximum NYI is 7 centuries."[308]

The conclusion, based on the aforementioned technical analysis, therefore, is that "the history of the Veil of Manoppello could be related to that of the Veil of Veronica, the relic of the face of Christ that the Christian tradition binds to his Passion and death."[309]

The Image of Divine Mercy

When Jesus appeared to Sister Faustina Kowalska, a rather uneducated Polish nun, on February 22, 1931, He instructed her to paint the image of Him that she saw and to encourage a devotion to His Divine Mercy. On that day, as Sister Faustina tells it, she was in Our Lady of Mercy convent in Plock, Poland. She "saw the Lord Jesus clothed in a white garment. One hand was raised in the gesture of blessing, the other was touching the garment at the breast. From beneath the garment slightly drawn at the breast, there were emanating two large rays, one red, the other pale. In silence I kept my gaze fixed on the Lord; my soul was struck with awe, but also with great joy. After a while, Jesus said to me: 'Paint an image according to the pattern you see, with the signature: Jesus, I trust in You. I desire that this image be venerated, first in your chapel, and [then] throughout the world.'"[310]

---

[308] Ibid. Page 13

[309] De Caro, Liberato; Matricciani, Emilio; and Fanti, Giulio, A Comparison Between the Face of the Veil of Manoppello and the Face of the Shroud of Turin. Heritage 2019, Received December 2018, Accepted January 22, 2019, Published January 24, 2019. www.mdpi.com/journal/heritage. Page 345.

[310] Kowalska, Saint Maria Faustina, Diary - Divine Mercy in My Soul. Marian Press, Stockbridge, MA. 2016. First published in 1987. From the Original Polish Diary,

Sister Christine, another nun at the convent, noted that "the rays of light from the window were visible that night, and attracted the attention of people standing on the other side of the street, implying that it was a 'physical' appearance, rather than an interior vision."[311]

Sister Faustina Kowalska

Sister Faustina was confused as to what she should do next. She couldn't paint, wasn't acquainted with anyone who could, and had no money to commission an artist. So, while in Vilnius, she confided in Fr. Michael Sopocko who was her spiritual director and confessor. He did what just about anyone would do under these circumstances. He ordered her to undergo psychiatric testing to make sure that she was not psychotic or delusional. The test confirmed that

---

Zgromadzenie Siosr Matkj Boxej Milosierdzia,ul. Zytnia 3/9, 01-014 Warszawa, Poland. 1981. Diary 47-48, Page 24.

[311] Wikipedia, Divine Mercy Image. https://en.wikipedia.org/wiki/Divine_Mercy_image#First_Painting. August 2021. Page 2.

she was not and Fr. Sopocko provided her with guidance on how to fulfil Jesus' request regarding the painting.

Fr. Sopocko commissioned Eugene Kazimirowski, a local artist, to paint the image under the direction of Sister Faustina, but things didn't go quite as smoothly as Faustina, Sopocko or Kazimirowski had envisioned. "When she saw the first offering, Faustina was not happy and told the artist to repaint the face because the rendering just did not look right to her. Ten times he was forced to repaint the face of Jesus. He threatened to quit and agreed to stay on only after being cajoled by Sopocko.

The current version of the painting was completed in 1934 and was still not to Faustina's liking. "When she first saw the image, she wept in disappointment, asking the Lord Jesus, 'Who will paint You as beautiful as You are?' But Jesus told her"[312] that it is in His grace and not the beauty of the color or the brush that the greatness of the image lies. With those comforting words, Faustina finally approved Kazimirowski's tenth rendering.

Though there are several noteworthy features of the original Divine Mercy image, three aspects are most significant, and they are unique to the original image. These features were discussed previously, but they merit another mention here. The first relates to God's mercy which is represented by the blue and white rays. "No one can see where they start, and no one can see where they end. They're unmeasurable."[313]

The second feature visually describes how Divine Mercy is given freely. "In the original image, Jesus is opening up His alb. In

---

[312] The Divine Mercy: On This Day, the Divine Mercy Image Was Revealed. https://www.thedivinemercy.org/articles/day-divine-mercy-image-was-revealed. February 22, 2024.
[313] Lambert, Aaron, Jesus, I Trust in You: The History and Mystery of the Divine Mercy Devotion, The Archdiocese of San Francisco, March 28, 2024. https://sfarchdiocese.org/jesus-i-trust-in-you-the-history-and-mystery-of-the-divine-mercy-devotion/. Page 2.

the other paintings of Divine Mercy, He's simply pointing, or touching, at best. But in the original image, he's lifting His alb, and he's giving it. That's Divine Mercy,"[314] Daniel DiSilva, founder of the Original Divine Mercy Institute explained. "God gives it. It's not taken from Him. It is a giving. It's a true gift."[315]

The third aspect of the original image is Jesus' downward gaze. Sister Faustina did not provide this detail to the painter, but it is there. "That feature came from Jesus Himself," DiSilva explained. "She didn't give the direction for the downward gaze, but the downward gaze was there, and [Faustina] asked Jesus, 'Why, in the painting, are your eyes downward cast?' And Jesus' answer was, 'My gaze in the painting is similar to my gaze from the cross.' Only in the original masterpiece is His gaze downward. Why is it important? Because if He's looking for us, He's looking for us at the foot of the cross. That's where we're supposed to be to receive His mercy. And that's a big deal."[316]

No scientific testing needed to be done to confirm how the image appeared on the canvass. It was obviously painted by Polish artist Eugene Kazimirowski. And no date-testing was needed to verify its age as the tenth version of the image was completed in 1934 and finally accepted by the visionary after a mystic consultation with Jesus. Photographic testing, however, was performed and the process produced a startling result. That will be the subject of the next section.

---

[314] Ibid.
[315] Ibid.
[316] Ibid. Pages 2-3.

CHAPTER X

SCIENTIFIC STUDIES PRODUCE THEORIES ON THE CREATION OF THE IMAGE ON THE SHROUD

As has been detailed throughout these chapters, several breakout groups of scientists have followed the STURP Study findings with independent research into various aspects of the Shroud. One area of study focused on how the image on the Shroud, the actual burial cloth of Jesus, may have been produced. These scientists have come to be known as the Yahoo Shroud Science Group.[317] In the course of their work, they have not rejected the force

---

[317] BBC News Magazine, How Did the Turin Shroud Get Its Image, (4. It Was Made by Some Kind of Energy Release) June 19, 2015.
https://www.bbc.com/news/magazine-33164668. Page 7.

of the *Resurrection* of Jesus of Nazareth as a potential source of the image creation. They noted that the "hypotheses correlated to an energy source coming from the enveloped or wrapped Man, [and] others correlated to surface electrostatic discharges caused by an electric field"[318] must be considered despite the invocation of processes not currently known to science, but nevertheless could occur during a resurrection from the dead.

One of the researchers, University of Padua professor, Giulio Fanti, found that "the image might have been burnt into the upper layers of the cloth by a burst of 'radiant energy' – bright light, ultraviolet light, X-rays or streams of fundamental particles – emanating from the body itself."[319] Fanti recalls the accounts of the Transfiguration of Jesus from Luke 9:29. "…and as He was praying, the appearance of his countenance was altered, and his clothing became dazzling white."[320] One version of the same text, taken from the NIV Bible, states that "his cloths became as bright as a *flash of lightning*."[321] Fanti proposed that science should at least test the theory of "whether artificial sources of such radiation can produce a similar result on linen."[322]

For years, Shroud researchers have been inundated with a series of enigmas, some of which may never be explained. At least five of these were reviewed during the 1978 STURP study and three of those five were plausibly explained. The three with plausible scientific explanation follow:

---

[318] Ibid.
[319] Ibid.
[320] Holy Bible, The New Testament, The Great Adventure Bible, Revised Standard Version, Second Catholic Edition, Ascension Press, West Chester, PA. 2006. Luke 9:29. Page 1350.
[321] Holy Bible, The New Testament, Luke 29:9, NIV (New International Version), https://www.bible.com/bible/111/LUK.9.29-31.
[322] BBC News Magazine, How Did the Turin Shroud Get Its Image, (4. It Was Made by Some Kind of Energy Release) June 19, 2015.
https://www.bbc.com/news/magazine-33164668. Page 7.

"**Enigma #1: The Image is Only on the Uppermost Surface of the Fibrils** – If the image formation came about through chemicals, then it would not explain how the image only appears on the uppermost surface of the fibrils. By their makeup, chemicals penetrate beyond the surface of the fabric.

Enigma #2: The Image Shows the Whole Body – Chemicals cannot explain how a perfect 3-dimensional image became evenly distributed on the cloth – especially on parts that did not come into contact with the corpse. Thus, something other than chemicals must be the cause of the image on the Shroud.

Enigma #3: The Image Was Not Produced by Vapors – Vapors from chemicals, or from the corpse itself, do not explain how the image is present on parts of the body where the cloth clearly did not touch the body (i.e. areas on either side of Christ's projected nose).

Dr. John Jackson, the leader of the 1978 scientific team that studied the Shroud, received his Ph.D. in Physics in 1972 from the Naval Postgraduate School with a dissertation on theoretical Cosmology. He continued his research work on the Shroud post-STURP and provided plausible explanations for these three mysteries. "Jackson deduced that vacuum UV radiation is the only possible explanation for the image's formation. 'Light radiation is needed to transform a linen into a "perfectly photographically sensitive material,"'[323] Jackson explained. The amount of light needed to create the image on the Shroud of Turin would require "several billion watts of light radiation," Jackson noted, "which exceeds the maximum output of any source of UV radiation known today. If the

---

[323] Magis Center, How Did the Shroud of Turin Get Its Image? (Hint: Think Radiation.), May 27, 2019. https://www.magiscenter.com/blog/how-did-shroud-turin-get-image#:~:text=The%20formation%20of%20the%20Shroud%E2%80%99s%20image%20would%20take,of%20any%20source%20of%20UV%20radiation%20known%20today. Page 4.

accompanying heat energy had been present, the cloth would have vaporized in less than 1/40 billionth of a second."[324]

In 2010, Dr. Paoli DiLazzaro, a physicist and Chief of Research at ENEA – Italian National Agency for New Technologies, Energy and Sustainable Economic Development, Applications of Radiation, validated Jackson's theory. DiLazzaro and his team concluded, "In particular, vacuum ultraviolet photons account for the very thin coloration depth, the hue of color and the presence of image in linen parts not in contact with the body. Obviously, it does not mean the image was produced by a laser. Rather, the laser is a powerful tool to test and obtain the light parameters suitable for a shroud-like coloration."[325]

While Enigma's one, two and three have plausible scientific explanations, enigmas four and five fall into the realm of the miraculous, according to the researchers. Those enigmas follow:

Enigma #4: The Double Image – The discovery of an image on the front and on the back of the Shroud carries with it the implication that "the cloth collapsed into and through the body."[326] Science is at an absolute loss to explain how this could have happened. It would have required that "the body became mechanically transparent, causing the cloth to collapse into it. If the cloth did collapse into the body, then the ultraviolet light would have completely surrounded the body. This would produce a double image on both the front and the back of the cloth, but nothing on the fibers in the middle."[327]

Enigma #5: You Can See Inside the Body, Like an X-ray – The circumstances under which the image on the Shroud was made enabled the bones of the hand to be visible through the flesh. In other words, both the flesh and the bone are visible in the Shroud image of

---

[324] Ibid.
[325] Ibid.
[326] Ibid. Page 5.
[327] Ibid.

the hands, implying once again, that "the Shroud became mechanically transparent, and that the cloth collapsed into and through this body. If it had not done so, the image would only be of the outside of the body."[328]

Fr. Robert J. Spitzer, S.J., Ph. D., of the Magis Center of Reason and Faith, admits that the current laws of physics are unable to explain how a body in some state of decomposition might emit a burst of "vacuum ultraviolet radiation", or how that body could become "mechanically transparent and emit light from every three-dimensional point within it."[329] He notes, however, that it is "reasonable to infer that there is some transphysical cause for the emission of this kind of radiation." The body of Jesus was changed at

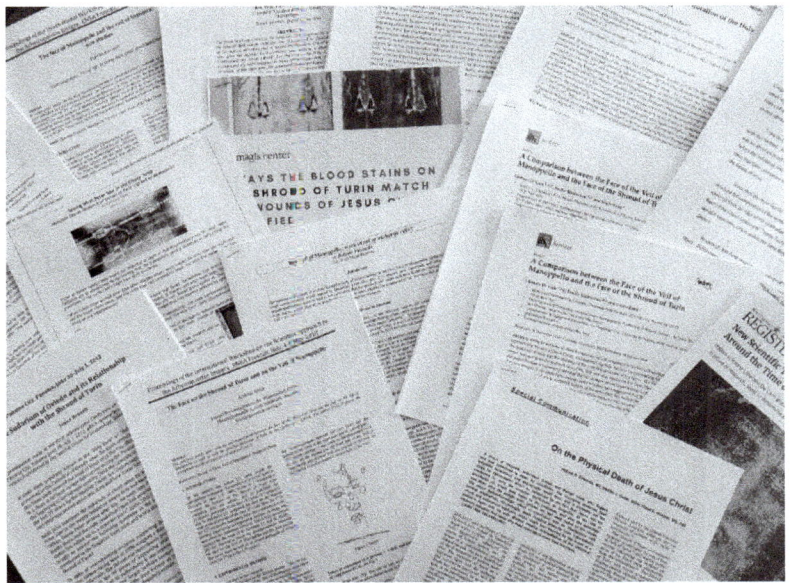

Some of the over one hundred peer reviewed scientific research studies written in the last 20 or so years and used by the author in writing this book.

---

[328] Ibid.
[329] Ibid.

the point of Resurrection. What was once a physical body was transformed into a glorified transphysical body, Spitzer explained. The evidence of this is found in the New Testament, where it is written that post-resurrection, Jesus was able to pass through doors like a ghost but had a body that his followers could touch; one that was able to consume food, and these features are not characteristic of ghosts.

PART III

THE TRUTH AND THE FAITH

CHAPTER XI

THE FOUR IMAGES ARE ONE

O ver the centuries, there have been hundreds if not thousands of paintings and other depictions of Jesus from statuary to film. Hollywood has portrayed Him in a variety of ways in movies and documentaries. He has been depicted as white, European, and of Middle Eastern descent. His hair has been long, short, curly and straight. His beard has been forked, single, double, or triple pointed. His eyes have been brown, hazel and blue. He was depicted as tall and not so tall, thin and not so thin.

Despite the conjecture and speculation, four images have been left to the world and each of them may hold the key to the actual physical appearance of Jesus. The Shroud, the Sudarium of Oviedo, the Veil of Manoppollo and the original Image of Divine Mercy, all seem to have the 'handprint' of God on them, yet all four look so different in appearance. At least that's how it appears to the naked eye. In reality, however, that is not the case.

It can't be overstated that the Shroud is the most studied and tested cloth in the history of the world. The Sudarium and the Veil have also been subjected to specific scientific and analytical examination. Using the Shroud as a control, the Sudarium, the Veil and the original Image of Divine Mercy, were part of a comparative analysis to ascertain points of congruity and points of difference between them. The results are rather shocking.

The Sudarium of Oviedo is Compared and Contrasted with the Shroud of Turin

Blood Stains and Type

Monsignor Ricci was the first to suggest a connection between the Shroud of Turin and the Sudarium of Oviedo, and his scientific studies have contributed important information about the similarities between them. He published the findings in two books; *L'Uomo della Sondone e Jesu* (Milan 1965), and *La Sindone Contestata, Difesa, Spiegata* (Rome 1992). In these two volumes, Ricci "highlights the exact matches in a number of areas of the Shroud and the Sudarium

Ricci first noted that the bloodstains on the Shroud and those of the Sudarium correspond very closely. The size and shape of the nose, the beard, the forehead, and blood stains on the back of the neck,"[330] are near matches from one cloth to the other.

Both the Sudarium and the Shroud are stained with type AB blood, a rather uncommon blood type outside of the Palestine area. Perhaps more stunning, the size and position of the stains on the two cloths are eighty percent congruent with each other. But if the two cloths covered the same body, wouldn't the stains be one hundred percent congruent? Janice Bennett explained why the twenty percent

---

[330] Khan, Arif, The Sudarium of Oviedo and the Shroud of Turin, The Review of Religions, https://www.reviewofreligions.org/11770/the-sudarium-of-oviedo-and-the-shroud-of-turin/. May 19, 2015. Page 2.

variation exists. Research shows that there are two drops of blood on the left eyebrow of the man of the Sudarium that are not present on the Shroud. It is entirely possible that blood droplets on the face were absorbed by the Sudarium, and that the bleeding was subsequently stemmed by the pressure of the cloth to the face, prior to the body being covered with the Shroud. In fact, at the 1994 International

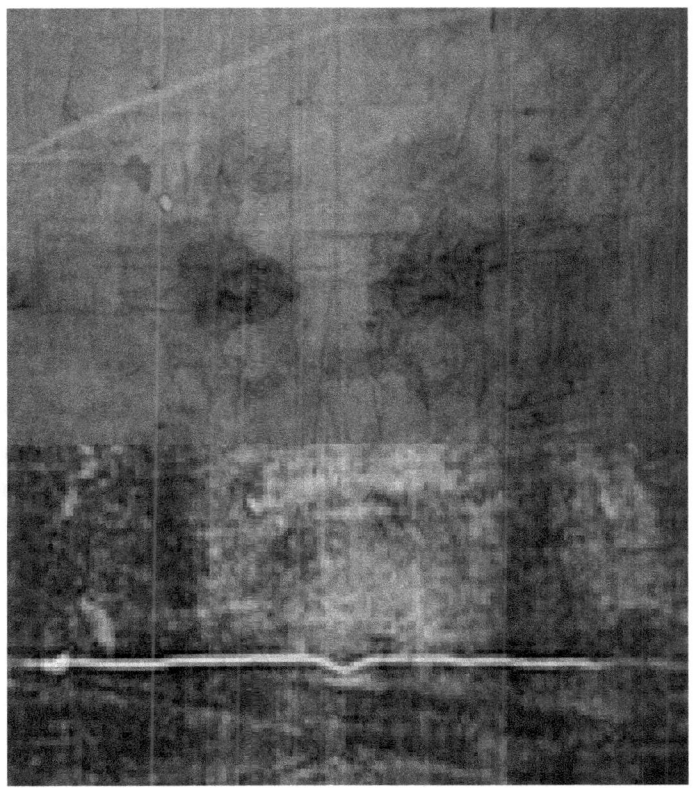

The overlapping image of the Shroud of Turin (bottom portion), and the Sudarium of Oviedo (top portion), showing the many points of congruence between the two images.

Congress in Oviedo, Dr. Jose Villalain, professor of Forensic Medicine at the University of Valencia, noted that "the Sudarium would have been used to cover the face while in transit, and when in the tomb it would have been removed prior to the Shroud being used...There is evidence that as the body was carried to the tomb the Sudarium was held to the face of the man. Actual finger marks are visible on the cloth which corroborate this."[331] The evidence further shows that the headwounds responsible for those stains on each cloth were produced from a crown of thorns.

Polarized Image Overlay

Dr. Alan Whanger and his wife compared the blood stains on the Sudarium and the Shroud of Turin utilizing a technique they developed known as Polarized Image Overlay. "The frontal stains on the Sudarium show seventy points of coincidence with the Shroud, and the rear side shows fifty."[332]

Janice Bennett, presenting at the First International Conference on the Shroud of Turin in Panama City, Panama in 2012, explained other similarities between the two cloths. "A simple superimposition of the photographs of the two linens shows surprising morphological similarities."[333] Regarding the facial features, the length of the nose is exactly eight centimeters (approximately 3.15 inches) on each cloth. Both the Shroud and the Sudarium show evidence of swelling on the right side of the nose about mid-way down from the bridge. "The nasal cavities and wings appear as though similar pressure had been exerted on them." There is evidence of bruising on the right cheek of each cloth. "The position and size of the mouth coincide with similar flows of blood along the beard from the post-mortem pulmonary edema."[334]

---

[331] Khan, Arif, The Sudarium of Oviedo and the Shroud of Turin, The Review of Religions, https://www.reviewofreligions.org/11770/the-sudarium-of-oviedo-and-the-shroud-of-turin/. May 19, 2015. Pages 3-4.
[332] Ibid. Page 2.
[333] Bennett, Janice, The Sudarium of Oviedo and its Relationship with the Shroud of Turin, A presentation made at the First International Conference on the Shroud of Turin, Panama City, Panama, June 30 – July 1, 2012. https://www.shroud.com/pdfs/bennettpantxteng.pdf. Page 9-10.
[334] Ibid.

Dust on the Nose

Both the Sudarium and the Shroud contain ground particles and dust on the nose in rather high concentrations. "Scholars have speculated that this was due to the Roman tradition whereby the condemned man carried his own cross to the place of crucifixion." This theory conforms to Gospel accounts that Jesus was struggling to carry the cross, and likely stumbled and fell along the way to Golgotha. Of course, because His arms were tied to the cross beam, he would have been unable to break his fall resulting in injury to the face and nose.

Pollen

The research of Dr. Max Frei not only confirmed the presence of pollen on the Shroud and Sudarium, but "was able to identify pollen specific to certain regions of the world and create a map of areas in which the Shroud of Turin had been. The results matched the history of the Sudarium, with samples found from Oviedo, Toledo, North Africa and Jerusalem."[335]

Professor Avinoam Danin, of the Hebrew University of Jerusalem, was able to narrow the pollen traces on the Shroud to "plants growing in a restricted area around Jerusalem and could date back to the time of Jesus. Two pollen grains of this same species were also found on the Sudarium."[336]

Aloe and Myrrh

Electron microscope expert, Felipe Montere, identified residue on the Sudarium as most likely being aloes and myrrh. The Scriptures, specifically the Gospel narrative of John, notes that Nicodemus and Joseph of Arimathea prepared the body of Jesus with

---

[335] Khan, Arif, The Sudarium of Oviedo and the Shroud of Turin, The Review of Religions, https://www.reviewofreligions.org/11770/the-sudarium-of-oviedo-and-the-shroud-of-turin/. May 19, 2015. Pages 3.
[336] Ibid.

aloes and myrrh. Both substances were also present on the Shroud of Turin.

Facial Features

Finally, it has been confirmed through scientific testing that both cloths covered the face of a man who had long hair, a moustache, and a beard, was tortured and ultimately crucified. All of the aforementioned evidence amounts to an extraordinarily high probability that the Shroud of Turin and the Sudarium of Oviedo were in Jerusalem around the time of the first century and that they were used to cover the same body.

Conclusions

It is likely that the Sudarium was in contact with the Shroud, and that provides "strong, independent evidence for the authenticity of the Shroud of Turin…The two cloths authenticate and validate each other and together they provide a strong case for being the original burial cloths of Jesus."[337] When all known historical and Scriptural accounts, are factored into the scientific findings and conclusions, it can be reasoned with a high degree of certainty, that the Shroud of Turin and the Sudarium of Oviedo were the cloths used to wrap the postmortem body of Jesus of Nazareth following His crucifixion.

The Veil of Manoppello is Compared and Contrasted with the Shroud of Turin

When making a comparison of the Holy Face as it appears on the Veil of Manoppello it is necessary to note the similarities as well as the differences between the two cloths. A visual study of the Veil reveals that the image appears on both sides of a highly transparent Veil comprised of very fine yarn. The image on the front is similar to that on the back but is not a mirror reflection. At first sight, many

---

[337] Ibid. Pages 5-6.

brushstrokes seem evident, and the image appears to be an artist's painting, "but after a detailed analysis some characteristics appear that may speak in favor of a supernatural hypothesis of the image formation."[338]

Microscopic and spectroscopic studies, however, simply exclude the use of various painting techniques making both the formation of the image as well as the nature of the image substantively unclear.

Adding to the mystery are some similarities found between the face on the Shroud of Turin, and that of the Veil, and these have drawn considerable interest in recent years. Attempting to provide some answers, Sister Blandina Paschalio Schlomer, a Trappistine nun,

Overlapping image of the Shroud of Turin and the Veil of Manoppello showing the many points of congruence.

---

[338] Jaworski, Jan S. and Fanti, Giulio, 3-D Processing to Evidence Characteristics Represented in Manoppello Veil. Research Paper. https://www.shroud.com/pdfs/jaworski.pdf. 2008. Page 1.

superimposed the two images on transparent foils, and the resulting composite was studied extensively by Heinrich Pfeiffer and Andreas Resch. Pfeiffer, who studied at the Art Students League of New York and continued his studies at the Pennsylvania Academy of Fine Arts, and Resch, who is a director, screenwriter, author and film critic from Berlin, Germany, noted that "ten congruence points…were used to perfect adjustment of both images one to another."[339]

The research team concluded that "not only a general appearance, but also some details of the face in both images are consistent….These include the shape and size of the face as well as some marks of wounds like a swelling on the right cheek." There were also notable differences between the two images that includes "the very evident bloodstain having the characteristic shape of a reversed '3' on the front of the Shroud face [which] is not present on the Veil face."[340] Jan Jaworski and Giuilo Fanti, co-authors of the report *3-D Processing to Evidence Characteristics Represented in Manoppello Veil*, believe that a painter copying the Shroud face would have certainly included this sign. Fanti believes that the omission of this mark indicates that the face on the Veil was produced before that of the Shroud. This theory supports the possibility of the image on the Veil being produced during Veronica's encounter with Jesus.

Other differences include the superficial character of the image on the Shroud which appears only on the very top of the cloth's fibers, something not duplicated on the Veil. "The Veil's image is composed of bring-substances of different colors, but still unknown," whereas the Shroud's image is in "monochromatic yellow to light brown color corresponding to chemical changes (a fast ageing) of linen fibers. The Shroud's image is not made of bring-substances, but the color derives from carbonyl groups formed in a dehydration of the

---

[339] Ibid. Page 2
[340] Ibid.

polysaccharides layer out of the linen fibers, which is not the case of the Veil's image."[341]

The final difference between the two cloths is the dimensionality. The Shroud has very clear three-dimensional qualities about it while the Veil has only very weak three-dimensional qualities evident in the hollow of the eye sockets and at the flattened end of the nose.

When exposed to the most sophisticated 3-D technology available, the Brice 4.0, "a number of characteristic details and marks of wounds known from the Shroud's images can be recognized in similar areas on the Veil's image. Marks of the wounds include: a swelling of both eyebrows and a crosscut of the left eyebrow; a triangular-shaped wound on the right cheek close to the nose; a swelling of the yoke bone below the left eye; a swelling below the right eye; the swollen nose and a deformation of the nose septum with the bruised cartilage; and a swelling of the upper lip. Other characteristic marks on the Shroud face which can be easily identified [on the Veil] include: a forked beard, a hairless area between the lower lip and the beard, an enlarged left nostril, a few strands of hair at the top of the forehead, and maybe also a transverse streak across the forehead, which is however, not clear in the images [of the Veil]."[342]

Based on the scientific comparison of the qualities of the Veil and the Shroud, it would appear highly likely that the two images are of the same person and one image was made before death while the other is a postmortem image of the crucified man. Sister Blandina Paschalis Schloemer began her research on the similarities between the Shroud and the Veil in 1979, after reading German books which stated that the two images had the same dimensions. This didn't seem to be true based on her own observations, so she began to study the two cloths to prove they did not reflect the same image. From 1979

---

[341] Ibid. Pages 2-3.
[342] Ibid. Page 5.

until 1991, her research was limited to comparisons of photographs and photocopies. But in 1991, Sr. Blandina "was able to make the first slides of natural size, and after placing one on top of the other, there appeared a perfect match of the wounds and other particulars...the images were derived from the very same source."[343]

The twenty-seven "panels which demonstrated the full convergence of the two images"[344] were presented in 1998 at the conference on the "Face of Faces" held at Rome. "Those panels now form the Exhibit "Penuel" at the Shrine of Manoppello."[345]

Findings

Following their 2018 scientific analysis comparing the face on the Veil of Manoppello to the face of the Shroud of Turin, researchers Liberato DeCaro, Emilio Matricciani and Giulio Fante noted that the faces on the two cloths overlap quite convincingly. "Thus," the trio concluded, "in our opinion, it is possible to conclude that the two images are related. In particular, the right cheek's profile of the two faces is very similar....It still remains unsolved how the faces of both the Shroud and the Veil were impressed on the fabric,"[346] or how the colors appeared on the Veil of Veronica.

What does it all mean? In a 2009 interview with the official magazine of *Il Volto Santo di Manoppello*, Sr. Blandina, who has chosen a life as a hermit to focus on her research of the image on the Veil, summed it up beautifully. "In the beginning it was not my

---

[343] Redzioch, Wlodzimierz, An Interview with Sr. Blandina Paschalis Schloemer, The Holy Face of Manoppello Blogspot. July 1, 2010. https://holyfaceofmanoppello.blogspot.com/2010/07/interview-with-sr-blandina-paschalis.html. Page 2.
[344] Ibid. Page 3.
[345] Ibid.
[346] De Caro, Liberato; Matricciani, Emilio; and Fanti, Giulio, A Comparison Between the Face of the Veil of Manoppello and the Face of the Shroud of Turin. Heritage 2019, Received December 2018, Accepted January 22, 2019, Published January 24, 2019. www.mdpi.com/journal/heritage. Page 354.

intention to seek out the Holy Face and to remain in Manoppello…Jesus is present in the Eucharist everywhere. However, in the Veil of Manoppello, He does something more: He shows Himself…God incarnate has an individual and unique Face, and this Face I can only contemplate at Manoppello."[347]

The Veil of Manoppello is Compared and Contrasted with the Sudarium of Oviedo

Scientific research and analysis conducted over the past thirty or so years has convincingly demonstrated the connection between the Shroud of Turin, the Sudarium of Oviedo and the Veil of Manoppello. It could be logically assumed that, if the image on the Veil and the stains of the Sudarium are closely related to the image on the Shroud, that they must be similarly associated with each other. And they are! The cloths have many points of congruity even though the Shroud bears the image of a dead man, the Sudarium contains the associated blood stains of that same dead man, and the Veil of Manoppello holds the image of a man that is very much alive.

It was a Capuchin friar by the name of Domenico da Cese who became one of the first to recognize that there were facial features on the Veil of Manoppello that matched those of the Shroud of Turin. It was the Trappist nun Blandina Paschalis Schlomer, however, who developed an overlay technique that was used to compare the Shroud image to the Veil image. This so-called 'superimposition' proved that both cloths showed an image of the same person. Schlomer later applied the same superimposition technique to the Sudarium of Oviedo and the Veil of Manoppello and realized the exact same result.

Schlomer's research produced at least ten points of congruence between those two cloths, including: "a cut between the two teeth visible on the cloth; a piercing of thorns between the middle and end of the left eyebrow; a stain over an injury of the right eyebrow; a diagonal line

---

[347] Ibid. Pages 2-3.

which is congruent with a bright red line in the [Veil] of Manoppello; and configuration at the nose caused by a blow from a cudgel. There are parallel dark lines and a bright triangular line, the tip of which points downwards; a horizontal line which is interrupted in places and delineates the lower boundary of the break in the middle of the nose; abraded and crushed tip of the nose; injury to the upper lip. One can see dark points in a straight line which projects slightly beyond the lip line from these possible puncture sites. An injury to the upper lip itself is also visible; trace fluid which begins precisely at the site of the pupil. The eye appears to be injured by thorns; [and]; injury caused by thorns on the right cheek in the geometric form of a trapezoid with the tip pointing downwards."[348]

The Image of Divine Mercy is Compared and Contrasted with the Shroud of Turin and Sudarium of Oviedo

To this point, the comparisons between the cloths are of cloths that are Acheiropoieta, a medieval Greek term meaning 'made without hand. They are considered to be Christian icons or relics which are said to have come into existence miraculously; not created by a human. The image of Divine Mercy, however, was certainly made by human hands. It is a painting that was commissioned by Fr. Michael Sopocko in 1934 and painted by Eugene Kazimirowski in Vilnius at the direction of Sr. Faustina Kowalska, based on her recollection of her vision of Jesus in 1931. And the image was painted upon the request made by Jesus to Faustina. Though Faustina made the artist change the painting ten times, it was Jesus, when the nun was still dissatisfied with the artists rendering, who told Faustina that the tenth painting would suffice.

---

[348] The Face of Christ, Website, Byssus and Pure Linen: Comparing the Cloths. https://www.sudariumchristi.com/en/tomb/compare.htm. Page 2.

This cross section of the image of Divine Mercy and the image from the Shroud of Turin demonstrates the perfect alignment of the two images.

To say, based upon this brief introduction, that it would have been easy for the painter to use the Shroud of Turin as a point of reference as he painted the image would be understandable. Yes, that would be a reasonable assumption, except that neither sister Faustina nor Eugene Kazimirowski, had ever seen the Shroud of Turin. They had never laid eyes on a photograph of the Shroud, and it is quite possible that they had never even heard of the relic. Kazimirowski painted the image of Jesus, using as his only reference, Sr. Faustina's recollection of what Jesus looked like in the vision that she had of Him almost three years earlier.

It was Fr. Serafin Michalenko who first noticed the similarity between the original Divine Mercy image and the Shroud of Turin. Upon his discovery, he asked Professor Zbigniew Treppa, from the Division of the Anthropology of Visual Representation at the University of Gdansk, to undertake a scientific analysis of the two images. Michalenko's 1990s request was honored by the professor who undertook anthropological studies of the two faces. The results were stunning.

According to Professor Treppa, the results show "a complete convergence with such characteristic facial points as the middle part of the eyebrows; the base of the nose; the cheekbones, jaws, the wings of the nose; and the beginning of the upper and lower lip and chin."[349]

Zbigniew later analyzed the same details by observing the images in three different dimensions using a model created by Professor Miniaro in 2002, that was based on the measurements of the Veil of Oviedo and the Shroud of Turin. "I put all three images on each other, and it turned out that the eight points determining the most characteristic feature of the face perfectly matched."[350] Treppa discovered the same match when overlaying the full body of the Shroud with the full-length body of the original Divine Mercy painting. Treppa estimates that in order for Michalenko to achieve that match without benefit of today's technology would have required him to paint over "a thousand face images to finally get the proportions such as the ones on the Shroud. This means that we cannot talk about accidental action here."[351]

On April 6, 2024, The Christ Cathedral Campus was the site of a discussion led by Fr. Robert Spitzer, S.J., PhD., a foremost expert on the proof of faith through science, and Adriana Acutis, a renowned researcher on the Holy Shroud of Turin. The pair led a conversation on Eucharistic miracles, the subject of the next chapter, and the relationship between the Holy Shroud and the Divine Mercy Image. Speaking to the circumstances of the painting of the Divine Mercy image and the many points of congruence between it and the Shroud, Acutis noted, "The artist of this painting is not Kazimirowski, but Jesus."[352]

---

[349] YouTube Video, What Happens When This Painting is Matched with the Shroud of Turin? Length = 14:11.
https://www.youtube.com/watch?v=Ije0GkSKohk. 2021.
[350] Ibid.
[351] Ibid.
[352] Ponsi, Lou, The Holy Shroud, the Divine Mercy Image and Eucharistic Miracles. Orange County Catholic, https://www.occatholic.com/the-holy-shroud-the-divine-mercy-image-and-eucharistic-miracles/. April 23, 2024. Page 2.

CHAPTER XII

THE SHROUD, THE VEIL OF MANOPPELLO, THE SUDARIUM OF OVIEDO, AND EUCHARISTIC MIRACLES

It was late April, in the year 29 A.D., and Jesus had just fed the five thousand near the Sea of Tiberias on the other side of the Sea of Galilee and walked on water to meet his disciples who were headed by boat to Capernaum. His popularity was growing by leaps and bounds and he drew large crowds everywhere. The very next day a great many of his followers crossed the sea in search of Jesus and found him in Capernaum. Jesus said to them, "'Very truly, I tell you, you are looking for me, not because you saw signs, but because you ate your fill of the loaves. Do not work for the food that perishes, but for the food that endures for eternal life, which the Son of Man will give you. For it is on him that God the Father has set his seal.' Then they said to him, 'What must we do to perform the works of God?' Jesus answered them, 'This is the work of God, that you believe in him whom he has sent.' So they said to him, "What sign are you going to give us then, so that we may see it and believe you? What work are you performing? Our ancestors ate the manna in the wilderness; as it is written, 'He gave them bread from heaven to eat.' Then Jesus said to them, 'Very truly, I tell you, it was not Moses who gave you the bread from heaven, but it is my Father who gives you the true bread from heaven. For the bread of God is that which comes down from heaven and gives life to the world.'"[353]

When the Jews began to complain about him Jesus said to them, "'I am the bread of life. Your ancestors ate the manna in the wilderness, and they died. This is the bread that comes down from heaven, so that one may eat of it and not die. I am the living bread that came down from heaven. Whoever eats of this bread will live forever; and the bread that I will give for the life of the world is my flesh.' The Jews then disputed among themselves, saying, 'How can this man give us his flesh to eat?' So Jesus said to them, 'Very truly, I tell you, unless you eat the flesh of the Son of Man and drink his blood, you have no life in you. Those who eat my flesh and drink my blood have eternal life, and I will raise them up on the last day; for my flesh is true food and my blood is true drink. Those who eat my flesh and drink my blood abide in me, and I in them. Just as the living Father sent me, and I live because of the Father, so whoever eats me will live because of me. This is the bread that came down from heaven, not like that which your ancestors ate, and they died. But the one who eats this bread will live forever. He said these things while teaching in the synagogue at Capernaum.

When many of his disciples heard it, they said, 'This teaching is difficult; who can accept it?' But Jesus, being aware that his

---

[353] Holy Bible, The – New Testament, The Word on Fire Bible, The Gospels. New Revised Standard Version. John 6:27-33. Brandon Vogt, General Editor. Word on Fire, Park Ridge, IL. 2020. Pages 494-495.

disciples were complaining about it, said to them, 'Does this offend you? Then what if you were to see the Son of Man ascending to where he was before? It is the spirit that gives life; the flesh is useless. The words that I have spoken to you are spirit and life….Because of this, many of his disciples turned back and no longer went about with him. So Jesus asked the twelve, 'Do you also wish to go away?' Simon Peter answered him, 'Lord, to whom can we go? You have the words of eternal life. We have come to believe and know that you are the Holy One of God.'"[354]

Jesus was not speaking metaphorically when he told His followers that they must eat His Flesh and drink His Blood. When some followers began to leave, He didn't walk His comments back. Nor did He endeavor to explain. Rather, He looked at the twelve and asked if they wanted to also leave. That is not the demeanor of someone who misspoke or spoke metaphorically.

Almost a year had passed since Jesus performed the miracle of feeding the five thousand. It was now the start of Passover, April 6, 30 A.D. and Jesus looked forward to sharing the meal with his disciples. It was during this meal that Jesus would empower the world with the gift of the Holy Eucharist. "When the hour came, he took his place at the table, and the apostles with him. He said to them, 'I have eagerly desired to eat this Passover with you before I suffer; for I tell you, I will not eat it until it is fulfilled in the kingdom of God.' Then he took the cup, and after giving thanks he said, 'Take this and divide it among yourselves; for I tell you that from now on I will not drink of the fruit of the vine until the kingdom of God comes. Then he took a loaf of bread, and when he had given thanks, he broke it and gave it to them, saying, 'This is my body, which is given for you. Do this in remembrance of me.' And he did the same with the cup after supper,

---

[354] Holy Bible, The – New Testament, The Word on Fire Bible, The Gospels. New Revised Standard Version. John chapter 6, select passages between verses 41-70. Brandon Vogt, General Editor. Word on Fire, Park Ridge, IL. 2020. Pages 495-496.

saying, 'This cup that is poured out for you is the new covenant in my blood.'"[355]

With those words, Jesus gave us Himself, Body and Blood, Soul and Divinity, so that we will have Him with us always, even to the end of the age. As was the case with many of His early followers, however, there are many today who don't believe that Jesus lives in the Eucharist. Catholics believe that the priest, who stands in persona Christi, performs this miracle during that part of the Holy Mass known as the Transubstantiation. Church doctrine teaches that it is at that moment that the ordinary bread and wine are converted into the actual Flesh and Blood of Jesus Christ. But even among Catholics only sixty-four percent believe that the host is the true Body and Blood of Christ, according to a September 29, 2023, report issued by the Catholic News Agency.

Since the year 750 A.D., however, there have been over one hundred approved Eucharistic miracles confirmed by science and recognized as authentic by the Catholic Church. These miracles, to which science simply refers as inexplicable, not only prove that the Eucharist is the true Body and Blood of the risen and living Christ but does so in a way that provides a mysterious connection to the Shroud of Turin and the Sudarium of Oviedo. This chapter will examine just a few of those miracles.

Buenos Aires, Argentina

It was August 18, 1996, at 7:00 P.M., and Fr. Alejandro Pezet had just finished distributing Holy Communion to his congregation, when he was approached by a woman who told him that she had seen a host that had been abandoned in a candle holder at the base of a crucifix on the right side of the church. The priest followed the woman to the location of the abandoned host. It appeared to have been lodged

---

[355] Holy Bible, The – New Testament, The Word on Fire Bible, The Gospels. New Revised Standard Version. Luke 22:14-21. Brandon Vogt, General Editor. Word on Fire, Park Ridge, IL. 2020. Page 422.

in a largely unused candle holder for some time, and consequently was very dusty. Fr. Pezet carefully removed it with the intention of consuming it, but it was so dirty that he decided to dispose of it by placing it in a bowl of water, the prescribed method for disposal of discarded Eucharists. Eucharistic minister Emma Fernandez was asked to tend to the task and did so.

Almost a week later, on Monday, August 26, Fr. Pezet went to the Church's Blessed Sacrament Chapel to pray, when Emma Fernandez informed him that something strange was taking place at the tabernacle. Upon inspection, Fr. Pezet found that the host that had been discarded in the water a week earlier, was turning red. A blood-like substance was coming from the host. Over the following weeks, the red substance grew in quantity. Fr. Pezet moved the bowl containing the host to the other tabernacle in the presbytery.

"Archbishop, Jorje Bergoglio (who later became Pope Francis) commissioned a professional photographer to document this supernatural process as it unfolded. The first photos taken on August 26, show a small round glass dish with a round undissolved host, but with dark spots surrounded by a bright red liquid. The photos taken on September 6 show that the dark sections had grown in size, and even more red liquid was interspersed with the liquid of a ruddy brown color. The original round outline of the host was still discernable."[356]

In 1999, Fr. Pezet was granted permission from the archbishop to have the host and the liquid analyzed scientifically. The analysis was part of a blind study, meaning that the lab was not notified how the material came to be, or what it was thought to be. They simply extracted a sample of the bloody material, sealed it for forensic analysis, and sent it off to the lab.

The analysis determined that the material was human blood, type AB. Shockingly, "the human DNA would not yield a genetic profile. No

---

[356] Carpenter, John S., *He Is Alive: Science Finds Jesus*, Page Publishing, Inc. New York, 2018. Page 145.

scientist could explain how that was even possible."[357] The lack of genetic profile was a stunning revelation made more improbable by the fact that the blood type was the same type that appeared on the Shroud of Turin and the Sudarium of Oviedo. Recall that neither of those cloths yielded a genetic profile either. Jesus, of course, was conceived of the Holy Spirit. As such, He had DNA only from His Mother Mary.

This story gets even more interesting. The lab noted that the sample also contained flesh, so the tissue was given to another expert for analysis. "Dr. Frederick Zugibe, a heart specialist and forensic pathologist in New York, received the first sample. Highly respected, investigative Australian journalist Mike Willesee and Australian lawyer and researcher Ron Tesoriero flew to New York to film the test results on April 20, 2004. Looking up from his microscope, with no background information obtained at all, Dr. Zugibe explained what he was seeing, 'This looks to be of human origin. It is flesh, and I can see white blood cells. It is definitely heart tissue from the left ventricle wall, not too far from a valvular area. It's the part of the heart muscle that makes the heart beat. The left ventricle pumps blood to all parts of the body. This heart muscle has lost its striations, and there is the presence of intact white blood cells. The heart muscle is inflamed. There has been recent injuries like those that I see in cases where somebody has been beaten severely around the chest. The white blood cells indicate injury and inflammation. Well, there are a lot of them, all intact."[358]

Lanciano, Italy

This Eucharistic miracle, perhaps the first on record, occurred in 750 A.D. and involved a priest who had a difficult time believing that the transubstantiated host was truly the Body and Blood of the risen Lord. As he celebrated Mass one day, at the moment of

---

[357] Ibid.
[358] Ibid.

consecration where the priest elevates the host, he noticed the "round white wafer was instantly surrounded by a ring of visible flesh. At the same moment, the consecrated wine in the chalice on the altar formed into five jellylike pellets of human blood. The astonished priest and congregation at once begged God to forgive them for their weak faith and recent doubts." [359]

The miraculous host was carefully encased for the purpose of preserving it. However, without preservatives, and in a non-airtight container, the miraculous host disintegrated, leaving behind the ring of flesh. The five pellets of blood, though hardened on the outside, were still liquified on the inside. In the year 750, science did not have the means to test the liquid to determine its origin. Neither did it have the ability to identify blood type or other significant details about the fleshy substance. In 1971 however, it did. That is when Professor Edwardo Linoli, an anatomy and pathological histology expert, was granted permission to perform an examination on the material.

It was determined that the blood was human, and the type was "AB both in the blood and flesh samples. The blood was shown to contain the same minerals, chemicals, and proteins as fresh human blood taken the same day – even though this blood was 1,221 years old in 1971! The five unequal portions of blood weigh the same altogether as each pellet weighs separately (15.85 grams)."[360] Let that sink in for a minute. The unequal parts of blood each weigh the same as the other, and the total weight of all the blood samples is the exact same weight as any one of the parts. Science cannot explain this, but Church theologians have always contended that any fragment of the Eucharist contains the same amount of living flesh and blood as is contained within the entire Eucharist. This miracle simply provides proof.

---

[359] Ibid. Page 71.
[360] Ibid. Page 72.

The Eucharist from 750 AD is still preserved with the 1273-year-old blood. AFC photo, CC BY-SA 3.0 <https://creativecommons.org/licenses/by-sa/3.0>, via Wikimedia Commons

The professor continued his examination and found that "the tissue was actually the muscle of the heart. The tissue is neither dead nor mummified but considered to still be living tissue because the commission determined that it responded rapidly to all the clinical reactions distinctive of living beings"[361]. The samples from the

---

[361] Ibid. Pages 72-73.

Eucharistic miracle from Lanciano, Italy have been unchanged even from 1971 and remain in the same condition as they were in 750.

Legnica, Poland

He was distributing Holy Communion to the congregation at the Christmas Mass, December 25, 2013, when the priest accidentally dropped a consecrated Host on the floor. In accordance with the procedure at St. Hyacinth's Shrine in Legnica, Poland, the Host was placed in a bowl of holy water to dissolve.

By mid-January 2014, however, the wafer was only partially dissolved, and a red substance appeared on it. The parish priest notified Bishop Stefan Cichy, who formed a committee to study the matter. The Committee obtained the services of two forensic departments of medicine, one from a university in Wroclaw and the other from a university in Szczecin. The university specialists studied the samples independently. The results were stunning. The Department of Forensic Medicine stated:

"In the histopathological image, the fragments of tissue have been found containing the fragmented parts of the cross striated muscle. The whole sample is most similar to the heart muscle with alterations that often appear during agony. The genetic researchers also indicated that the origin of the tissue is human."[362]

The blood type from this Eucharistic miracle, like all the others, was type AB. Newly installed Bishop Kiernikowski needed no more convincing than that to know that a Eucharistic miracle had taken place in his diocese. In January of 2016, "he presented the matter to the Vatican's Congregation for the Doctrine of the Faith. In April, in accordance with the Holy See's recommendations, he asked parish priest Andrzej Ziombrze to prepare a suitable place for the Relic so that the faithful could venerate it.

---

[362] Ibid. Page 154.

What Does It All Mean?

There is so much to unpack here that it merits repeating. The discarded host in South America began to ooze human blood when placed in water. The blood is of the same type found on the burial cloths of Jesus - type AB. No genetic profile could be determined. The sample contained human flesh. There was heart tissue from the part of the heart that pumps blood to the rest of the body. The tissue was from a heart that was in distress, having undergone a severe beating. White blood cells were present and "white blood cells can only exist if they are fed by a living body. This means that the heart was alive at the moment this sample was collected.

The story is the same for the Eucharistic miracle in Lanciano, Italy, and for the one in Legnica, Poland. In fact, the realities are the same for all one hundred plus Eucharistic miracles that have been approved and sanctioned by the Catholic Church.

Scientists have no explanation for any of this. It defies all logic, and everything known to science. According to Dr. Maria Elzbieta Sobaniec-Lotwska, one of the experts who examined the sample from Sokolka, "No technology from NASA could possibly do this. It is 100 percent fake proof." Fr. Spitzer, President of the Magis Center for Reason and Faith, added, "We can't duplicate it. Now, of course, that speaks volumes, and that is I think really important to combine with the other two hosts. At the very same time they said we know this is not a process, that it's a living tissue, but that living tissue is in the process of death."

While science may be baffled by these documents, a person of faith doesn't need science to explain what is happening here. They can see very clearly how all these things, the Veil of Manoppello, the Sudarium of Oviedo, the Shroud of Turin, the Image of Divine Mercy, and the plethora of Eucharistic miracles from around the globe, are all interconnected, and can all be traced back to one man in history: Jesus Christ, the living God.

Conclusion

*"To one who has faith, no explanation is necessary.
To one without faith, no explanation is possible."*
                                             St. Thomas Aquinas

Is the Veil of Manoppello the cloth that Veronica used to wipe the face of Jesus as He carried His cross to Golgotha? Are the Shroud of Turin and the Sudarium of Oviedo His actual burial cloths? Science cannot answer these questions with any definition, but neither can science claim that these relics are not associated with Jesus, and in 2022, David Rolfe offered the British Museum one-million-dollars to prove the Shroud was a fake. On February 8, 2024, Myra Adams, the executive director of the National Shroud of Turin Exhibit, took to the podium to announce a one-million-dollar challenge to anyone who can recreate the Shroud of Turin using only tools and techniques of the fourteenth century. Despite a universal clamor for free money, no one has taken advantage of the offers.

Rather than proving the Shroud a fake or showing how it could have been reproduced, that cloth, and the other relics that are the subject of this book, are instead the source of extraordinary miracles. Recounted below very briefly, are examples of the miracles associated with these relics.

The Veil of Manoppello

The French revolution raged on, and in 1849, the Pope sought refuge in Gaeto. From there, in an effort to invoke divine protection, he ordered that Veronica's Veil be displayed to the public between Christmas and Epiphany. "On the third day of this extraordinary exhibition, the unexpected happened. A soft light surrounds him, transforming the event into a striking miracle. This divinely inspired manifestation sets off a chain reaction among the faithful and the curious, leading to a collective manifestation of incredible spiritual intensity that lasts for three hours."[363] For not only was the Veil of Manoppello illumined by divine brilliance, but any reproductions touched to the original during the miracle of illumination were also touched by the aura subsequently providing their own light.

The Shroud of Turin

She was only eleven years old in 1954, but Josie Wollam lay in a hospital bed dying of a severe bone disease. Doctors at the facility in Gloucestershire, England could not explain how osteomyelitis had impacted both her hip and her leg, or how she acquired the abscesses in her lung. Regardless, they had to explain to the girl's grief-stricken mother, that there was nothing they could do to help little Josie, and through the tears she was given the last rites of the church. While the doctors seemed to give up hope, little Josie never did. She had heard that a local group was holding a lecture on the Shroud of Turin and that she knew she would be healed if only she could see the sacred relic.

Josie's mother complied by contacting Captain Leonard Cheshire, a coordinator of the event, who had a photograph of the face on the Shroud sent to Josie at the hospital. Simply holding the image put Josie into partial remission of the bone disease, and two weeks later the girl returned home. Josie still couldn't walk, but insisted that if she could just see the Shroud and be near it, she would be totally cured.

So impressed was Cheshire by the little girl's faith that he arranged to take her to Turin where the Shroud was kept, though still under the ownership of former King Umberto II of Portugal. "Once

---

[363] Relics, "The Veil of Veronica" or "Holy Face": A Relic Venerated in Rome Since Antiquity. https://relics.es/en/blogs/relics/veil-of-veronica#:~:text=The%20legend%20surrounding%20this%20relic%20dates%20back%20to,on%20the%20fabric%20when%20she%20picked%20it%20up. Pages 5 – 6.

there, the rolled-up Shroud was placed across the arms of her wheelchair. Josie gently and respectfully placed her hand onto the shroud – and she was healed"[364] instantly and completely.

Thirty-five-year-old Josie walked freely into the Cathedral in Turin for the public exhibition of the Shroud in 1978. No longer bound to a wheelchair and no longer under the death sentence of cancer. While there, "she told Father Peter Rinaldi that after her healing she had lived a normal working life, was married and had a daughter of her own."[365]

The Image of Divine Mercy

His family was very religious. In fact, his mother had a very special devotion to Divine Mercy - always had. But Brendan O'Neill was a successful businessman from Ireland and had little time for such things. When he did find time for the occasional prayer however, like his mother, he would find himself praying to Saint Faustina.

Brendan had promised his mother that he would read Faustina's diary one day, a book she had gifted him sometime earlier, but he just never had the time to fulfill that promise. For some reason, he did take the time to inscribe his name on the inside front cover however, and because his intentions were good, he always kept the book in his car when traveling for business. Despite that constant companion, business reading always became his priority, even on those trips.

One day, while traveling to Dublin on business, his car was stolen. Taken along with it was Faustina's diary, his overnight bag, personal items such as his golf clubs, and his business papers. Three days later, Brendan received a phone call from an old friend in Dublin, who told him that someone had thrown an overnight bag in his back

---

[364] Heggadon, Geoff, Healing Miracles of the Shroud of Turin, Works by Faith Ministries. https://www.worksbyfaith.org/healing-miracles-of-the-shroud-of-turin/. November 28, 2012. Pages 1-2.
[365] Ibid. Page 2.

yard. The only thing in it was the Diary of St. Faustina, which had Brandan's name and contact information inside.

Brendan retrieved the bag and the book and promptly put the book into his car, realizing that his reading it was now a matter of fate. Like before, however, his good intentions were never realized. But then one night, the unthinkable happened again. While parked in a public car park, his car was stolen once more…with the diary in it. He reported the theft to the Guards and several days later, they contacted Brendan to tell him his car had been found, but that it had been set afire. "Not only was the car burnt to a cinder, but everything that was in it was burned to a cinder as well, except for one item which they said was totally unbelievable, a book that they found on the remains of a seat that had not a screed of upholstery left on it, and nothing else in the car was recognizable.

The Guards could not believe that any book could survive in what they said must have been a fire that raged at 2000 degrees. Brendan had a number of books and papers in the car, all of which had been incinerated in the fire, but there on the remains of a seat was the diary of St. Faustina, burned around the edges which meant it had caught fire like everything else, but the fire stopped when it reached the text, which was the message of Divine Mercy."[366]

Brendan could only stare at the charred wreck. That's when he heard the voice, "How long are you going to keep me waiting," the same question Jesus asked of Faustina. Shortly thereafter, Brendan entered the seminary, and today, as a priest, has devoted his life to the service of Christ.

Experts can't describe how an ordinary book could survive a raging inferno. Doctors can't enlighten us as to how a little girl could be cured of terminal cancer by touching a cloth. Science is at an

---

[366] DivineMercy.org Website, The Miracle of Brendan O'Neill, Divine Miracles in Action, Miracles of Divine Mercy. https://www.divinemercy.org/elements-of-divine-mercy/miracles.html. 2024. Page 1.

absolute loss to explain how a Polish artist could paint an image that is an exact match for the image on the Shroud, while getting his only direction from a nun who said that Jesus told her to paint the image of Him that was revealed to her during an apparition. And scientists cannot explain how the Holy Eucharist, on over one hundred occasions, has turned to flesh and blood, containing living distressed heart muscle tissue, with type AB blood - the same blood type that appears on the Shroud and the Sudarium, all while leaving no genetic profile.

But for millions of people around the world, the experts, the scientists and the doctors, simply don't *need* to explain it.

APPENDIX A

Traditional Catholic Prayers to the Holy Face
and
The Chaplet of Divine Mercy

Traditional Catholic Prayers to The Holy Face
"'Nothing whatsoever will be refused to us' through the Holy Face"

PRAYER TO THE SACRED HEAD OF OUR LORD, SEAT OF WISDOM

WISDOM of the Sacred Head, guide me in all my ways.
O Love of the Sacred, consume me with Thy fire.
Three Glorias, in honor of the Divine Will, Memory and Understanding.
O Seat of Divine Wisdom, and guiding Power, which governs all the motions and love of the Sacred Heart, may all minds know Thee, all hearts love Thee, and all tongues praise Thee, now and forever more.

Imprimatur: Jacobus Canonicus Carr, Pro Epo Liverpolitano

PRAYERS OF REPARATION TO THE HOLY FACE OF JESUS

O Blessed Face of my kind Savior, by the tender love and piercing sorrow of Our Lady as she beheld Thee in Thy cruel Passion, grant us to share in this intense sorrow and love so as to fulfill the Holy Will of God to the utmost of our ability. Amen.

Mother Maria-Pierina

CROWN OF THORNS PRAYER

DEAR LORD, I am grieved when I consider Thy sad condition when Thou wore the Crown of Thorns upon Thy holy Head. I desire to withdraw the thorns by offering to the Eternal Father the merits of Thy Wounds for the salvation of sinners. I wish to unite my actions to the merits of Thy Most Holy Crown, so that they may gain many merits, as Thou hast promised. Amen.

Prayer based on a revelation by Our Lord to Sr. Chambon

OFFERING OF THE HOLY FACE TO APPEASE GOD'S JUSTICE AND DRAW DOWN MERCY UPON US

ETERNAL Father, turn away Thine angry gaze from all guilty people whose faces have become unsightly in Thy eyes. Look instead upon the face of Thy Beloved Son, for this is the Face of Him in Whom Thou art well pleased. We now offer Thee this Holy face, covered with shame and disfigured by bloody bruises, in reparation for the crimes of our age, in order to appease Thy anger, justly provoked against us. Because Thy Divine Son, our Redeemer, has taken upon His head all the sins of His people that they might be spared, we now beg of Thee, Eternal Father, to grant us mercy. Amen.

Archconfraternity of the Holy Face

PRAYER TO THE HOLY FACE
Long Version

O Jesus, Who in Thy cruel Passion didst become the "Reproach of men and the Man of Sorrows," I worship Thy Divine Face. Once it shone with the beauty and sweetness of the Divinity: now for my sake it is become as the face of a leper. Yet in that disfigured Countenance I recognize Thy infinite Love, and I am consumed with the desire of loving Thee and of making Thee loved by all mankind. The tears that streamed in such abundance from Thine Eyes are to me as precious pearls which I delight to gather, that with their infinite worth I may ransom the souls of poor sinners.

O Jesus, Whose Face is the sole beauty that ravishes my heart, I may not behold here upon earth the sweetness of Thy Glance, nor feel the ineffable tenderness of Thy Kiss. I bow to Thy Will—but I pray Thee to imprint in me Thy Divine Likeness, and I implore Thee so to inflame me with Thy Love, that it may quickly consume me and I may soon reach the Vision of Thy glorious Face in Heaven. Amen.

Short Version

Jesus, Who in Thy bitter Passion didst become 'the reproach of men and the Man of Sorrows', I venerate Thy Holy Face on which shone the beauty and gentleness of the Divinity. In those disfigured features I recognise Thine infinite Love, and I long to love Thee and to make Thee loved. May I behold Thy Glorious Face in Heaven! Amen.

CANTICLE TO THE HOLY FACE OF JESUS

Dear Jesus! 'tis Thy Holy Face
Is here the start that guides my way;
Thy countenance, so full of grace,
Is heaven on earth, for me, to-day.
And love finds holy charms for me
In Thy sweet eyes with tear-drops wet;
Through mine own tears I smile at Thee,
And in Thy griefs my pains forget.
How gladly would I live unknown,
Thus to console Thy aching heart.
Thy veiled beauty, it is shown
To those who live from earth apart.
I long to fly to Thee alone!
Thy Face is now my fatherland, —
The radiant sunshine of my days, —
My realm of love, my sunlit land,
Where, all life long, I sing Thy praise;
It is the lily of the valley,
Whose mystic perfume, freely given,
Brings comfort, when I faint and fail,
And makes me taste the peace of heaven.
Thy Face, in its unearthly grace,
Is like the divinest myrrh to me,
That on my heart I gladly place;
It is my lyre of melody;
My rest — my comfort — is Thy Face.
My only wealth, Lord! is Thy Face;
I ask naught else than this from Thee;
Hid in the secret of that Face,
The more I shall resemble Thee!
Oh, leave on me some impress faint
Of Thy sweet, humble, patient Face,
And soon I shall become a saint,
And draw men to Thy saving grace.
So, in the secret of Thy Face,
Oh! hide me, hide me, Jesus blest!
There let me find its hidden grace,

Its holy fires, and, in heaven's rest,
Its rapturous kiss, in Thy embrace!

                        St. Therese of Lisieux, August 12, 1895

PRAYERS OF VENERABLE LEO DUPONT

O adorable Face of my Jesus, so mercifully bowed upon the tree of the Cross on the day of Thy Passion, for the salvation of men, now again, incline in Thy pity toward us poor sinners; cast upon us a look of compassion and receive us to the kiss of peace. Amen.

O Lord Jesus Christ, in presenting ourselves before Thy Adorable Face, to beg of Thee the graces we most need, we beseech Thee, to give us above all things the disposition of never refusing at any time to do what Thou requirest of us by Thy commandments and divine inspirations. Amen.

PRAYER OF BLESSED POPE PIUS IX

O my Jesus, cast upon us a look of mercy; turn Thy Face towards each of us, as Thou didst to Veronica; not that we may see It with our bodily eyes, for this we do not deserve, but turn It towards our hearts, so that, remembering Thee, we may ever draw from this fountain of strength the vigour necessary to sustain the combats of life. Amen.

PRAYER OF POPE CLEMENT VI

O God, Who dost enlighten us with the light of Thy Countenance, and Who, to reward the loving kindness of St. Veronica, didst leave us the impression of Thy Face on her veil as a remembrance, grant that through Thy Cross and Passion, we may one day fearlessly look upon Thy Face, when Thou wilt come to judge the living and the dead.

    Almighty and Eternal God, through Whose grace the image of Thy Holy Face doth shine forth radiantly to Thy devout people, grant us, we beseech Thee, the remission of our sins, and direct all the thoughts, words, and actions of those who confide in Thy Mercy, Who livest and reignest with the Father, in unity of the Holy Ghost, one God, world without end. Amen.

PRAYER OF ST. AUGUSTINE TO THE HOLY FACE

I appear before Thy Holy Face, O my Saviour, laden with my sins and the penalties they have brought upon me. What I suffer is far less that

I deserve, for although conscious of the justice of my punishment, I cease not to commit fresh sins every day. I sink beneath Thy scourges, yet I do not amend my ways; my heart is full of bitterness, still my obstinacy in evil remains ever the same. My life is spent in misery, and I do not correct myself. When Thou chastisest me, I make Thee great promises, which, as soon as Thou liftest up Thy hand, I forget.

I come now to make to Thee, O God, a sincere confession of my sins. I declare in Thy presence that if Thou show not Thy mercy to me, I shall surely perish. Grant me, my Saviour, what I beg of Thee, since of Thy pure goodness Thou hast drawn me out of nothingness to put me into a state wherein I can pray to Thee. Amen.

Hail, Adorable Head, crowned with thorns and struck with a reed for us!

Hail, worshipful Face, spit upon and smitten for us!

bleeding Face, O Face divine, be every adoration Thine!

LITANY OF THE HOLY FACE
Here are both abbreviated and complete versions of the Litany of the Holy Face

Introductory Prayers:

Dear Lord, through the Sorrowful and Immaculate Heart of Mary I (we) offer Thee these prayers in reparation for the sins which offend God the most in these modern times – the sins of blasphemy and the profanation of Sunday and Thine Holy Days of Obligation. Amen.

Our Father … Hail Mary … Glory Be …

Prayer to offer the Holy Face of Jesus to God the Father:

Almighty and Eternal Father, since it has pleased Our Divine Saviour to reveal to mankind in modern times the power residing in His Holy Face, we now avail ourselves of this treasure in our great need.

Since our Saviour Himself promised that by offering to Thee His Holy Face disfigured in the Passion we can procure the settlement of all the affairs of our household, and that nothing whatsoever will be refused to us, we now come before Thy throne.

Eternal Father, turn away Thy angry gaze from our guilty people whose face has become unsightly in Thine eyes. Look instead upon the Face of Thy Beloved Son; for this is the Face of Him in Whom

Thou art well pleased. We now offer Thee His Holy Face covered with blood, sweat, dust, spittle and shame, in reparation for the worst crimes of our age, which are atheism, blasphemy and the desecration of Thine holy days.

We thus hope to appease Thy anger justly provoked against us. The All-Merciful Advocate opens His mouth to plead our cause; listen to His cries, behold His tears, O God, and through the merits of His Holy Face, hearken to Him when He intercedes for us poor miserable sinners.

Litany (abbreviated version)

I salute Thee, I adore Thee and I love Thee, O adorable Face of Jesus, my Beloved, noble Seal of the Divinity! outraged anew by blasphemers. I offer Thee, through the heart of Thy blessed Mother, the worship of all the Angels and Saints, most humbly beseeching Thee to repair and renew in me and in all men Thine Image disfigured by sin.

O Adorable Face which was adored, with profound respect, by Mary and Joseph when they saw Thee for the first time, *(* have mercy on us)*

O Adorable Face which ravished with joy, in the stable of Bethlehem, the Angels, the shepherds and the Magi, *(*)*

O Adorable Face which transpierced with a dart of love in the Temple, the saintly old man Simeon and the prophetess Anna, *(*)*

O Adorable Face which filled with admiration the Doctors of the Law when Thou appeared in the Temple at the age of twelve years, *(*)*

O Adorable Face which possesses beauty always ancient and always new, *(*)*

O Adorable Face which is the masterpiece of the Holy Ghost, in which the Eternal Father is well pleased, *(*)*

O Adorable Face which is the ineffable mirror of the Divine Perfections, *(*)*

O Adorable Face of Jesus which was so mercifully bowed down on the Cross, on the day of Thy Passion, for the salvation of the world! Once more today in pity bend down towards us poor sinners. Cast upon us a glance of compassion and give us Thy peace.

O Adorable Face which became brilliant like the sun and radiant with glory, on the Mountain of Tabor, *(*)*
O Adorable Face which wept and was troubled at the tomb of Lazarus, *(*)*
O Adorable Face which was rendered sad at the sight of Jerusalem, and shed tears on that ungrateful city, *(*)*
O Adorable Face which was bowed down to the ground in the Garden of Olives, and covered with confusion for our sins, *(*)*
O Adorable Face which was covered with the sweat of blood, *(*)*
O Adorable Face which was struck by a vile servant, covered with a veil of shame, and profaned by the sacrilegious hands of Thine enemies, *(*)*
O Adorable Face which by Its divine glance, wounded the heart of St. Peter with a dart of sorrow and love, *(*)*
Be merciful to us, O my God! Do not reject our prayers, when in the midst of our afflictions, we call upon Thy Holy Name and seek with love and confidence Thine adorable Face.
O Adorable Face which was washed and anointed by Mary and the holy women and covered with a shroud, *(*)*
O Adorable Face which was all resplendent with glory and beauty on the day of the Resurrection, *(*)*
O Adorable Face which is hidden in the Eucharist, *(*)*
O Adorable Face which will appear at the end of time in the clouds with great power and great majesty, *(*)*
O Adorable Face which will make sinners tremble, *(*)*
O Adorable Face which will fill the just with joy for all eternity, *(*)*
O Adorable Face which merits all our reverence, our homage and our adoration, *(*)*
O Lord, show us Thy Face, and we shall be saved!
O Lord, show us Thy Face, and we shall be saved!
O Lord, show us Thy Face, and we shall be saved!

Litany (complete version)

Lord, *have mercy on us.*
Christ, *have mercy on us.*
Lord, *have mercy on us.*
Christ, *hear us.*
Christ, *graciously hear us.*

Holy Mary, *pray for us.*
O Adorable Face, which wast worshipped with a profound respect by Mary and Joseph, when they beheld It for the first time, *(* have mercy on us)*
O Adorable Face, which delighted the angels, the shepherds, and the Magi in the stable of Bethlehem, *(*)*
O Adorable Face, which wounded the holy Simeon and Anna the prophetess with love, *(*)*
O Adorable Face, which was bathed with tears in Thine holy infancy, *(*)*
O Adorable Face, which called forth the admiration of the doctors of the law when Thou appearedst in the temple at the age of twelve, *(*)*
O Adorable Face, white with purity, crimson with charity, *(*)*
O Adorable Face, more beautiful than the sun, more gracious than the moon, more brilliant than the stars, *(*)*
O Adorable Face, fresher than spring roses, *(*)*
O Adorable Face, more precious than gold, silver, and diamonds, *(*)*
O Adorable Face, whose look was ravishing, and grace charming, *(*)*
O Adorable Face, whose trait is characterised by nobleness, *(*)*
O Adorable Face, contemplated by angels, *(*)*
O Adorable Face, principal work of the Holy Ghost, in Whom the eternal Father was pleased, *(*)*
O Adorable Face, delight of Mary and St. Joseph, *(*)*
O Adorable Face, ineffable mirror of Divine Perfection, *(*)*
O Adorable Face, whose beauty is always old, and yet new, *(*)*
O Adorable Face, which appeasest the wrath of God, *(*)*
O Adorable Face, which maketh devils to tremble, *(*)*
O Adorable Face, treasure of grace and benediction, *(*)*
O Adorable Face, exposed in the desert to the inclemency of the weather, *(*)*
O Adorable Face, burnt with the heat of the sun, and bathed in sweat, *(*)*
O Adorable Face, whose expression was always divine, *(*)*
O Adorable Face, whose modesty and mildness attracted the just and the sinner, *(*)*

O **Adorable Face**, which bestowed a holy kiss on the children after having blessed them, *(*)*
O **Adorable Face**, troubled and weeping at the tomb of Lazarus, *(*)*
O **Adorable Face**, brilliant as the sun, and radiant with glory on mount Thabor, *(*)*
O **Adorable Face**, saddened at the sight of Jerusalem, and weeping over that ungrateful city, *(*)*
O **Adorable Face**, bent to the ground in the garden of Olives, and bearing the confusion of our sins, *(*)*
O **Adorable Face**, which was covered with bloody sweat, *(*)*
O **Adorable Face**, kissed by the traitor Judas, *(*)*
O **Adorable Face**, whose sanctity and majesty terrified the soldiers, and caused them to fall on their faces, *(*)*
O **Adorable Face**, struck by a servant, covered with the veil of ignominy, and profaned by sacrilegious hands, *(*)*
O **Adorable Face**, soiled with spit, and bruised with blows, *(*)*
O **Adorable Face**, whose divine look wounded the heart of St. Peter with grief and love for Thee, *(*)*
O **Adorable Face**, humiliated for us in the tribunal of Jerusalem, *(*)*
O **Adorable Face**, which preserved Thy usual calmness when Pilate pronounced the sentence of death, *(*)*
O **Adorable Face**, covered with sweat and blood, falling in the mud under the heavy weight of the cross, *(*)*
O **Adorable Face**, which deservedst our respect, homage, and adoration, *(*)*
O **Adorable Face**, wiped by a pious woman on the road to Calvary, *(*)*
O **Adorable Face**, whose forehead was crowned with thorns, *(*)*
O **Adorable Face**, whose eyes were filled with tears and blood, *(*)*
O **Adorable Face**, whose divine lips tasted vinegar and gall, *(*)*
O **Adorable Face**, whose hair and beard was blackened by the executioners, *(*)*
O **Adorable Face**, which became like to a leper, *(*)*
O **Adorable Face**, whose incomparable beauty was obscured by the frightful cloud of the sins of the world, *(*)*
O **Adorable Face**, covered with the sad shades of death, *(*)*
O **Adorable Face**, washed and perfumed by Mary and the holy women, and covered with a winding sheet, *(*)*

O Adorable Face, covered in the sepulchre, *(*)*
O Adorable Face, all resplendent with glory and beauty at the day of the Resurrection, *(*)*
O Adorable Face, all glistening with light at the moment of the Ascension, *(*)*
O Adorable Face, concealed in the Eucharist, *(*)*
O Adorable Face, which will appear at the end of time, in the clouds, with great power and majesty, *(*)*
O Adorable Face, which will make sinners tremble, *(*)*
O Adorable Face, which will fill the just with joy for eternity, *(*)*
Lamb of God, who taketh away the sins of the world, *pardon us.*
Lamb of God, who taketh away the sins of the world, *hear us.*
Lamb of God, who taketh away the sins of the world, *have mercy on us.*
Let us pray.

 salute, adore, and love Thee, O Jesus, my Saviour, covered with new insults by blasphemers, and offer Thee, in the heart of the divine Mary, as an incense and perfume of agreeable odour, the homage of Angels and all Saints, praying Thee humbly, by the virtue of Thy Holy Face, to repair and re-establish in me and all mankind Thy image disfigured by sin.

I salute, adore, and love Thee, O Adorable Face of Jesus, my well beloved, noble impression of the Godhead. I devote myself to Thee with all the powers of my soul, and humbly pray Thee to stamp in my heart all the traits of Thy divine resemblance. Amen.

Oh Jesus, through the Merits of Thy Holy Face, have pity on us and on the whole world! (3 times)

Both the long and short versions of this prayer were composed by Sr. Mary St. Peter. Recommended to be recited on Tuesdays and Sundays, particularly in front of the Blessed Sacrament.

CHAPLET OF DIVINE MERCY
Optional Opening Prayer
(especially at the 3:00 hour, the hour of Jesus' death)

(Opening Prayer - on the first 3 beads after the Cross of the Rosary)

You expired Jesus, but the source of life gushed forth for souls and the ocean of Mercy opened up for the whole world. O Fount of Life, O unfathomable Divine Mercy, envelop the whole world and empty Yourself out upon us.

O Blood and Water, which gushed from the Heart of Jesus, as a fountain for us, we trust in You. (3 times)

The Lord's Prayer
Our Father, Who art in heaven, Hallowed be Thy Name.
Thy Kingdom come, Thy Will be done, on earth as it is in Heaven.
Give us this day, our daily bread,
And forgive us our trespasses,
as we forgive those who trespass against us.
And lead us not into temptation, but deliver us from evil.
Amen.

Hail Mary
Hail Mary full of Grace, the Lord is with thee.
Blessed are thou amongst women
and blessed is the fruit of thy womb Jesus.
Holy Mary Mother of God,
pray for us sinners now and at the hour of our death.
Amen

Apostle's Creed
I believe in God, the Father almighty,
creator of heaven and earth.
I believe in Jesus Christ, his only Son, our Lord.
He was conceived by the power of the Holy Spirit
and born of the Virgin Mary.
He suffered under Pontius Pilate,
was crucified, died, and was buried.

He descended into the dead.
on the third day he rose again.
He ascended into heaven
and is seated at the right hand of the Father.
He will come again to judge the living and the dead.
I believe in the Holy Spirit,
the holy catholic Church,
the communion of saints,
the forgiveness of sins,
the resurrection of the body,
and the life everlasting.
Amen.

On the 'Our Father' bead of each decade pray:
Eternal Father, I offer you the Body and Blood, Soul and Divinity of Your dearly beloved Son, Our Lord Jesus Christ in atonement for our sins and those of the whole world.

On the 10 'Hail Mary' beads of each decade pray:
For the sake of His sorrowful Passion, have Mercy on us and on the whole world.
Repeat with the remaining decades: 1 "Eternal Father..." & 10 "For the sake...")

Closing Prayers
(At the end of the 5 decades)
Holy God, Holy Mighty One, Holy Immortal One, have Mercy on us and on the whole world. *(Repeat 3 times)*

Optional Closing Prayer
Eternal God, in whom Mercy is endless, and the treasury of compassion inexhaustible. Look kindly upon us and increase your Mercy in us, so that in difficult moments, we may not despair nor become despondent but with great confidence, submit ourselves to Your Holy Will, which is Love and Mercy itself. Jesus, I trust in you, Jesus, I trust in you, Jesus, I trust in you. Amen.

BIBLIOGRAPHY

Books:

Agreda, Mary of, Venerable. The Mystical City of God, Volume III, The Transfixion. Tan Books, Charlotte, NC, 1914, Translated from the Original Authorized Spanish Edition by Fiscar Marison (Rev. George J. Blatter), Begun in 1902.

Bennett, Janice, Sacred Blood, Sacred Image: The Sudarium of Oviedo – New Evidence for the Authenticity of The Shroud of Turin. Ignatius Press, San Francisco, CA. 2001.

Bini, Antonio, The Holy Face: From Manoppello to the World. Supplemento a "IL Volto Santo di Manoppello" Anno CI – n. 1, 2016.

Bishop, Jim, The Day Christ Died. Harper & Row, Publishers, New York, 1957.

Carpenter, John S., He Is Alive: Science Finds Jesus, Page Publishing, Inc. New York, 2018.

Goodier, Alban, Archbishop, The Passion and Death of Our Lord Jesus Christ. Sophia Institute Press, Manchester, NH. 2022, First Edition published by Burns Oates & Washbourne, London & Ireland. 1933

Guerrera, Vittorio, Fr. The Shroud of Turin: A Case for Authenticity. Tan Books and Publishers, Inc. Rockford, Il. 2001.

Guscin, Mark, The Oviedo Cloth. The Lutterworth Press, Cambridge, Great Britain. 1998.

Holy Bible, The - New Testament, The Great Adventure Bible, Revised Standard Version, Second Catholic Edition, Ascension Press, West Chester, PA. 2006.

Holy Bible, The – New Testament, The Word on Fire Bible, The Gospels. New Revised Standard Version. John 20:1-10. Brandon Vogt, General Editor. Word on Fire, Park Ridge, IL. 2020.

Hynek, R.W. MD, Science and the Holy Shroud: An Examination Into the Sacred Passion and the Direct Cause of Christ's Death. Freely translated from the Czech by Dom Augustine Studney, O.S.B. Benedictine Press, Pilsen Station, Chicago, IL. 1936.

Institute of St. Clement I, Pope and Martyr, The Eucharistic Miracles of the World. Eternal Life, Bardstown, KY. 2009. Kowalska, Saint Maria Faustina, Diary - Divine Mercy in My Soul. Marian Press, Stockbridge, MA. 2016. First published in 1987. From the Original Polish Diary, Zgromadzenie Siosr Matkj Boxej Milosierdzia,ul. Zytnia 3/9, 01-014 Warszawa, Poland. 1981.

Lavoi, Gilbert, Dr. The Shroud of Jesus and the Sign John Ingeniously Concealed. Sophia Institute Press, NH. 2023.

Mariani, Drew, Divine Mercy. Relevant Radio, P.O. Box 10707, Green Bay, WI, 2021.

O'Connell, Patrick, Rev. B.D. Columbian Fathers, Dalgan Park, Navan, Ireland, and Carty, Charles, Rev., Radio Press Society, St. Paul 1, MN, USA. The Holy Shroud and Four Visions: The Holy Shroud New Evidence Compared with the Visions of St. Bridget of

Sweden, Maria d"Agreda, Catherine Emmerich, and Teresa Neumann. Tan Books, Charlotte, NC. 2014, originally published 1974.

Serafine, Franco, Dr., A Cardiologist Examines Jesus: The Stunning Science Behind Eucharistic Miracles. Translated by Dr. Umberto Villa, B.S., M.B.B.S. and Fr. Brendan Purcell, M.A., S.T.L., Ph.D. Sophia Institute Press, Manchester, NH. 2021.

Verschuuren, Gerard, A Catholic Scientist Champions the Shroud of Turin. Sophia Institute Press, Manchester, NH. 2021.

Wilson, Ian, The Shroud: Fresh Light on the 2000-Year-Old Mystery. Bantam Books. Great Britain. 2010.

Zugibe, Frederick T. M.D., Ph.D., Pierre Barbet Revisited, Sindon, No. 8, December 1995.

Zuzolo, Mary Jane, Unveiling the Sixth Station of the Cross: Reparation to the Holy Face, Mother of All Devotions. Sophia Institute Press, Manchester, New Hampshire, 2024.

Internet:

Bennett, Janice, Simply Catholic, Face Cloth of Jesus' Burial: The Sudarium of Oviedo. Scott Richert, publisher. https://www.simplycatholic.com/about-us/. Page 3.

BibleVerseStudy.com, Roman Scourge, Roman Scourge & Flagellum, 2023, https://www.bibleversestudy.com/acts/acts22-roman-scourge.htm.

Blogspot, Holy Face of Manoppello, "In San Francisco Archbishop Cordileone Calls Attention to the Feast of Omnis Terra and the Veil Bearing te Holy Face of Jesus. January 26, 2024.
http://holyfaceofmanoppello.blogspot.com/.
DivineMercy.org Website, The Miracle of Brendan O'Neill, Divine Miracles in Action, Miracles of Divine Mercy.
https://www.divinemercy.org/elements-of-divine-mercy/miracles.html. 2024.

Downing, Ray, The Fabric of the Shroud of Turin, March 30, 2017.
https://www.raydowning.com/blog/2017/2/23/the-fabric-of-the-shroud-of-turin.

Encyclopedia Britannica, On-Line version. Stations of the Cross, Christianity. November 7, 2023, Written and fact checked by the editors of Encyclopedia Britannica and most recently revised and updated by Amy Tikkanen.
https://www.britannica.com/topic/Stations-of-the-Cross.

Gaspari, Antonio, Has Veronica's Veil Been Found?, Urbi et orbi Communications, November 1999. CatholicCulture.org, Inside the Vatican, Martin de Porres lay Domincan Community, KY. Trinity Communications, 2024.
https://www.catholicculture.org/culture/library/view.cfm?recnum=2856.
Heggadon, Geoff, Healing Miracles of the Shroud of Turin, Works by Faith Ministries. November 28, 2012.
https://www.worksbyfaith.org/healing-miracles-of-the-shroud-of-turin/.

Institute of St. Clement I, Pope and Martyr, The Eucharistic Miracles of the World, Presented by the Real Presence Eucharistic Education and Adoration Association, In. www.therealpresence.org.

Eternal Life, Bardstown, KY. 2009, Reprint 2022.

Khan, Arif, The Sudarium of Oviedo and the Shroud of Turin, The Review of Religions, https://www.reviewofreligions.org/11770/the-sudarium-of-oviedo-and-the-shroud-of-turin/. May 19, 2015.

Lambert, Aaron, Jesus, I Trust in You: The History and Mystery of the Divine Mercy Devotion, The Archdiocese of San Francisco, March 28, 2024. https://sfarchdiocese.org/jesus-i-trust-in-you-the-history-and-mystery-of-the-divine-mercy-devotion/.

Moorhead, Joanna, The $1M Challenge: 'If the Turin Shroud is a Forgery, Show How it Was Done', April 17, 2022, https://www.theguardian.com/world/2022/apr/17/the-1m-challenge-if-the-turin-shroud-is-a-forgery-show-how-it-was-done.

Naab, Kathleen, Seeing What Peter Saw in the Empty Tomb: Historian Shares Research on Shroud of Turin and Veil of Manoppello. Zenit.org., Servants for the Pierced Hearts of Jesus and Mary. https://www.piercedhearts.org/treasures/relics/shroud_veil_jesus.html.

Ponsi, Lou, The Holy Shroud, the Divine Mercy Image and Eucharistic Miracles. Orange County Catholic, April 23, 2024. https://www.occatholic.com/the-holy-shroud-the-divine-mercy-image-and-eucharistic-miracles/.

Redzioch, Wlodzimierz, An Interview with Sr. Blandina Paschalis Schloemer, The Holy Face of Manoppello Blogspot. July 1, 2010. https://holyfaceofmanoppello.blogspot.com/2010/07/interview-with-sr-blandina-paschalis.html.

Relics, "The Veil of Veronica" or "Holy Face": A Relic Venerated in Rome Since Antiquity. https://relics.es/en/blogs/relics/veil-of-veronica#:~:text=The%20legend%20surrounding%20this%20relic%20dates%20back%20to,on%20the%20fabric%20when%20she%20picked%20it%20up.

Rogers, Ray, Carbon 14 Dating Invalidated. BSTS Newsletter No. 61- Part 6 – n61Part6.pdf. https://www.shroud.com/pdfs/n61part6.pdf. Page1.

Sanctuary of the Holy Face website, Immaculate Conception Church, Nampicuan, Nueva Ecija, Philippines. http://www.holyfacenampicuan.com/.

Saunders, Fr. William, EWTN, How Did the Stations of the Cross Begin. 2023. https://www.ewtn.com/catholicism/library/how-did-the-stations-of-the-cross-begin-1155.

Stackpole, Robert, STD, Why So Many Images? Which One is Best?. https://www.thedivinemercy.org/articles/why-so-many-images-which-one-best.

The Catholic Exchange, Fr. Donald Calloway, MIC, The Miraculous Image of Our Lady of Las Lajas. March 29, 2017. https://catholicexchange.com/miraculous-image-lady-las-lajas/.

The Divine Mercy: On This Day, the Divine Mercy Image Was Revealed. https://www.thedivinemercy.org/articles/day-divine-mercy-image-was-revealed. February 22, 2024.

The Face of Christ, Website, Byssus and Pure Linen: Comparing the Cloths. https://www.sudariumchristi.com/en/tomb/compare.htm.

The Socratic Method, St. Thomas Aquinas, October 7, 2023, https://www.socratic-method.com/quote-meanings/thomas-aquinas-to-one-who-has-faith-no-explanation-is-necessary-to-one-without-faith-no-explanation-is-possible.

Turley, K.V. The Mysterious Holy Veil of Manoppello, Catholic Exchange. February 16, 2023. https://catholicexchange.com/the-mysterious-holy-veil-of-manoppello/.

WebMD, Editorial Contributors, Medically Reviewed by Debra Jaliman, MD on January 26, 2022. https://www.webmd.com/a-to-z-guides/hematidrosis-hematohidrosis

Wikipedia, John Chrysostom, https://en.wikipedia.org/wiki/John_Chrysostom.

Wikipedia, Saint Veronica. https://en.wikipedia.org/wiki/Saint_Veronica.

Wilson, Ian, Holy Faces, Secret Places. Doubleday, Garden City, Page 175. https://archive.org/details/isbn-9780385261050/page/175.

YouTube Video, Crucifixion: The Process and the Monstrous Logic Behind It. April 2023. https://www.youtube.com/watch?v=Emk21WbOFo0.

YouTube video, The Man of the Shroud Lecture Series, The Sufferings of the Man of the Shroud, Fr. Andrew Dalton, May 19, 2023. https://video.search.yahoo.com/yhs/search?fr=yhs-tro-freshy&ei=UTF-8&hsimp=yhs-freshy&hspart=tro&p=youtube+video%2C+the+sufferings+of+the+

man+of+the+shroud&type=Y219_F163_204671_102220#id=1&vid =27149d850f4e485514276857ab5387b1&action=click.

YouTube Video, The Origin of Crucifixion.

YouTube Video, The Significance of the Folded Napkin: Fairview Church of Christ, https://www.youtube.com/watch?v=dNy65pKZS34. May 30, 2023.

YouTube Who Do You Say I Am? A Shroud of Turin Documentary Blending Science and Faith, Patchwork Heart Ministry, https://video.search.yahoo.com/yhs/search?fr=yhs-tro-freshy&ei=UTF-8&hsimp=yhs-freshy&hspart=tro&p=youtube+video+who+do+you+say+I+am%3 F+A+shroud+of+turin+documentary+blending...&type=Y219_F163 _204671_102220#id=2&vid=cc7eba355eb83531d5687df304132472 &action=click. December 2023.

EWTN News Nightly, Veils of Veronica: Cloth Shows the Face of Jesus. YouTube Video. https://video.search.yahoo.com/yhs/search?fr=yhs-tro-freshy&ei=UTF-8&hsimp=yhs-freshy&hspart=tro&p=veils+of+veronica%3A+cloth+shows+the+fa ce+of+Jesus%2C+EWTN+News+Nightly+youtube+video&type=Y 219_F163_204671_102220#id=1&vid=203a01630e97e46f335b8eab 94ec6164&action=click. May 1, 2020.

YouTube video, Why Did Jesus Fold the Cloth That Covered His Face in the Tomb? Catholic Bellator, https://www.youtube.com/watch?v=L7San7bOSD0.

Periodicals:

Saunders, William Fr., How did the Stations of the Cross Begin? Arlington Catholic Herald, March 10, 1994. https://www.ewtn.com/catholicism/library/how-did-the-stations-of-the-cross-begin-1155.

Journal of the American Medical Association (JAMA), Edwards, William D.; Gabel, Wesley J., MDiv; Hosmer, Floyd E. MS, AMI, On the Physical Death of Jesus Christ. JAMA, March 21, 1986, Vol. 255, No. 11. Pages 1455-1463.

Scientific Research Publications

Bennett, Janice, The Sudarium of Oviedo and its Relationship with the Shroud of Turin, A presentation made at the First International Conference on the Shroud of Turin, Panama City, Panama, June 30 – July 1, 2012. https://www.shroud.com/pdfs/bennettpantxteng.pdf.

De Caro, Liberato; Matricciani, Emilio; and Fanti, Giulio, A Comparison Between the Face of the Veil of Manoppello and the Face of the Shroud of Turin. Heritage 2019, Received December 2018, Accepted January 22, 2019, Published January 24, 2019. www.mdpi.com/journal/heritage.

Falcinelli, Roberto, The Veil of Manoppello: Work of Art or Authentic Relic? 2005. https://www.shroud.com/pdfs/roberto.pdf.

Fanti, Guilio, A Review of 3d Characteristics of the Turin Shroud Body Image, A research study presented to the Workshop Italy-Canada on 3D Digital Imaging and Modeling Applications of: Heritage, Medicine & Land. Padova, April 3-4, 2001. https://mail.google.com/mail/u/0/#inbox/FMfcgzQVxtrGXmrVSvSVPfvVWzFgqzsr.

Jaworski, Jan S. and Fanti, Giulio, 3-D Processing to Evidence Characteristics Represented in Manoppello Veil. Research Paper. 2008. https://www.shroud.com/pdfs/jaworski.pdf.

Resch, Andreas, The Face on the Shroud of Turin and on the Veil of Manoppellp, Proceedings of the International Workshop on the Scientific Approach to the Acheiropoietos Images, ENEA Frascati, Italy, May 4-6, 2010.
http://www.acheiropoietos.info/proceedings/ReschWeb.pdf.

Videos, DVDs:
Brault, Russ, Shroud Encounter, CSI: Jerusalem – Where Science, History and Faith Meet to Explore the Mystery of All Mysteries.

Rolfe, David, The Shroud of Turin, New Expanded Edition. The four films: The Silent Witness, Shroud of Turin, Shroud, A Grave Injustice. Ignatius Press, 2017.

YouTube Video, What Happens When This Painting is Matched with the Shroud of Turin? Length = 14:11.
https://www.youtube.com/watch?v=Ije0GkSKohk. 2021.

ABOUT THE AUTHOR

Paul F. Caranci is a public speaker and the author of fifteen published books. He is a third-generation resident of North Providence, RI and has been a student of history for many years. He served as RI Deputy Secretary of State for eight years and was elected to the town council where he served for almost seventeen years. He has a BA in political science from Providence College and has completed several masters' level courses toward an MPA from Roger Williams University.

Together with his wife Margie he founded The Municipal Heritage Group in 2009. He is an incorporating member of the Association of Rhode Island Authors (ARIA) and is a member of the board of the RI Publication Society. Paul also served on the boards of the RI Heritage Harbor Museum, and the RI Heritage Hall of Fame. He is past chairman of the Diabetes Foundation of RI where he served on the board for over fifteen years. He also served on the Board of Directors of the American Diabetes Association, Rhode Island Affiliate.

During his tenure on the town council, Paul's efforts to successfully pass laws and implement health policies earned him several public health awards including the James Carney Public Health Award from the RI Dept. of Health, an advocacy award from the American Cancer Society, the advocate of the year award from the Diabetes Foundation of RI and an advocacy award from the American Diabetes Association.

In 2015, Paul was awarded the Margaret Chase Smith American Democracy Award for Political Courage, the highest honor awarded by the National Association of Secretaries of State, for his undercover role in exposing political corruption in his hometown of North Providence. His undercover work with the FBI, in breaking up what a federal judge called a criminal empire, is the subject of Paul's seventh book, Wired: A Shocking True Story of Political Corruption and the FBI Informant Who Risked Everything to Expose It.

Another of Paul's books chronicles daily life for World War II prisoners held at Dachau, Germany's oldest and most brutal concentration camp. The Nazi regime programmed every activity to inflict the most physical and psychological pain possible. The sadistic nature of the camp commanders is portrayed through the eyes of Fr. Jean Bernard, A Catholic priest from Luxembourg imprisoned at Dachau for using the Catholic Film Agency to denounce the inhumane policies of the Nazis. This remarkable true story is a must read for lovers of history and World War II enthusiasts.

In 2023, Paul collaborated with award-winning mystery-thriller novelist Julien Ayotte to write In The Shadows of Vietnam: The Gallant Life of Father Philip Salois. This story of an unlikely war hero turned priest captures Fr. Phil's life-saving journey from the jungles of Vietnam to his award-winning work with the priests at La Salette ministering to Vietnam veterans suffering from PTSD. This is the awe-inspiring true story of the life of a gentle giant, a man who received the Silver Star for his acts of valor in Vietnam, and a man who has merited the highest distinction for his service, from veterans' organizations to religious and civic groups alike.

Four of Paul's books were awarded special recognition. The Hanging & Redemption of John Gordon: The True Story of Rhode Island's Last Execution (The History Press, 2013) was voted one of the top five non-fiction books of 2013 by the Providence Journal. Scoundrels: Defining Corruption Through Tales of Political Intrigue in Rhode Island (Stillwater River Publications, 2016) was the winner of the 2016 Dorry Award as the non-fiction book of the year. The Promise of Fatima: One Hundred Years of History, Mystery and Faith

(Stillwater River Publications, 2017), and I Am The Immaculate Conception: The Story of Bernadette of Lourdes (Stillwater River Publications, 2018), were named finalists in the International Book Awards in 2018 and 2019 respectively.

The movie rights to four of Paul's books, The Hanging & Redemption of John Gordon: The True Story of Rhode Island's Last Execution, The Promise of Fatima: One Hundred Years of History, Mystery and Faith, I Am The Immaculate Conception: The Story of Bernadette of Lourdes, and Terror in Wichita: A True Story of One Woman's Courage and Her Will to Live (Stillwater River Publications, 2020) have been sold to a Hollywood production company and may one day be featured on the big screen.

Paul and his wife Margie have two adult children and four grandchildren.

OTHER BOOKS BY THE AUTHOR
Order Form
Please use the following form to order additional copies of:

North Providence: A History & The People Who Shaped It ($20.00)

The Hanging & Redemption of John Gordon: The True Story of Rhode Island's Last Execution ($20.00)

Award Winning Real Estate Sales in a Declining Market ($10.00)

The Essential Guide to Running For Local Office ($15.00)

Monumental Providence: Legends of History on Sculpture, Statuary, Monuments and Memorials ($20.00)

Scoundrels: Defining Political Corruption Through Tales of Intrigue in Rhode Island ($20.00)

Wired: The Shocking True Story of Political Corruption and the FBI Informant Who Risked Everything to Expose it ($23.00)

The Promise of Fatima: One Hundred Years of History, Mystery & Faith ($20.00)

I Am The Immaculate Conception: The Story of Bernadette And Her Apparitions At Lourdes ($20.00)

Heavenly Portrait: The Miraculous Image of Our Lady of Guadalupe ($20.00)

Terror in Wichita: A True Story of One Woman's Courage and Her Will to Live ($20.00)

Before the End of the Age: Signs of the Coming Chastisement ($23.00)

Darkness at Dachau: The True Story of Father Jean Bernard ($20.00)

Ear Candy: The Inside Story of Foxes & Fossils, America's #1 Cover Band ($25.00)

In The Shadows of Vietnam: The Gallant Life of Father Philip Salois ($20.00)

_____ (Qty) _____ (Title) x _____ (Price) = $_____

_____ (Qty) _____ (Title) x _____ (Price) = $_____

_____ (Qty) _____ (Title) x _____ (Price) = $_____

_____ (Qty) _____ (Title) x _____ (Price) = $_____

_____ (Qty) _____ (Title) x _____ (Price) = $_____

Total for Books: $_____ + Postage** $_____ = Total Cost $_____

**Postage: Please add $3.50 for the first book and $1.50 for each additional book ordered.

Payment Method:
_____ Personal Check Enclosed (Payable to PMC Associates, LLC)

_____ Charge my Credit Card

Name: _____ Billing Zip Code: _____

Visa _____ Master Card _____ Other _____

Card Number: _____ Exp. ___/___ CSC (3-digit code) _____

(Order Form Continues on the next page)

Ship My Books To:

Name: _____

Street Address: _____

City: _____ State: _____ Zip Code: _____

Phone: _____ Email: _____

Do you want the author to sign the book? Yes_____ No_____

Special Signing Instructions: IE. To Whom do you want the book signed? Do you want the author to include a message or just sign his name? Etc.

_____
_____
_____
_____
_____

Mail Your Completed Order Form to:

Paul F. Caranci
26 East Avenue
North Providence, RI 02911
You May also order using the author's email address at: municipalheritage@gmail.com or by calling 401-639-4502.

Visit the Author's Website at www.paulcaranci.com.
You may also order books directly from the website.

www.ingramcontent.com/pod-product-compliance
Lightning Source LLC
Chambersburg PA
CBHW071111160426
43196CB00013B/2535